EVERYDAY ECONOMICS

EVERYDAY ECONOMICS

A User's Guide to the Modern Economy

STEVE COULTER

agenda
publishing

First published in 2017 by Agenda Publishing

Agenda Publishing Limited
The Core
Science Central
Bath Lane
Newcastle upon Tyne
NE4 5TF
www.agendapub.com

ISBN 978-1-911116-35-6 (hardcover)
ISBN 978-1-911116-36-3 (paperback)

British Library Cataloguing-in-Publication Data
A catalogue record for this book is available from the British Library

Printed and bound in the UK by CPI Group (UK) Ltd, Croydon, CR0 4YY

CONTENTS

PREFACE AND ACKNOWLEDGEMENTS

This is a book about economics for non-economists. It requires no grounding in economics at all – just, hopefully, a lively interest in the world around and an ability and willingness to think about things logically and systematically. It is aimed at students in the humanities and the social sciences who are likely to encounter some economics in their work and studies, and thereby perhaps want to know a bit more about the economy without needing to sign up for a lot of mathematical-sounding economics modules. As such, it tries to place economics in its real-world, political context, and for this reason it may even appeal to trained economists wanting a rounder view of their discipline.

Hopefully, all kinds of readers will find something of interest in the book and will be left with a desire to know more. It is for this reason that copious references are provided, not just to support various assertions and data points but also to guide readers towards further sources that may be of interest. As well as laying out how economists approach the topics examined here, the book also tries to serve as a guide to past and current debates and controversies in economics. Although mildly critical of some of the tenets of neoclassical economics, it does not consciously take sides in any of these debates but aims to instil in readers a curiosity to learn more about the economy and what economists have to say about it.

A great many people assisted in the writing of this book. In particular, I would like to thank my publisher at Agenda, Alison Howson. In addition, Waltraud Schelkle, Bob Hancké, Nick Barr, Michael Beveridge, Darren Acheson and several anonymous reviewers read all or part of the manuscript and gave immensely helpful comments. Any errors are mine, of course. Pieter Tuytens, Marina Cino-Pagliarello, Chrysa Papalexatou, Frieder Mitsch, Dimitrios Koutsoupakis and Sarah Watters provided invaluable research assistance. Finally, my greatest debt and fondest appreciation go out to Sunita and Lucas, to whom this book is dedicated.

1

ECONOMICS: WHAT IS IT GOOD FOR?

1.1 Introduction

It must have been a fairly toe-curling moment. Opening a new academic building at the London School of Economics and Political Science (LSE) in 2008, as
the financial crisis was raging unchecked, Queen Elizabeth II asked her academic host a cutting question: "Why did none of you see this coming?" Her
Majesty's comment, and the awkward embarrassment with which it was greeted,
was reported around the world as an emblem of the inability of the economics
profession to prepare the world for disaster.

Were these accusations fair? Yes and no. No, because economists are not
omniscient and, the mini-industry of economic forecasting notwithstanding,
cannot predict the future. The claim of economists that they are (social) scientists is often mocked by "real" scientists studying applied natural phenomena,
as opposed to the behaviour of unruly human beings. Yet some of these are
equally poor at making predictions about disruptive occurrences in their own
realms: seismologists cannot predict earthquakes; meteorologists can make reliable weather forecasts only for the next few days; and so on.

But, on the other hand, yes; because the financial crisis was an extraordinary
event that shook the discipline of economics to its core, exposed some of its
central tenets as wishful thinking and revealed a stunning level of complacency
on the part of leading members of the profession, including highly paid analysts
in government and financial institutions. Among the most searing criticisms was
that modern economics was addicted to abstract theorizing and thereby irrelevant to the everyday concerns of ordinary mortals. This was not merely sniping
from the sidelines. Leading economists and financial insiders felt the same way.
Just before he quit his job, the president of the European Central Bank (ECB),
Jean-Claude Trichet, complained in exasperation that, "as a policymaker during
the crisis, I found the available [economic and financial] models of limited help.

In fact, I would go further: in the face of the crisis, we felt abandoned by conventional tools."[1]

The crisis and its aftermath have prompted much soul-searching among economists,[2] as well as ridicule from many commentators (although applications to university economics courses shot up). Methods have been questioned, theories and models rethought and the data re-interrogated. Public policy, grounded in economic theory, has been retooled to ensure the crisis will not happen again, although few really believe we have seen the last of such shocks. Economics, albeit chastened, continues. And this is surely a good thing, because trying to make sense of how modern economies work is profoundly important. Moreover, it is a task well suited to economists, as they possess many of the intellectual tools needed to do this.

For economics is a practical discipline that brings much-needed rigour to the analysis of questions that are fundamental to everyday life – in particular, how to produce a fair and prosperous society, given finite resources. Most people are dimly aware of the "big" questions of economic management: how to control inflation, create jobs and foster growth. But many do not appreciate how much more there is to the field than that. Economics, especially the field of microeconomics, also deals with many of the particular challenges and opportunities of existence at a very human and immediate level, such as getting and keeping a job, making the most of an education, buying the right house, staying healthy, getting goods from producers to the shops, financing a retirement – and many other things besides.

In a lot of ways economics is at its most interesting and engaging when it considers these subjects, which are also probably the things that matter most to people on a daily basis. Economics provides a way of thinking about life and how to make the most of it that is both distinctive and a good guide to public policy. It helps to make sense of a world that is both familiar and strange, but in a way that offers a unique, yet rigorous, perspective. This book looks at a lot of these issues by throwing light on some of the fascinating study and research that economists have undertaken over the years. It does this by taking areas of everyday life experienced by individuals – work, education, health, welfare, housing, shopping and finance – and explaining how these work in economics terms. By making economics understandable – hopefully – through an explanation of the things most people encounter personally on a day-to-day basis, the book is intended to show how relevant economics is to important aspects of everyday concern.

More humility from economists is required, however, and it is perhaps also a good thing if their knowledge and understanding are shared out a little bit more. The trouble is that, in the hands of professional economists over the years, economics has come to be associated with grand, abstract theorizing and an arrogant ambition to make human beings conform to conceptions of behaviour that strike many people as remote and unrealistic. Economics is possibly at its worst when it comes to rigid worldviews and overconfident forecasting, when it is prone to over-promise and under-deliver. It is at its best when it is about problem solving and shedding new light on familiar conundrums.

The crisis and its aftermath have given rise to two big questions about economics that are also the central themes of this book: what use is economics if it cannot predict the next destructive shock, or even explain previous ones; and what can be done to make it seem more relevant to the experiences of individuals? Answering the first question is pretty straightforward. The rest of this introductory chapter tries to show that economics offers an extremely powerful set of tools for comprehending the modern world. If understood as a particular way of thinking about human affairs, rather than a set of iron laws, it can help us to restrain our more destructive, short-sighted impulses to help build prosperous, cooperative societies. This will be easier to achieve, however, if economists open up and make more effort to explain themselves.

The second question is therefore more challenging, and is the focus of the rest of the book. To outsiders, economics often seems lost in its own impenetrable world of dogmas and abstractions. To those not steeped in the advanced maths required to read academic papers in economics journals, the subject can often seem like a private game played between aloof figures uninterested in everyday problems of wider concern. To the men or women in the street, the methods and concerns of economists can seem baffling and irrelevant. Can, they may well ask, all these models and equations help me get an affordable mortgage, or tell me why my daughter's school is underperforming? Why do the latest gadgets get so much cheaper if you wait a few months after they are introduced in the shops before buying them? What are my taxes being spent on, and how do I know if they are spent well?

To be fair, plenty of economists, particularly those working in microeconomics, the branch of the subject concerned with the behaviour of individuals and firms, are actively considering these problems. And they regularly come up with policy suggestions based on their research that improve our lives. The trouble is, this study is conducted in a way that is largely inaccessible to those directly affected by the problems being put under the microscope by economists. Possibly the most off-putting thing about modern economics that contributes hugely to this gulf in understanding is its seeming inability to theorize human beings in a way that seems realistic to real people. Two conceptual strategies are generally adopted, neither of which particularly recommend economists' methods to the layperson. One is to simply abstract the behaviour of large numbers of individuals up to the macro level, so they are treated as members of groups rather than individual subjects, and examined according to collective dynamics. The other is to consider people as individuals but to assign to them a number of assumptions about their motivation and behaviour in order to render them predictable: that they are rational, self-interested "utility maximizers", for example.

But this can look bizarre. Economics appears then to view people either as faceless cogs in a machine or, at the other extreme, atomized and self-absorbed individuals relentlessly pursuing their own ends and indifferent to the needs of the group. In a key sense, people should ideally be conceptualized as both at the same time. It is only if you assume the former that can you easily aggregate individual behaviour to the group, and only if you suppose the latter that this aggregate behaves predictably.

The financial crisis demonstrated well how individuals affect, and are affected by, the wider economy of which they are an intrinsic part. The crisis had numerous causes, among them institutional and policy failings by governments and regulators. Some observers note that major financial crises erupt roughly every 70 years and are probably an inevitable part of modern capitalist economies. Governments elected by us, the voters, stripped away much of the regulation stopping reckless behaviour by banks. So perhaps we simply need to learn to live with the consequences of our actions?

But behaviour by individuals played its part too. Private debt, particularly in the form of mortgages for housing, spiked in the years leading up to the meltdown, and once the banking crisis was under way people responded by pulling out their savings, producing a run on the banks. What was individually rational and understandably self-interested behaviour produced, collectively, a financial and economic crisis that affected everyone through its destructive impact on jobs, incomes and life prospects.

This is not, of course, to say that if only a few more people had economics degrees or read *The Economist* magazine then the foolish behaviour leading up to the crisis would not have happened. But it is entirely possible that a greater awareness of the consequences of certain actions might lead to better decisions in future, with beneficial outcomes.

So, we have a couple of challenges. One is to try to provide an entry point to economic thought. The other is to build on this to guide readers through aspects of the economy they are likely to encounter and to render these more explicable by using economics to explain them. What is needed, therefore, is an account of economic life that combines explanatory power and simplicity with a focus on activity from the ground up. A book about "everyday economics", in other words.

The seven thematic chapters that follow this one each deal with an aspect of everyday life and try to explain them by using economics: why education is important; how to get and keep a job; buying and owning a home; the economics of health; why we need a welfare state; shopping and consumption; and how finance works. Each chapter begins with an examination of foundational explanations from microeconomics, usually the mainstream "neoclassical" view.

They are then critiqued and expanded upon as alternative explanations are introduced, before moving on to the macro level with a look at how governments and the international economy have an effect. Finally, we conclude with a look to future developments, and how economics can contribute to explaining these.

But, before we get to that stage, it is worth delving more into the earlier discussion of what economics is about and how it treats us as individuals. The next section will try to dispel any lingering doubts about the value of economics by clarifying what it can and cannot (and does not try) to do. It also sheds some light on how economics works as an intellectual exercise. The final section of the chapter returns to the question of the individual and the group in economics by showing how economic thought has wrestled with this conundrum since at least the days of Adam Smith. Far from dismissing individuals as cyphers or automata, economists have generally placed them at the centre of their analysis. But let us first settle exactly what economics is for.

So what use is economics?

Two and a half centuries of thinking by economists have accumulated a fairly reliable set of explanations of the various facets of what makes societies materially successful: why some countries get richer and others stagnate; why inflation is often, but not always, a bad thing; where and when markets are successful in allocating resources, and when governments should step in; why education boosts economic growth; and so on. But economics is also sometimes best thought of as a method, or approach, rather than an established body of facts. This method generally consists of a reliance on data, coupled with a set of assumptions about human behaviour (that we tend to respond to incentives, for example), from which theories, or models, are constructed.

The popular *Freakonomics* and *Undercover Economist* series of books offer an amusing and eye-opening set of vignettes about familiar, everyday life: why estate agents should not be trusted, why crime rates rise and fall and what makes a perfect parent, for example. Fun though they are, they can also usefully be read as books about social science methodologies. The exhaustive testing of the data against prevailing assumptions about the causes of social problems, married with economists' own perceptions of what causes people to act in the way they do, throws new light on familiar problems. This book takes this approach, and runs with it by looking to explain everyday challenges we encounter alongside the quirky, paradoxical ones. It also tries to explain the whole economy, rather than focusing on particular parts.

Economics is above all a practical academic discipline, and therefore one that can illuminate important public policy problems in unexpected ways.

Take one example: the rise of antibiotic-resistant superbugs. The World Health Organization (WHO) warns that the overuse of antibiotics is causing new strains of bugs to evolve that are resistant to even the most powerful drugs. If this continues, once routine operations will become impossibly risky and we will all be vulnerable to potentially fatal infections.[3]

On the face of it, this sounds like a problem for medicine, not economics. Scientists just need to develop better drugs to trounce the bugs and all will be fine. But they are not doing this. Why? Economics offers several possible reasons. The first thing to remember is that most drugs are researched, tested and brought to market by private companies. Governments can alter the conditions under which this is done, through regulation and the direct funding of scientific research, but when we are talking about private companies we are concerned above all with the operation of a *market*, a set of interactions in which buyers and sellers come together to agree on the price and quantity of a good to be supplied.

At the moment, the market for the development of effective new antibiotics is failing.[4] Developing these drugs costs billions of dollars, and private companies are not sure that they will be able to recoup the costs of doing so because of fears over licensing, piracy and so on. So, it is basically a problem of *incentives*. Companies respond to a range of incentives, depending on the market they are in and how they are governed internally. But prominent among them is the requirement to make a profit for their owners, who provide their capital. This can lead to short-termism: if tackling superbugs is not profitable within their timeframe, they may direct their research money elsewhere.

The problem of incentives is also apparent at the other end: us individuals, who use and, it seems, overuse antibiotics by pressuring doctors to prescribe them for harmless sniffles. This problem is also known as the "tragedy of the commons", and it arises when individuals share a common resource (public health, in this case) but act to maximize their own benefit and, in doing so, end up depleting that resource for everyone. This may happen when people get well but fail to complete the course of antibiotics, which then allows resistance to build up in the bacteria they are supposed to be fighting. Think of public health as a benefit (as well as a responsibility) to all of us in common but to no one in particular. As the costs of bacterial resistance are not directly and immediately experienced by those responsible for it through antibiotics overuse, there is no incentive to use them responsibly.

So, at all levels, incentives operate to exacerbate the problem of too much thoughtless drug consumption leading to drug-resistant bugs, which then becomes a problem that is difficult to tackle. Elinor Ostrom, so far the only woman and the only political scientist to have been awarded the economics Nobel Prize, has suggested that the "tragedy of the commons" could be overcome by assigning property rights to encourage people to use resources responsibly.[5]

Failing that, the incentives system can be altered by governments and other actors, so policy-makers, advised by economists, now advocate subsidizing research into drugs and restricting their use.

Paying attention to incentives, as economists do, can also suggest links between apparently unrelated areas of public policy. Feminists have used the tools of economics to explain why harsh divorce laws not only trap women in bad marriages but may also adversely affect fertility rates. As the penalties for divorce have been reduced in recent years with the liberalization of divorce laws, the costs of possibly entering into a bad marriage have also been reduced. This makes the decision to marry an easier one to take for couples who want children in a marital setting. This has been shown to produce an increase in marital fertility and a decrease in out-of-wedlock fertility. Since children tend to do better when raised by (happily) married couples, the outcome is arguably good for society as well as women liberated from unhappy marriages.[6]

Much of modern economics is therefore, at bottom, the study of how economic "agents" (people, firms, etc.) pursue their wants in an environment in which they face numerous constraints. As Lionel Robbins, one of the fathers of neoclassical economics, has put it: "Economics is the science which studies human behaviour as a relationship between given ends and scarce means which have alternative uses."[7]

Fine, but what *use* is economics? Why is it worth knowing about? Well, it has plenty of uses. It shows policy-makers, those people in charge of our world making important decisions that affect our lives, what happens to economies and societies if you alter them without thinking things through. Why one allocation of resources over another will produce a different outcome. What the range of possibilities is if a country quits the European Union, say, or cancels its international trade deals. Economists are not perfect, and their forecasts should always be taken with a large grain of salt, but we have yet to come up with an unambiguously better way of analysing how what we do in the present helps us prepare for the future.

Economists advise governments, businesses and regulators. Yes, some were also advising the banks that blew up in the financial crisis. But there were many more toiling away in academia and government flashing warning signs and pointing out that inequality and other social ills were getting worse while trying to devise ways to tackle them. And by focusing sometimes on our baser instincts, such as selfishness and short-sightedness, economics makes us think about the design of institutions intended to protect us from opportunism, free-riding and recklessness. Above all, economics is extremely interesting. It addresses big, contentious topics with methods that are relatively objective and so can be used by researchers with different agendas who may nevertheless reach similar conclusions about how the world works.

The problems with economics

Mainstream economics has come in for much flak in recent years, and not just because of the failure to predict the financial crisis. Many people from within the profession are also questioning fundamentally how it is done. John Aldred, a sceptical Green economist, describes most economists as "policy entrepreneurs" who peddle a narrow and simplistic method to serve vested interests and political ends.[8] This seems a bit harsh, but it would be a mistake to ignore where mainstream economics has possibly gone wrong. Complaints about economics generally fall into three categories: that economics is too complicated, with a lot of difficult-looking maths in it; that it is not even very realistic, let alone "scientific", as it claims to be; and that its view of human nature is dour and narrow. There is a little bit of truth in all these jibes. Let us examine each of these criticisms in turn.

1. *Economics is too complicated and mathematical.*

There's not much point in denying this one; economics *is* complicated. But this is to be expected, because its subject matter is the interaction of millions of individuals in local, national and international economies. Being human, most of these individuals have fairly similar motivations. They want to get on in life. But in doing so they will interact with other individuals with different, perhaps conflicting, goals, and they do this in an environment not of their own choosing. Equally, there will be many instances when cooperation will evolve to generate mutually agreeable outcomes. Analysing and describing this is incredibly complicated, and so economists generate economic *models* to explain what is going on. These sacrifice some realism for explanatory power and generalizability.

Dani Rodrik, a Harvard economist, has likened economic models to fables, as they allow us to portray the world in a highly simplified fashion, highlighting a couple of salient features that clarify for us what we want to investigate.[9] Fables also have a moral to them, akin to a policy implication arising from what the model shows us. A model is therefore a useful intellectual device that allows economists to specify their hypotheses and the method by which data should be applied to test these, from which the conclusions will follow. As for the maths content, most models in economics are highly mathematical, as this allows arguments to be stripped down to their basic principles, which helps to clarify for researchers the causal mechanisms and unstated assumptions at work. This is a reasonable justification, although critics of modern economics argue that the complex maths is too often deployed to camouflage the lack of realism in economic modelling.

Another concern is that the growing application of "big data" – vast datasets gleaned from statistical agencies and things such as web use – can obscure the truth and lead economists astray by instilling a false sense of security in what the numbers indicate. The problem with big datasets is that they may show what is happening but be unable to explain why, so they can only ever function as the initial motivation for further investigation. The application of data to knotty problems can be illuminating, but needs to be done with care to avoid controversy.

Possibly the best example of the ability of the ostensibly dry discipline of economics to shock is a revisionist history of slavery in the United States published in 1974 by two economic historians, Robert Fogel and Stanley Engerman. In *Time on the Cross*, Fogel and Engerman used extensive data allied with economic theory to portray slavery in the antebellum South not as economically backward but as a highly efficient capitalist institution.[10] The book had a big impact, as its data suggested conclusions that appeared to explode various myths: that black farmhands were lazy (on average, they were more productive than white agricultural workers); that it destroyed black families (the family unit remained the basic unit of social organization under slavery); and that slavery was inefficient (Fogel and Engerman claimed Southern farms performed better than free farms in the North). Most contentiously, they argued that, although slavery may have been exploitative, it was not automatically abusive, as the master would have viewed his slaves as valuable property. This naturally upset civil rights activists, although it also undermined some of their opponents' arguments that the South had gone to war mainly to defend states' rights rather than preserve what was argued was an already defunct system on the verge of being abandoned.

The authors' reliance on statistics came in for fierce attack, however, with critics assaulting the book's ahistorical assumption that slaves would have been guided by "rational" economic motivation (as opposed to fear of the whip), and even that they were productive farmhands because they had internalized a "Protestant work ethic". To many, *Time on the Cross* is remembered, not particularly fondly, as an interesting but alarming warning about the perils of extrapolating too much from data alone.

2. *Economics is not a science, nor even very realistic.*

Another key criticism of modern economics is that merely devising models and applying mathematical techniques to them does not make economics realistic or scientific. Robert Heilbroner, an economist who tried to emphasize historical and psychological factors in his theories, argues that economics, unlike the natural sciences, enacts few testable hypotheses and relies instead on a "vision" of how the world operates.[11] The mathematical models economists construct to justify and expound this vision bear scant relationship to the real world, Heilbroner argues.

If so, this may have contributed to the blind spot many economists had about the financial crisis (although practical businesspeople, and politicians, were scarcely more prescient). At its worst, the economics profession prefers mathematical elegance to reality and assumes all factors, or variables, can be subsumed into its models. The models used by a lot of banks and many academics in the run-up to the crisis made questionable assumptions about individual rationality and self-correcting markets based on inadequate datasets fuelled, moreover, by blissful ignorance about the previous history of financial and housing crashes, which come around with startling regularity. Matthew Watson, a political economist, is sharply critical of many in the economics profession, who reacted to the crisis not by abandoning their models but by shifting the blame onto other things, such as profligate governments that gave in to pressure groups and spent too much on welfare.[12]

To be fair, though, not all economists thought like this, and plenty of them, such as Hyman Minsky, sounded early warnings about what proved to be the key ingredients in the crisis: bloated housing markets, soaring private debt and inadequate banking regulation.[13] One potential problem identified by Rodrik is that a lot of modern economics has actually moved on from grand theorizing and is now more about problem solving. Models are constructed that illuminate particular challenges in public policy, such as how to sell off mobile telecoms spectra, or boost incomes in developing countries, but there are fewer systematic attempts to integrate these together to explain how the economic world functions holistically. These discrete explanations produce what are called *partial equilibria*, in that they produce a stable solution for one part of the system so long as the rest of the system is held largely constant.

But it is very difficult to integrate these pieces of the jigsaw together to provide what is known as a *general equilibrium* model, which might come in useful for sounding warnings about crises, as the individual models may use incompatible assumptions and putting them together introduces feedback effects that descend into chaos. For example, many general equilibrium models of the economy focused on fundamental inputs into production, such as labour, trade or capital, and so were primarily concerned with broad economic functions, such as service or manufacturing industries. High finance was often peripheral to these models, despite what proved to be the banking industry's pivotal contribution to the financial crisis. This may be compounded by the fact that, in spite of this fragmentation of economics into discrete topics, many of its practitioners still insist upon applying universal laws rather than approaching problems on a case-by-case basis.[14]

A further problem faced by modern economists has been that they have difficulty directly verifying the implications of their models – how they impact, and are impacted by, the behaviour of individuals. Macroeconomists, who try to explain how the economy works as a system, increasingly refer to the "microfoundations" of their models by plugging into these some standard assumptions about how people behave and trying to show how these determine the bigger – that is, macro – picture. A very tidy way of doing this is to assume that people are "rationally selfish". Economists make this assumption not necessarily because they share a cynical or unduly simplistic view of human beings but because their models work best with a small number of consistent and not too unrealistic assumptions. If you introduce too many variables into a model, such as some people behaving in one fashion when x is happening, and others differently when y, *but not z*, is in place, then the model becomes far too complicated.

An example of a macroeconomic theory built on micro-foundations is that of "rational expectations". This holds that people will base their present and future behaviour on experiences about the past, and has been used to critically model responses to attempts by governments to grow the economy through cutting taxes or increasing spending, often done just before elections. The Nobel-Prize-winning Chicago economist Robert Lucas has argued that people would observe that prior attempts to do this had simply produced higher inflation and so they would demand higher wages to replace their lost earning power.[15] Their expectations about the result of expansionary policies would therefore be the cause of the inflation that would nullify the effect of the government stimulus, bringing everyone back to square one.

One concrete result of this theory has been the creation of independent central banks, as governments try to depoliticize monetary policy by "tying their hands" to avoid this wasteful exercise. This is a good example of how a field of economics grounded in an apparently abstract and alien set of assumptions can generate good public policy. Inflation has remained lower since the move to independent central banks from the late 1980s, although these are not the only factors at play here and low inflation is not the be-all and end-all.

3. *Economics has a narrow and unrealistic view of human beings and their behaviour.*

Of all the social sciences, economics is the one that is most oriented towards the individual. To be clear, though, it is interested in individuals in a methodological sense, as a good place from which to start when trying to understand complex social systems, rather than in a normative sense to do with prioritizing individual rights, although this conclusion can certainly follow from much economic analysis.

But the way economics regards individuals has inspired controversy and is in the process of being rethought. As already mentioned, the study of human behaviour requires a number of simplifying assumptions to be made in order for explanatory models to work without being drowned in complexity. This entails a rather stripped-down view of what governs human behaviour. The main assumptions are that people are (a) self-interested (they act to maximize their *utility* and have a clear plan for doing so), (b) rational (consistent) and (c) atomized (they act as if others are just "nature" and do not respond to their actions). Assuming these things about people provides for the theorist the enormous benefit of making them predictable, which keeps unnecessary complexity in check.

The avatar for this bundle of assumptions is known is *Homo economicus*, and he or she forms the basis for much of economists' thinking about how individuals behave. If *Homo economicus* has a name, it would probably be Robinson Crusoe, from the Daniel Defoe novel about a shipwrecked man eking out a solitary living on a desert island. Such is the power of *Homo economicus* that many political scientists use him in their theories, although sociologists, who emphasize the importance of groups over individuals, have a more community-minded mascot: *Homo sociologicus.*

Homo economicus has a set of goals, or preferences, and acts always to maximize his utility function (if a consumer) and profit (if a producer). Interaction with others with different utility functions can be analysed using game theory, a powerful technique that enables the modelling of dynamic, repeated interactions between individuals subject to various assumptions about their goals and strategies. The *Homo economicus* concept obviously trades off a psychologically shallow conception of a human being for conceptual clarity and simplicity, essential for building parsimonious theory that can then be generalized to explain other segments of economic life. But there is just enough of a combination of realism (most of us are self-interested to a certain extent, at certain times) and theoretical generalizability to have made it a powerful intellectual tool in the hands of mathematically minded economists.

Homo economicus crops up in unexpected places. Gary Becker, the Chicago economist whose interest in applying economics to domestic topics inspired the *Freakonomics* authors, Steven Levitt and Stephen Dubner, has even modelled a marriage as the search for a partner in an imperfect market.[16] Becker views the possibility of marriage as being in permanent suspension as both parties remain open to better opportunities. In other words, the higher we rate our own marriageability, the longer we are prepared to hold out for Mr or Mrs Right. Not very romantic, perhaps, but, given that most people end up getting hitched to their social and aesthetic equals, how far from the truth is this?

Yet, for some this all goes a bit too far. Daniel Cohen, a French economist, argues that adoption of the Darwinian, selfish view of human nature embodied in *Homo economicus* not only is unrealistic but has impoverished our understanding of society.[17] Why, Cohen asks, if people are utility maximizers have decades of economic growth since the 1960s not made them happier? Others object that *Homo economicus* is taken as a given, existing somehow outside the economic process and unchanged by it. In reality, points out the American economist John Davis, humans have multiple identities that change over time.[18] The economy does not exist in splendid isolation but has political dimensions. Governments intervene in markets, and human beings have views about non-economic concerns, which they express through voting and participation in civic life. Other social scientists and historians have long recognized this, but some economists seem resistant to embracing a more three-dimensional view of humanity.

So, all in all, economists cannot really win, can they? On the one hand, they are accused of being unrealistic and ignoring how the real world works; on the other, that they can only ever explain segments of reality but not provide useful warnings about systemic failings such as banking crashes. Economists try to explain things from the ground up, by starting with individual people, but run into flak when their conception of these necessarily becomes abstract and their predictions uncertain. This is not a new concern. Economics has been wrestling with these dilemmas since its foundation as a serious topic of study in the eighteenth century. The next section looks at how it has tried to develop a methodology for approaching these problems and a set of explanations for making sense of the ever-changing reality of economic life.

1.2 How economists deal with the individual in the economy

Economics sometimes looks as though it is uncomfortable with individuals by the way it abstracts them into something unrealistic and unrecognizable. In fact, what it is doing is to integrate the study of individual and group behaviour over matters of mutual well-being. Max Weber, the great German sociologist often regarded as the father of modern social sciences, argued that *social* phenomena can be explained by showing how they result from *individual* actions.[19] These actions could, in turn, be analysed through reference to the intentional states that motivate the individual actors. In other words, explanations of the whole ("society" or "the economy") work only in so far as they are regarded as agglomerations of the purposive actions of its parts (individual people).

This is where the complexity escalates, however, as Weber's "methodological individualism" poses dilemmas over whether to focus on the individual actors themselves or to progressively abstract from these a set of more wide-ranging preoccupations to do with the macro-behaviour of larger groups and whole societies. In other words, focus too much on the former (individuals) and you risk having little interesting to say about the whole (individuals coming together as represented by the economy); but shifting attention upwards onto the economy as an overarching system entails making many simplifying assumptions about human behaviour that can produce unrealistically theoretical models that lead us astray. If there is a happy medium in between these two extremes then it is not obvious where it lies. This is the methodological dilemma that generations of economists have wrestled with as they try to offer theories about the economic world capable of marrying realism with explanatory power.

The classical school of political economy

The "classical school" emerged in eighteenth-century Britain as the country was in the early stirrings of profound changes that would eventually produce the Industrial Revolution and parliamentary democracy. It was known as the classical school of "political economy", reflecting the political and psychological interests of its founders, who included David Ricardo, John Stuart Mill and, most famously, Adam Smith.

Smith is often caricatured as championing selfishness and opposing government intervention. These conclusions may follow logically from his famous book, *The Wealth of Nations*, but they are not the whole story, and Smith also emphasized the social side of human beings in his other writings.[20] The classical political economists assumed that individuals were self-interested, but also that they were grouped into social classes – landowners, capitalists and workers – who competed and were unequal but whose collective interests could best be satisfied in a market society.

The market, to Smith and his contemporaries, was a system of private want satisfaction made up of individual private agents. Markets arose as the result of free exchange between profit-seeking individuals (Smith's "invisible hand") and developed according to their own logic and not the plans of any one individual, let alone politicians and governments. By acting selfishly, individuals unleashed the power of competition, which ensured that market agents strove to supply goods and services to the best of their ability and at the lowest price to beat their rivals. Market systems also allowed people to specialize in one or a few activities, which they then could become very good at through practice, lowering the cost and improving the quality of the goods they produced. Yet it was also through cooperation with others, coordinated through the market system, that the finished good incorporating the labour of all was produced. Market collaboration and competition, arising from individuals acting selfishly on their own behalf, therefore made everyone collectively richer.

As Smith put it in this famous quote: "It is not from the benevolence of the butcher, the brewer, or the baker, that we expect our dinner, but from their regard to their own interest. We address ourselves, not to their humanity but to their self-love, and never talk to them of our own necessities but of their advantages."

Two implications emerge from this analysis that have shaped the views of subsequent generations of economists. First is the idea of the self-regulation of the market. Left largely to their own devices, market arrangements would coordinate the activities of many individuals for the benefit of all. Private ends were ultimately the same as the public good. Of course, some individuals might have a difficult time, but this could not be helped. Many classical political economists cleaved to utilitarian philosophy, which argued that individual misfortune did not matter if society as a whole was made better off through letting market forces off the leash. Furthermore, the desire to avoid hardship would itself motivate people to try hard.

The second implication is the primacy of the market over society. Politics is downgraded and the market becomes the main ordering system for society. The state is conceived as an agent acting for private interest rather than with independent responsibility for public ends. In practice, this means that government should keep out of the way. State interference in the market would fail and, along the way, would wreck individual's incentives to work hard and prosper through their own efforts. Left to its own devices, on the other hand, the market would ensure that all of society's resources (its capital stock) would be fully employed, keeping everyone gainfully employed.

Box 1.1 Key terms

- *Utility.* The satisfaction gained from consuming a good or service. Utility generally rises with consumption (if I like apples, I will want more rather than fewer) up to a certain point (when I get stomach ache from eating too many), after which it diminishes.
- *Externalities.* A cost arising from a transaction that is not borne by whoever is making the transaction. These can be negative (my passive smoking from your cigarette habit) or positive (a next-door beehive whose bees pollinate my garden).
- *Public good.* A good supplied to everyone, whose use does not diminish it (e.g. clean air, national defence). A "market failure" may occur when public goods are undersupplied by the market, possibly justifying government action.
- *Rational choice.* The bedrock of neoclassical economics. It assumes that individuals always make prudent decisions in furthering their own interests, given the options available.

Classical political economy was a doctrine of its time. It described a society with a relatively limited number of mostly small firms struggling to build up their businesses and the beginnings of a gradual movement of people from farms to towns and factories. But by the middle of the nineteenth century industrial societies were becoming places of great poverty and inequality with some markets now dominated by big, powerful companies.

Karl Marx wrote from within the tradition of classical political economy but was perhaps capitalism's greatest critic, seeing within it the seeds of its own destruction.[21] He also conceived of individual action and autonomy in a very different way from the earlier political economists. While Smith based his theory on individuals building market society through their selfish but ultimately enlightened actions, Marx reversed the causality and saw individuals as part of larger social classes whose fates were determined by their position within the economy. Politics was, once again, subordinated to economics, being seen as merely the "superstructure" on top of the economic "base", which determined it. One particular class – the industrial working class, or "proletariat" – alone was equipped with agency, however, and its historic destiny was to overthrow capitalism.

Marx was prescient in understanding the incredible dynamism of capitalism and particularly the critical role of technological change. But he underestimated how political and social reforms would lessen the despair of the working classes and defuse their desire for revolution. Moreover, economies organized on Marxist lines have generally failed to prosper, probably because they underestimated the importance of economic incentives in motivating people and relied on an overly powerful state to run the economy.

The neoclassical school of economics

Neoclassical economists agree with classical political economists on a lot of things: the importance of markets and a view of individuals as self-interested, for example. But they refine this in many other important ways, presenting a more three-dimensional analysis of how people place a value on things, and providing economists with a powerful set of tools to analyse economic and social behaviour. In other words, neoclassical economics (henceforth NCE) is a metatheory, providing a set of rules that can be applied to the understanding of economic issues in a wide range of contexts. Such is its power and impact that most contemporary economists – including many who disagree profoundly with each other – could be described as neoclassicists.

NCE also takes individuals as its starting point. In fact, these now take centre stage, as it makes the economy much more about subjective wants and how these are satisfied than the objective organization of society. Although classical political economists believe the value of a good is determined by supply conditions, principally the cost of production, neoclassicists are also interested in how individuals use their time to achieve the ideal balance of consumption of goods and leisure – demand as following from supply conditions.

This opened the door to the technique of marginal analysis developed by Léon Walras, as much of the subject of economics began to revolve around finding the point at which the desire of consumers to consume intersected with the willingness of producers to produce.[22] Almost anyone who has ever glanced at an economics textbook will recognize the downward-sloping demand curve: as the price of something rises, we will want less of it. The supply curve, on the other hand, slopes upwards: when the price goes up, more will be supplied. At a certain point these curves coincide and we have the market price at which a given quantity of the good will be provided.

Because of the new focus on demand, NCE needed to develop a much more elaborate account of individual's desires and motivations that went beyond the classical focus on basic self-interest. A more precise conception of the individual was therefore devised, with individuals now viewed as atomized but rational consumers who sought to maximize their advantage (or "utility", as economists often call it) through various strategies. We have already encountered this individual: *Homo economicus.*

Moreover, in a world of finite resources there were increasingly obvious restraints on individuals' ability to do this. People were constantly faced with choices: about what to buy and forgo; how to divide their time between work and leisure; and so on. Individuals had to keep on making decisions regarding their utility maximization. This boiled down to the need to prioritize their wants and desires. From this economists derive a "preference ordering", which is the sequence in which individuals pursue their goals and the respective utilities they attach to these.

To explain all this NCE economists developed the concept of "rational choice". This is a set of assumptions underpinning a system of decision-making based on preference ordering, and, in principle, we can apply the rational choice method to almost any realm of everyday experience (thereby, to the alarm of some, making almost everything potentially about markets). Rational choice also provides a conception of individual choice that can be applied to group decisions, and this allows economists to begin to explain the workings of the entire economy, starting with individual preferences. As with classical political economy, the mechanism making this possible is the market. Markets allow unique prices to be set arising out of the voluntary actions of individuals, ensuring that the random strategies of producers and consumers coincide.

One of the attractions of this approach is that it, arguably, has a strong moral and ethical component: who could possibly object to a system that takes individual aspirations as its starting point? Even better, the Italian economist Vilfredo Pareto showed how individual preferences, reflected in the price mechanism, provided objective criteria for judging the efficiency of a particular income distribution.[23] Left to its own devices, the market would get us eventually to an equilibrium that is "Pareto-optimal", in the sense that any other allocation of goods and services would leave someone worse off and should be rejected. In other words, socially optimal outcomes could arise, via the market, of course, from individual actions. Collective welfare was therefore identified powerfully with individual choice, a clear argument for markets that rested on individualistic foundations.

Rethinking NCE: market failures, institutions, behaviourism
and political economy

NCE has proved to be very adaptable. Most economists begin their training with a grounding in it and many of its original tenets are still commonly accepted by economists today. But the theory has also evolved considerably as parts of it have come under scrutiny. Its inability to fully rebut some criticisms, in large part to do with the assumptions it makes about individual behaviour and motivations, has also led to something of a counter-revolution.

Let us start with some of the criticisms of NCE that it has managed to incorporate. In the 1920s some economists began to question assumptions about the supremacy of markets. The Cambridge economist Arthur Pigou identified a number of instances in which they failed to operate properly.[24] So-called "market failures" could arise over the undersupply of what are known as "public goods". These are things that are useful for society at large (such as clean air, national defence or industrial training) but not necessarily in the interests of anyone in particular to provide (people being selfish, remember).

Public goods have several characteristics, including "non-rivalry" (my breathing clean air does not detract from you doing so as well) and "non-excludability" (if the air is clean, I cannot stop you enjoying it).[25] These features entail a potential "free-rider problem", whereby the fact that the good may be enjoyed by those who did not contribute to its creation makes it hard to levy the charges needed to pay for it. Another species of market failures is known as "externalities", which arise because some economic activities cannot be priced properly by the market, leading to either their *over*production (a negative externality, such as pollution) or *under*production (a positive externality, such as basic scientific research that does not lead directly to a commercializable invention). Market failures may provide a rationale for governments to intervene in the market to rescue us from our selfishness and short-sightedness, for example by subsidizing health insurance and taxing pollution.

Later on, other economists such as George Akerlof[26] and Joseph Stiglitz[27] have pointed to information problems inherent in most transactions that undermine markets. Markets work best when everyone has access to the same information. But information is generally available asymmetrically, in that one side – buyer or seller – usually knows more than the other. For example, used car dealers will know more about the actual state of the vehicle they are selling than the buyer and will inflate the price beyond what the car is worth. Again, acting perfectly rationally, people buying life insurance may know more about their own health (their 40-a-day cigarette habit, for example) than they are prepared to reveal. In these circumstances markets may cease to work properly: people may shun used car dealers, despite the bargains probably to be had there; sick people may go without health insurance. These failures present a possible justification for government intervention in the market (Chapters 2, on education, 4, on healthcare, and 8, on welfare, discuss a number of government responses to market failures and information problems in these areas).

But the most sustained and far-reaching critiques of NCE have been directed towards its assumptions about individuals being atomized, rationally self-interested beings. These attacks began with economists of the Austrian school, associated particularly with Friedrich von Hayek. Hayek agreed that markets created order through the price mechanism.[28] Far from this being the result of individuals rationally following their self-interest, however, it arose largely through a spontaneous order created by the diverse but often short-sighted strategies of individuals responding to a wide range of motivations, mediated through the institution of the market.

Hayek's great rival, the Cambridge economist John Maynard Keynes, also took issue with the idea of self-ordering markets as well as assumptions of rationality in individuals.[29] Keynes largely invented the field of macroeconomics (the idea of looking at the economy as an entire national or international system) but grounded this partly in his conception of investors and businesspeople as being guided by emphatically non-rational "animal spirits" in their actions. Keynes warned that these investors were prone to bouts of excessive fear or optimism that could interrupt the flow of funds into the economy, causing booms and busts (Chapter 5, on finance, examines this in more detail).

On the other hand, Keynes also rejected the idea, implicit in the neoclassical approach, that the whole economy was, analytically, the sum of its parts. This mistake led in the 1930s (and again, arguably, following the financial and Eurozone crises of 2008–10) to policy prescriptions urging governments to "live within their means" just like any household. Keynes saw that what was rational individually was collectively disastrous. One person's spending was another's income, so if everyone decided to be frugal at the same time the economy would collapse through lack of demand for the goods and services that are its lifeblood (the real-world impact of a lack of demand on unemployment is explored in Chapter 3, on work).

There were also economists who, while generally pro-market, rejected the neoclassical emphasis on individuals and their tastes and looked elsewhere for the foundations of economic organization. Joseph Schumpeter, Vienna-born but not identified with the Austrian school per se, emphasized the crucial role of entrepreneurs in driving wealth creation.[30] These dynamic, risk-taking individuals propelled economic development through a process of "creative destruction", whereby dynamic new firms drove out stale, old ones. Although entrepreneurs were undoubtedly self-interested they were driven by a range of other motivations as well, thought Schumpeter (Chapter 5, on education, has more to say about the importance of science and innovation to the modern economy).

Another approach, known as transaction cost economics, views the neoclassical ideal of market exchange between utility-maximizing individuals as missing the point about how the economy really functions. The real action takes place inside and between organizations, such as firms, which exist to manage the "friction" arising from economic activity. Ronald Coase, its founder, famously derided the neoclassical view of markets as "cavemen exchanging nuts and berries on the edge of the forest", reflecting his view that markets are not always flat, decentralized venues for exchange but can also be characterized by hierarchies of transactions taking place inside firms.[31] Coase's insight has led economists to regard firms as important organizations in their own right, rather than as the passive agents of markets, focusing attention in turn on how individuals (owners, managers, workers) operating within them behave in the face of incentives and constraints.

Others, such as the economic sociologist Thorstein Veblen, stressed that individuals, even if ostensibly rational and self-interested, nevertheless operate within the confines of institutions – rules and customs governing behaviour.[32] Studying institutions can help explain a wide range of things in economics, from why firms exist instead of there just being one big market to why some countries grow more rapidly than others.

Behave yourself

But it is possibly with "behaviourist" economics that the attack on individual rationality has really begun to hit home. Behaviourism builds a model of the economy from the ground up through its concern with how individuals actually behave. This is reflected in its methodology, which is inductive (in that it begins with empirical evidence and builds theory from the observable implications of this), as opposed to much of the rest of economics, which uses deductive methods (starting with a set of theoretical axioms and then seeking to apply these to real-world problems).[33]

Behaviourists are therefore at liberty to conduct experiments, rather than trawling through data or making theoretical assumptions and searching for ways to prove these, and this has opened up the field to other experts, including psychologists, to peer into people's minds to see how economic decisions are actually made. The result has been to challenge many of the assumptions of NCE about rational, self-interested individuals, and behavioural economics has shot to greater prominence since the financial crisis as it offers a wealth of clues as to why individual market traders, house buyers and consumers acted like lemmings in piling up so much debt.

Several important insights result. One is the concept of "bounded rationality", associated with the economist Herbert Simon.[34] As the term implies, people try to be rational, but the sheer complexity of the world limits their horizons and so they fall back on established routines and social conventions. NCE tends to operate on the assumption that individuals' preferences and the options available to them are both given – that is, they know what they want and how to get it. But we may not know what we want until we see it, and new options may be thrown up by the decision-making process itself (the important insights behavioural economics has for healthcare, retailing and welfare are explored further in Chapters 4, 7 and 8).

Other human motivations besides self-interest may also therefore be important: things such as loyalty, reciprocity and altruism. The Israeli psychologists Daniel Kahneman and the late Amos Tversky take this further by exploring some of the ways in which people who might generally consider themselves to be rational are in fact conditioned to behave instinctively and therefore often irrationally.[35] For example, they may be overconfident about their abilities, or what the future holds for them. They could be loss-averse, in that they value an object more when giving it up than when acquiring it, and prone to overreacting to new information and underreacting to existing information. Some economists have taken these insights still further by teaming up with neuroscientists to peer into the human brain to see what actually takes place there when we absorb information and make decisions. The insights generated by these kinds of investigations could be very useful in indicating to policy-makers the situations when people might behave rationally, and when they might follow their own instincts or go with the herd, as happens in property and stock market booms.

Box 1.2 Famous behaviourist experiments

The new focus on psychology has made economists more open to the idea of using experiments to develop their theories. These have tended to undermine the view of people as rational, sovereign consumers, although economists do not always agree on the extent of this or why. One such experiment, described in the *Freakonomics* book, concerned an Israeli daycare centre where staff had devised a system of fines to discourage parents from picking up their children late. They assumed that the cost of the fine would deter this and staff would get to leave work on time. But the opposite happened, and more parents picked up their kids late. The researchers concluded that some parents may have thought that the fines made it seem acceptable to flout the rules on pick-up times. This experiment underlines that human interactions are not merely transactions but usually have a social element to them. The financial incentive did not augment the moral imperative to pick up the kids on time – it replaced it – with the result that some parents thought they could "buy" extra time at the daycare centre when it suited their schedule. In another experiment, cited in Thaler and Sunstein's book *Nudge*, one-half of a group of students were given nice mugs and the other, mugless, half were asked to state how much they would pay their colleagues to buy them. On average (and this experiment has been repeated many times), those with the mugs valued them twice as much as those without. What this shows is that people are loss-averse, in that giving something up is deemed twice as bad as never having had it in the first place. If so, then calculating an individual's utility function is more complex than NCE allows.

But the key point about behavioural economics and its offshoots is really that it throws a big spanner into the works in terms of calculating individuals' utility functions, which will not necessarily stem objectively from their preference ordering, as the neoclassicists suppose. This casts further doubt on the neoclassical reliance on markets as the main ordering principle of the economy, as these may be dysfunctional. The economics journalist John Cassidy points out that irrational behaviour in situations in which individuals are presumed to behave rationally, such as financial markets, can explain a number of recent economic calamities, including the dot-com boom of 1999 as well as the financial crisis.[36]

One of the real beauties of behavioural economics, however, is that it can offer a wealth of simple, reality-based policy suggestions. Indeed, it has spawned its own sub-school of public policy, with "nudge" units springing up in many governments in honour of one of the first books to popularize the field, by Richard Thaler and Cass Sunstein.[37] Nudge economists encourage policy-makers to work with people's hidden biases in order to get them to do sensible but difficult or counter-intuitive things, such as exploiting people's lethargy by getting employers to auto-enroll workers in pension schemes on the assumption that even those who did not really want to save for a pension will opt to stick with them.

Behaviourist economics sounds like a breath of fresh air, but does it take individualism too far? One criticism is that it is possibly just a little *too* micro. So it is very difficult to extend behaviourism to build a model of the whole economy, which would be very useful. Some critics of nudge economists are also uncomfortable about the idea of manipulating people into doing what politicians want.

What about politics? The return of political economy

Like much of the micro-scale, public-policy-oriented economics of today, behaviourism also has little to say about the relationship between markets and society. This is a core concern of many political economists who are intent on investigating the impact of capitalism on democracy by analysing how societies, governments and institutions interact with the market. Modern political economists in many ways return the study of the economy to the days of Smith and Mill through their interest in how societies and economies are organized holistically around the needs of each other, rather than the former being dominated by the latter. Many are quite critical of the assumptions and implications of neoclassical – and also some heterodox – economics.

In particular, they take issue with the idea of the market as a conceptual abstraction and something assumed to be the natural order of things. This tends to ignore the fact that markets, even in the "free-market" United States, are in fact heavily regulated and therefore subject to political intervention. Ben Clift, for example, maintains that capitalism is a dynamic social order, not a static equilibrium, and is continually being reinvented through political interference.[38]

But who gets to determine this? Economists often ignore issues of power within the economy. Susan Strange, another political economist, argues that the rules of the global economy are shaped by the most powerful actors – the richest countries and larger firms – for their own benefit.[39] Other political economists are less pessimistic and point out that domestic politics and social groups shape the organization of the economy in numerous ways. This helps explains why countries such as Sweden still have more generous welfare states and less inequality than the United Kingdom and the United States, even though they operate in the same global market. Political economy theories can also shed light on why people may be more powerful when acting in groups (for example, in trade unions, or other interest organizations) than as sovereign consumers, as NCE suggests.[40]

Political economists therefore bring a different intellectual toolbox to the study of the modern economy – one based on concepts of power, institutional structure and legitimacy – in contrast to the methodological individualism of NCE. It is perhaps not surprising, therefore, that they often reach different conclusions. These debates will be explored further in the chapters to come.

Conclusion: what we have learnt

This introductory chapter has tried to spell out why the discipline of economics, for all its flaws, is one worth studying and taking seriously. The body of knowledge accumulated over at least two and a half centuries of economic thought, together with the advanced methodologies developed, make for a powerful set of tools for analysing economic life. Indeed, observing how economists have wrestled with the task of integrating the study of individual behaviour into a macro theory of the whole surely reveals the flexibility of the discipline in dealing with different challenges. Responding to the excesses of rational choice, economics is in some ways returning to the concerns of the political economists of the eighteenth century, in its renewed interest in individual psychology and concern with society as a whole.

The major objections to the current discipline examined in the chapter – that it is too difficult, too abstract and takes an unrealistic view of human nature – have, I hope, been partly – although probably not completely – answered. As economists slowly absorb the lessons of the financial crisis and its aftermath, they will hopefully continue to refine their methods, and perhaps do a better job of explaining their conclusions.

Notes

1. Speech to the ECB central banking conference, Frankfurt, 18 November 2010.
2. For a good and accessible guide to the emerging debate among economists, see D. Coyle (ed.), *What's the Use of Economics? Teaching the Dismal Science after the Financial Crisis* (London: London Publishing Partnership, 2010).
3. If this sounds alarmist, take a look at some WHO publications on this, starting with World Health Organization, *Global Action Plan on Antimicrobial Resistance* (Geneva: WHO Press, 2015), available at www.who.int/antimicrobial-resistance/publications/global-action-plan/en (accessed 14 March 2017).
4. A. Alanis, "Resistance to antibiotics: are we in the post-antibiotics era?", *Archives of Medical Research* 36:6 (2005), 697–705.
5. E. Ostrom, *Governing the Commons: The Evolution of Institutions for Collective Action* (Cambridge: Cambridge University Press, 1990).
6. A. Alesina & P. Giuliano, "Divorce, fertility and the shot gun marriage", Working Paper no. 12375 (Cambridge, MA: National Bureau of Economic Research [NBER], 2006).

7. L. Robbins, *An Essay on the Nature and Significance of Economic Science* (Auburn, AL: Ludwig von Mises Institute, 1932).
8. J. Aldred, *The Skeptical Economist: Revealing the Ethics inside Economics* (Abingdon, UK: Earthscan, 2009).
9. D. Rodrik, *Economics Rules: The Rights and Wrongs of the Dismal Science* (Oxford: Oxford University Press, 2015).
10. R. Fogel & S. Engerman, *Time on the Cross: The Economics of Negro Slavery* (New York: Norton, 1974).
11. R. Heilbroner, *Worldly Philosophers: The Lives, Times and Ideas of the Great Economic Thinkers* (London: Penguin Books, 2000).
12. M. Watson, *Uneconomic Economics and the Crisis of the Model World* (Basingstoke, UK: Palgrave Pivot, 2014).
13. H. Minsky, *Stabilizing an Unstable Economy* (New York: McGraw-Hill, 2008).
14. J. Madrick, *Seven Bad Ideas: How Mainstream Economists Have Damaged America and the World* (London: Vintage Books, 2015).
15. R. Lucas, "Expectations and the neutrality of money", *Journal of Economic Theory* 4:2 (1972), 103–24.
16. G. Becker, "A theory of marriage", in T. W. Schultz (ed.), *The Economics of the Family: Marriage, Children and Human Capital*, 299–344 (Chicago: University of Chicago Press, 1974).
17. D. Cohen, *Homo Economicus: The (Lost) Prophet of Modern Times* (Cambridge: Polity Press, 2014).
18. J. Davis, *The Theory of the Individual in Economics: Identity and Value* (Abingdon, UK: Routledge, 2003).
19. M. Weber, *Economy and Society* [1922], 2 vols, G. Roth & C. Wittich (eds) (Berkeley, CA: University of California Press, 2013).
20. A. Smith, *The Wealth of Nations* (London: Strahan and Cadell, 1776); and A. Smith, *The Theory of Moral Sentiments* (London: Millar, 1759).
21. A fine introduction to Marx's life and works is G. Steadman-Jones, *Karl Marx: Greatness and Illusion* (London: Penguin Books, 2016).
22. L. Walras, *Elements of Pure Economics* [1877] (Abingdon, UK: Routledge, 2010).
23. V. Pareto, *Manual of Political Economy* [1927], A. Schwier & A. Page (eds) (New York: Augustus M. Kelley, 1977).
24. A. Pigou, *The Economics of Welfare* [1920], 2 vols (New York: Cosimo Classics, 2006).
25. P. Samuelson, "The pure theory of public expenditure", *Review of Economics and Statistics* 36:4 (1954), 387–9.
26. G. Akerlof, "The market for lemons: quality, uncertainty and the market mechanism", *Quarterly Journal of Economics* 84:3 (1970), 488–500.
27. J. Stiglitz, "The contribution of the economics of information to twentieth-century economics", *Quarterly Journal of Economics* 115:4 (2000), 1441–78.
28. F. Hayek, *Individualism and the Economic Order* (Chicago: University of Chicago Press, 1948).
29. J. M. Keynes, *The General Theory of Employment, Interest and Money* [1936] (Whitefish, MT: Kessinger Publishing, 2010).
30. J. Schumpeter, *History of Economic Analysis* [1954] (Oxford: Oxford University Press, 1996).
31. R. Coase, "The nature of the firm", *Economica* 4:16 (1937), 386–405.
32. T. Veblen, *The Theory of the Leisure Class* (New York: Modern Library, 1934).
33. For a good survey of behaviourist and other heterodox economic approaches, see D. Coyle, *The Soulful Science: What Economists Do and Why It Matters* (Princeton, NJ: Princeton University Press, 2007).
34. H. Simon, "Organization and markets", *Journal of Economic Perspectives* 5:2 (1991), 25–44.
35. D. Kahneman, *Thinking, Fast and Slow* (New York: Farrar, Straus & Giroux, 2011).

36. J. Cassidy, *How Markets Fail: The Logic of Economic Calamities* (London: Allen Lane, 2009).
37. R. Thaler & C. Sunstein, *Nudge: Improving Decisions about Health, Wealth and Happiness* (London: Penguin Books, 2009).
38. B. Clift, *Comparative Political Economy: States, Markets and Global Capitalism* (Basingstoke, UK: Palgrave Macmillan, 2014).
39. S. Strange, *States and Markets*, 2nd edn (London: Continuum, 1998).
40. M. Olson, *The Rise and Decline of Nations: Economic Growth, Stagflation, and Social Rigidities* (New Haven, CT: Yale University Press, 1982).

2

KNOWLEDGE IS POWER: EDUCATION AND TRAINING

Nothing is more purifying on earth than wisdom.
bhagavad gita

Key questions

- What is human capital, and why are people's education levels linked closely to their performance at work?
- Why is a nation's prosperity so closely related to how well educated and skilled its workers are?
- Are narrow, specialized skills better than general ones, and how can we ensure these fit with people's aspirations and the needs of employers?
- Should those who benefit most from higher education pay for it themselves?

Summary

It is a fact that better-educated societies tend to be richer and happier. Highly skilled and educated workers are simply more productive and efficient, benefiting the economy and society in general, as well as leading more fulfilling and financially rewarding careers themselves. Yet there can still be problems supplying the right kinds of skills, and this presents a dilemma for governments and employers. Education and training are expensive, so who should pay for it: the individuals who stand to directly benefit from it, their employers, or society at large? Furthermore, technological change is profoundly affecting the world of work and putting a premium on workforces with ever more specialized skills. Governments are increasingly realizing the importance of research and innovation in universities and encouraging entrepreneurship, so should learning and education be geared towards the interests and needs of employers?

Main topics and theories covered

The division of labour and the gains from specialization; skills and productivity; the skills of the future; the economics of innovation.

2.1 The economics of education

Philosophers and poets have long extolled the value of learning. Now economists are getting in on the act, pointing to the substantial material benefits that stem from having a good education system and getting the right number of people through it. And, for many parents in developed countries, a good schooling for their children, followed hopefully by university, has become something of an obsession. Likewise, governments nervously eye league tables of educational attainment and steal policies from countries at the top. Yet education is expensive, time-consuming and difficult to get right. We have all probably been served enough coffee by recent graduates in shops and cafes to know that its benefits are long-term and uncertain. So why is education so important?

The short answer, backed by copious research across many countries,[1] is that it almost always materially benefits the individuals who undergo it as well as the societies they live in. Stripping out the effects of inherited wealth, the richest people in Western countries tend also to be the best educated. National and local economies blessed with highly trained workforces tend to grow more rapidly and find it easier to shift into higher-value industries. In almost all cases this more than justifies – sometimes by a significant multiple – the cost of the education to either the individual concerned or the society that bears some or all of the cost of it. Moreover, there are also plenty of intangible, non-economic, benefits to education that contribute to individual and national well-being. Well-educated people are generally healthier than the norm and levels of education are strongly correlated with good things such as civic engagement and political stability.[2] They vote more, volunteer more and commit less crime, although they are not necessarily happier.

This is all very well, of course, but individuals face complex choices about how much education to undergo. While undertaking a certain level of basic education is a legal requirement (most Organisation for Economic Co-operation and Development [OECD] countries mandate full-time schooling up to the age of at least 16), many people opt to top this up with additional years in the classroom, and probably university or an apprenticeship as well. They may have both mate-rial and non-material motives in mind. Accordingly, economics has tended to view education simultaneously as an investment (in our future productive capa-bilities) and as something that we consume (placing more emphasis on current, personal enjoyment of education).[3] We each attach utilities to our educational goals: the net value (taking account of the costs involved in getting educated) we place on improved earning potential; or the personal satisfaction and cultural kudos we get from being able to quote Lorca or read ancient Greek.

It is, nevertheless, increasingly economic imperatives – particularly the impact of changing technologies generating demand for new skills – that drive education policy. Governments have long associated education and technical know-how with prosperity and security. When Russia launched Sputnik, the world's first satellite, at the height of the Cold War in 1957, the US govern-ment reacted by passing the National Defense Education Act, committing it to a massive increase in education and science spending. Now, in a similar vein, intensifying global economic competition is encouraging governments to nur-ture domestic drivers of competitiveness. Education and research are viewed as a key component of this, and policy-makers increasingly talk of the "knowledge economy", or the "learning society". Better comparative statistics showcasing the countries with the best educational results provide convenient role models for less successful nations to copy policies from. The learning society therefore encourages all sections of economy and society to respond to the challenge. Individuals are encouraged to get as much education as they can manage or afford. Firms are urged to enhance the knowledge base of their businesses to stay ahead of low-cost competition. Governments strive to invest in their countries' educational facilities and ensure that as many people as possible are in education at any one time.

So, education and economics obviously go together. But do knowledge and learning boil down merely to material prosperity, or are other things important here? This chapter examines these dilemmas facing individuals at each stage of the education system, from schools to universities and technical training. It suggests ways to approach the question of what education is for, and looks at how govern-ments try to reconcile the individual and collective costs and benefits of learning.

Educate to accumulate

Education seems to be a no-brainer for all concerned. But in considering its eco-nomic, let alone cultural, value we still need to weigh up a number of factors. The critical question is probably: how much is the right amount of education? Most observers agree that, in complex modern societies with labour markets

demanding increasingly sophisticated workers, a certain minimum level of schooling is required even for quite basic, manual jobs. Moreover, for people to play their
part in society as active citizens, or simply to be able to vote, or read and pay their
own gas bill, basic numeracy and literacy are needed. Historically, the drive for
mass education (i.e. beyond that of a ruling elite) has always been suffused with
instrumentalist rationales such as these. When educational opportunities were
expanded for ordinary people in the United States and many European countries
in the late nineteenth century and early twentieth, it was to meet the needs of
industry for skilled labour. The 1950s and 1960s were marked by further mass
expansion that was motivated by more egalitarian concerns: the desire to further
equality of opportunity and social mobility. Current talk of the "knowledge economy" in the twenty-first century has again underlined the link between learning
and economic success, however.

Nevertheless, education is costly to provide and acquire, and therefore involves
trade-offs. Individuals considering investing their time and maybe money in extra
education (in other words, staying on at school or college beyond the statutory
minimum) will need to weigh up the "opportunity cost" represented by the earnings they will forgo while at college, as well as potentially the actual cost of fees and
living expenses, set against the improved earnings they can realistically expect to
accrue over their lifetimes from gaining the extra qualifications. Governments
also need to think carefully about the resources they devote to education and
training, as this is money that is thereby unavailable for other purposes (including leaving it with taxpayers). The sums involved are far from trivial. The OECD
estimates that rich countries spend around 5.2 per cent of their annual gross
domestic product (GDP) on it.[4] Education is typically the third or fourth biggest
item of public spending, behind the social security and health budgets.

Getting the economics of education right is therefore critically important.
And there is a further dilemma: how do we allocate, collectively and individually,
the costs of getting educated? Governments promoting the learning society to
individuals commonly emphasize the personal material benefits of staying on at
school or going to college. But, if most of these accrue to individuals, as governments suggest, then should they not bear the costs rather than taxpayers? And,
if this is the case, then why are governments even making the effort to encourage
people to get educated? Should this not be in their own best interests anyway?
To provide some answers, let us look at what economics has to say.

Education for work rather than play: human capital theory

The skills and knowledge of human beings have always been seen as an important part of the roster of advantages that successful nations possess.[5] Adam

Smith argued that the division of labour in market society allows individuals scope to develop their talents to the full as economic specialization ensures these will be put to good use. The standard NCE explanation of education comes from human capital theory (HCT), developed by the Chicago economist Gary Becker, which takes a highly instrumental view of education and training.[6] The purpose of these in HCT is to provide future workers with skills that will be useful to them in the labour market. A higher level of skills raises people's productivity, which in turn increases the profitability of the firm they work for, meaning that they can command a higher wage – a win-win situation for both parties. Investing in skills is therefore similar to investing in new capital equipment, except that the skill cannot be sold or transferred to another person. Moreover, high skills produce "network effects" that benefit others nearby; by learning to operate my company's computer system properly I boost the productivity of my colleagues as well as my own.

Box 2.1 Key terms

- *Human capital.* The skills and knowledge acquired by individuals, which help to determine their productivity and can be boosted by training.
- *Network effects.* When one user of a good has an effect (normally positive) on the value of that product to other users.
- *Positional good.* A good whose value depends on its scarcity and exclusivity.

HCT sees people as rational utility maximizers; they will calculate in their own minds whether the investment of time, effort and money into acquiring these skills is worth it in terms of extra earnings and job satisfaction. HCT can seem coldly materialistic to those who value learning for its own sake but there are probably many situations that approximate to this. Suppose that you are a recent graduate working for a financial services company in an already well-paid job. But you want to get ahead and are considering taking study leave to pursue either a specialist one-year master's degree in finance or a two year master's in business administration, a more general business degree possessed by a lot of senior executives. These are very expensive courses in terms of fees as well as time off from paid employment. HCT suggests you will invest in your education, and if necessary borrow to finance it, up to the point at which you estimate that the rate of return to the education exceeds the cost.

Note the assumptions here. First, that you are well informed about the relative costs and benefits of either degree compared with doing neither. This implies that you have already formed realistic expectations about your career path. Of course, highly paid finance professionals would probably have a good idea about all this, and there are numerous league tables of business and finance schools with detailed information about graduate salaries and employment, so this is probably OK. The second assumption is that you are able to borrow against future earnings to finance the next step of your education. Again, a good MBA or MSc will probably pay for itself in the end despite the huge expense, and banks, knowing this, will be happy to lend to you.

But what about a kid from a poor background with only basic schooling trying to choose from among a range of apprenticeships? Can she make an equally informed choice about her future prospects? The economics of information suggest she would be less likely to make a good decision about this as the choices are less clear-cut. Notions of bounded rationality and bounded willpower drawn from behavioural economics also suggest she is unlikely to be in a position to make the best decision, or summon the fortitude to act upon it. And would financial markets be willing to underwrite a loan to her to do this? With a more uncertain but probably less lucrative future ahead of her, and less information available about her ability to thrive in the labour market, possibly not. But we need apprentices in industry as well as finance people – right? In this case, the government may have to take a view on the desirability of our school leaver doing this and maybe step in to help by co-funding her. "Market failures", which are what happens when some of the assumptions of NCE break down, may thereby provide an important rationale for state involvement in the education system at all stages.

And there is a third assumption underlying HCT of relevance to job-seekers. It is that getting more education endows you with a genuine, and not relative, advantage over other people in the labour market. Education can be viewed as a "positional" good that may confer benefits to a person only if she possesses more of it than others. This is known as the "screening hypothesis", because it suggests that employers "screen" candidates by educational background, as it is an easy way to differentiate between people of differing aptitude who appear equivalent in other ways.[7] The assumption is that it is the effort and commitment to get a higher qualification that sets the candidate apart, not any improvement to her human capital per se. So, if everyone in my firm has a bachelor's degree, then I may need to get a master's to stand out from the crowd and secure promotion, prompting others to follow suit. And so it goes on, until everyone has an MSc and we are all of equal status again.

Essentially, the screening hypothesis is sceptical that education, beyond the minimum needed to perform the job adequately, really adds much to an individual's productivity. It infers that education confers private benefits (I get the promotion as a reward for my costly efforts to stand out from the crowd), but not necessarily social benefits (my extra education has not necessarily made me more productive and might even be a waste of money). This has very different implications from HCT, which claims both private and public benefits to education and training. The screening hypothesis casts doubt on the wisdom of politicians' ceaseless efforts to improve education and suggests that individuals should bear the cost of education as they corner most of the benefits.

HCT has also been attacked by critics uncomfortable with its narrow focus on individual economic returns. Marxists allege that it ignores class and distributional issues, despite the labour market's central role in reinforcing and perpetuating these. Schooling and training systems that are already stratified by class simply prepare people for an unequal economic system.[8] Amartya Sen, an Indian-born Nobel laureate, criticizes HCT for treating individuals solely as a productive resource. Sen argues that utility, or well-being, is not derived solely from income but results from the intersection between the things we obtain from resources and the capabilities that lie in between – things that could be put to use to achieve social as well as economic goals.[9]

HCT is certainly not the whole story, but it does underline the important economic rationales for education, notably the idea that it is undertaken to make us richer and improve our social status. The next section examines the extent to which this is actually the case.

2.2 Education and growth: smarter and richer?

Let us move from the individual level to that of society as a whole in order to begin answering questions about how much to invest in education. In other words, how can we estimate its economic value? One way to do this is to turn to the macro-picture. Fortunately, there is ample evidence that education is good for the economy overall as well as the individuals who acquire a lot of it. Let us consider the link in more detail and think about the implications.

Surprisingly, economics has only relatively recently begun to include education in its models of how economies grow. The standard neoclassical "exogenous" growth model developed in the 1950s by Robert Solow saw the output of the economy as determined mainly by its capital, labour and technological inputs.[10] Although the quality of the labour force might vary according to its educational level, technology was usually the driving force in these models and was outside the control of governments. Paul Romer's "endogenous" growth model in the 1980s subsequently brought technology inside the model and under the influence of policy-makers.[11] The growth rate therefore became something that could be enhanced through better education, increasing the economy's ability to innovate through new ideas and technologies. Romer underlines the importance of good policy by relating individuals' decisions about how much to invest

Table 2.1 2015 ranking of countries in PISA scores for science

1	Singapore
2	Japan
3	Estonia
4	Finland
5	Canada
6	Vietnam
7	China
8	South Korea
9	New Zealand
10	Slovenia
11	Australia
12	United Kingdom
13	Germany
14	Netherlands
15	Switzerland
~	~
20	United States

Source: OECD PISA scores, 2015.

to acquire knowledge to their social context. People stuck in an underdeveloped society in which the returns to being educated were low would rationally under-invest in education. Countries as a result could get caught in a low-level educa-tion trap, and it might fall to their governments to pull them out of it by investing in technology that required higher-skilled people to operate it.

Most economists now note a strong connection between levels of educational attainment and economic growth. Proving and elucidating this connection is not straightforward, however. Countries start from different places, and there are problems in defining education and measuring its quality. There may also be problems of causality; perhaps rich countries choose to spend more on educa-tion because their citizens demand it, but this investment is not the reason why they are rich.

Some major recent studies can now account for these factors, and they quan-tify a strong link between growth rates and educational test scores. These kinds of studies generally cross-reference country data on GDP per head with inter-national comparisons of cognitive skills to see if they are correlated. The main dataset is the OECD's PISA (Programme for International Student Assessment) scores, which compare attainment in reading, mathematics and sciences in most countries (see Table 2.1).[12] The relationship is strong and positive, in that coun-tries with high PISA scores tend to be richer and/or faster-growing, with clear indications that the former causes the latter.

In fact, one influential estimate suggests that a 47 point improvement on the PISA maths score, which was the average difference between top performers

Sweden and Japan in 2000, or between the average Greek student and the OECD average score, would add one whole percentage point to a country's GDP growth rate – a sizeable difference given that most advanced countries' growth rates are 1 to 2 per cent a year if they are lucky.[13] The OECD calculated in 2010 that bringing the PISA scores of all countries up to the level of Finland, that year's top performer, would boost the world economy by a staggering $250 trillion.[14] Rates of return on better education seem to be particularly strong for low-income countries, for those on lower levels of schooling and for women, indicating that the benefits are particularly striking if starting from a low base.

So, test performance is strongly correlated with economic success. Countries that neglect their human capital clearly do so at their peril. The question then is: how to maximize student attainment? Among the first things to note is that money does not appear to buy quality, and the quality of education should not be confused with paper qualifications. For example, the United States spends a lot on education and a large share of its population has degrees, but records only middling PISA scores. Finland, which regularly tops the PISA table, spends only around the OECD average.

Nevertheless, the raw PISA scores merely provide us with a ranking and do not settle dilemmas for us about which bits of the education system contribute most to growth. Is it better to have lots of university graduates, or devote funding to early years schooling? What kinds of skills and subjects yield the greatest economic returns? Rocket scientists, or education for all? Companion studies by the OECD indicate that, among rich countries, the rate of return to education spending is highest for primary education and then declines with age.[15] This may reflect social inequalities in schooling, which result in bright but poor kids falling behind early and never getting the chance to catch up. Yet in many countries spending is concentrated on secondary or, in the case of the United States, tertiary (university) education.

But, if quality of schooling is more important than raw spending, how can that quality be measured? Recent research by the World Bank suggests both still matter (it's hard to learn effectively if your school's roof is leaking over your head) but improvements to quality offer the best returns unless this is already very high. That means that things such as improving student–teacher ratios, for example, or hiring better-educated teachers can offer better returns than simply making children stay on longer in school.[16] The institutional environment outside the classroom is also a key factor. Education is less beneficial in countries lacking the rule of law, as this discourages entrepreneurship and pushes talented people into the black economy. Revealingly, countries with more engineering students grow more rapidly than countries with a lot of law students.[17]

All this theorizing about education has encouraged governments to think hard about improving their countries' systems. Parent pressure and lobbying by people working in education has added to this. The next section focuses on schools and what happens afterwards for people who do not move on to university.

2.3 Schools and vocational training

The arguments in the previous section about the private and public benefits of education are fairly compelling. Individuals stand to gain from honing their skills, and society at large benefits from encouraging them in this. But we also saw that delivering a "good" education system is not straightforward and expensive mistakes can be made. So, starting with primary and secondary or high schools – the bedrock of the system, which virtually everyone attends – how can we maximize quality to ensure that pupils are not wasting their time? And what about non-monetary factors? Remember that, as well as imparting skills useful in the labour market, we want schools to teach good citizenship to children and turn them into rounded human beings. Some of us may also want them to try to right the wrongs of society – to reverse inequalities of birth, for example, or tackle racism.

Economists interested in school performance tend to model it in a similar way to that of a firm, with a "production function" that compares the "input" into the school (the resources it has to work with) with its "output" (how well it does in educating its students).[18] These kinds of quantitative studies may offend those who decry the commodification of education but they have proved a useful tool in driving up quality and spotting situations when education systems perform badly – the low number of girls doing science subjects, for example, or underachievement among some minorities.

The main drawback of the model is that it is only as good as the data it relies upon. Measuring school inputs would seem to be straightforward, as there are readily available figures on school budgets, numbers of teachers, books, classroom sizes, for example. As pointed out earlier, however, the correlation between spending and outcomes appears to be quite weak, and it is not clear from the evidence what the crucial inputs are that drive up standards. Some educationalists claim class sizes are important, yet the successful Chinese system has large classes (38 students per class). Perhaps it is teacher quality? Finland employs highly qualified teachers on high salaries. But evidence from other countries (Singapore) shows it is no good having great teachers if they do not have enough time to prepare lessons.

Measuring outputs – pupils' performance – is equally hard. PISA scores may be the agreed international standard but they are quite crude, as they reduce

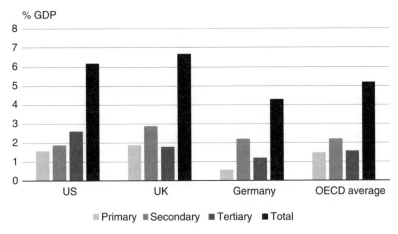

Figure 2.1 Spending by country and level of education
Source: OECD. Education spending at a glance 2014.

quality to a set of numbers, ignoring things such as how successful schools are at socializing their pupils. In any case, they do not tell us much about how to go about achieving high scores in the first place. Domestic tests such as SATs in the United States suffer from much the same drawback. Moreover, as the screening hypothesis suggests, we cannot even be sure how much education is really benefiting the individual student. Is all that schooling really enhancing your daughter's skills or is she just naturally able?

Finally, we should also not overlook the contribution of other factors outside the education process itself. Children do better if they have educated or affluent parents who read to them before bed and surround them with books and educational toys. The schools system is not usually in a position to alter this, although it may be able to compensate for it to some extent. Either way, measures of "quality" are not much use if they do not take into account such contextual factors. One way around this is to replace absolute attainment scores such as PISA with "value-added" scores, which, as the name suggests, measure how much a student's test score is improved by attending the school. Such tools could enable comparisons to be made between an elite grammar school, say, and a nearby school catering for students with special educational needs. But these scores are not perfect either, as they need large amounts of good-quality statistics to produce meaningful indications of variations in quality (see Figure 2.1, which indicates the different spending priorities of different countries).

The difficulty of defining and measuring quality has led policy-makers to look to economics for strategies to make schools perform better. One strategy is introducing competition into the system on the assumption that this will force schools to improve. After all, competition seems to benefit firms in a market, so why not schools? Schools could be treated as akin to firms, with the best ones given more resources and encouraged to expand. Schools in inner city areas with lots of poor kids could be handed extra teachers to compensate for their pupils' disadvantage, say. Pupils and parents in the state system could also be treated like consumers by giving them vouchers to "spend" on their chosen school with resources following the pupils, allowing good schools to expand and forcing weaker ones to close. Private schools can also be encouraged to operate along-side state schools for those willing and able to pay, forcing state schools to com-pete for middle-class pupils whose ambitious parents drive up standards. These approaches have been tried in a number of countries, such as Sweden and the United Kingdom, with some limited success.

Economics also provides reason for caution, however, and state supervision and provision of the school system remain the norm. There are numerous mar-ket failures in education, many of these concerning information. Children – or, more particularly, their parents – might not be very well informed about the quality, price and availability of local schools and so might make poor decisions about where to send their kids. This might be particularly so among less well-off parents who themselves have had a poor experience with their own education. More to the point, schools generally serve their local area. In an inner city it might make sense for parents to shop around as there will probably be good alternatives available. Competition makes a lot less sense in rural areas with maybe only one or two local schools.

Vouchers might seem as though everyone is being treated equally as anon-ymous consumers of education. In practice, though, there is little to stop schools "cream skimming" – admitting only the best students, who will get the best exam results and boost their status in the education "market". Given what we know about the scholastic advantages of having a middle-class back-ground and educated, professional parents, this can easily result in social segregation and spell an end to dreams about using education to fuel the meritocracy unless other measures are put in place to force schools to diver-sify their intakes.

Concerns about social justice therefore tend to reinforce arguments about efficiency. Education is seen as a key source of social advancement in a merito-cratic society; poor, but bright, kids need every opportunity to make the most of their skills and talents, and not wasting talent is a sensible economic strategy. Education is particularly important for social equity because children typically get only one chance at it. If they miss out on a good education their lives may be permanently disadvantaged. For the moment, then, the economics of the market has had a limited impact on how schooling is organized, and government regula-tion and provision remain the norm.

Training for the job: apprenticeships

Employers often complain that school leavers are not well prepared for the workplace as they lack practical skills (many say the same thing about graduates). A good bridge between school and work is to do an apprenticeship. These are training programmes that combine vocational education with training in the workplace for intermediate-skill occupations. Policy-makers in many countries have also developed tertiary-level (university-equivalent) apprenticeships.

The attraction of apprenticeships is that they offer a route into the workplace for youngsters who could benefit from extra training but are not academic and do not want to go to university. Governments like them because they are a good way of tackling youth unemployment. Many firms are enthusiastic because they are a low-risk way of meeting their skills needs, as they are usually under no obligation to hire the trainee permanently once the apprenticeship is over if things do not work out. Apprenticeships therefore strongly embody the idea of human capital formation as they are unambiguously aimed at developing the skills of trainees. But they arguably also have a useful social function in transitioning less academic school leavers into the workplace. Done properly – in other words, when not viewed as a source of cheap labour – apprenticeship programmes can perform these functions extremely effectively. Numerous studies have found that a high percentage of apprentices find employment immediately after finishing their training. A good proportion stay in the company where they trained, where they are rewarded with higher wages.[19]

Apprenticeships may offer lots of advantages but they are surprisingly hard to get right. In many countries, extensive government-sponsored apprenticeship programmes exist alongside stubborn skills shortages in key sectors such as construction and engineering. One problem with state-sponsored apprenticeship programmes is that governments are often not very good at spotting where skills shortages exist and may be under political pressure to expand apprentice numbers to massage youth unemployment figures. One analysis of training policy in the United Kingdom found that 94,000 hairdressing trainees were produced in 2010/11 for an industry with only 18,000 vacancies. By contrast, only 40,000 trained in building services engineering when there were double the number of vacancies in the sector.[20]

But there is a dilemma here. Certainly, the public provision of apprentices runs the risk that the government might not guess right. This suggests that getting employers to take the lead is vital. After all, the whole point of apprenticeships is that they induct school leavers into the workplace and equip them with a set of practical, job-related skills – something best done in the workplace. But this can give rise to a systemic problem, as it is not necessarily in the interests of any one company to provide them. Naturally, all companies have a *general* interest in improving the skill level of the economy, as it increases the choice of skilled workers among whom to recruit, which thereby keeps a lid on wages. They may still be unwilling to train, however, because of the risk their trainees could be poached by other firms that choose not to bother doing training, denying them the benefit of their investment.

So firms may find themselves in the odd and contradictory position of demanding action by governments to improve skills (even though governments are not necessarily very good at this) while taking no action themselves to help achieve this. In other words, although a high level of industry skills is an attractive goal for all concerned, it is not always easy to reach in practice, and industries in some countries can end up with an undersupply of skills.[21]

There are a couple of ways around this. Employers that are big enough to dominate their industry and so face little competition for skilled workers will still find it worthwhile to train. Smaller firms in some countries can also group together to develop their industry's skills needs collectively. German firms are particularly good at this, as chambers of commerce and other industry associations in Germany are well organized and powerful. They collaborate on a range of commercial activities (including research and development [R&D] and supply chain management as well as training) in a way that would probably be ruled illegal in countries such as the United States and Canada, which have more pro-market regulators who take a dim view of collaboration between competitors.

Membership of these networks is so important to their business strategies that German firms will not risk expulsion by poaching apprentices from competitors and so will do their own training, which they can then tailor precisely to their needs. The "collective action problem" concerning skills is thereby overcome. Germany's "dual" system of technical education combines theoretical instruction in schools with on-the-job training in the workplace, and is enormously effective; the country's technical skills regime is cited as a major reason for its dominance of high-value manufacturing export sectors such as machine tools and performance cars. Large firms at the head of supply chains are often happy to take on more trainees than they need in the knowledge that those they let go may still find employment with their suppliers, ensuring high-quality workmanship all the way down the line. Governments can encourage this by subsidizing employer-led training, financed either through general taxation or a training levy on all employers directed towards those that train.

Many countries have been promoting apprenticeships with substantial investment of public resources and by aspiring to the experience of Germany and its well-established tradition of apprenticeship training. For example, South Korea started in 2014 a dual system inspired by the German apprenticeship systems. China is also going in this direction.[22] Undoubtedly, therefore, apprenticeships offer a valuable route into the workplace for those who are not suited to university. The growing expense of higher education is also turning some students off, something that is explored next.

2.4 Universities and innovation

Debates about the value, purpose and funding of learning are possibly at their sharpest when it comes to higher education – colleges and universities. Some argue that even to discuss universities in a book on economics is to miss the point that these are places of learning for its own sake and socially necessary venues for free debate.[23] Others accept that universities have an economic rationale but point to their long-term role in producing knowledge rather than addressing the short-term needs of the market.

Teaching, promoting core values and the development of knowledge for its own sake remain key objectives of higher education. But these have been supplemented by the need to nurture human capital. For a long time, of course, a university education at one of the handful seats of learning was the preserve of the rich in need of a finishing school for their sons (women were not thought worth educating in great numbers until recently). From the 1960s onwards, though, the shift in economic activity from manufacturing to service industries has created a demand for a workforce equipped with sophisticated cognitive skills, such as critical thinking. Expanding state bureaucracies also required more skilled administrators. Thus began the expansion of higher education from being the preserve of the elite to a mass rite of passage securing entry to the professional middle classes. At the same time, universities began to be seen as generators of innovation and technology to power the modern economy. Between 2000 and 2012 the number of students enrolled in higher education at any one time more than doubled to over 100 million – an average annual growth rate of almost 7 per cent in student numbers.[24]

Governments have taken careful note, and over the last two decades universities have shifted from the periphery to the centre of policy agendas, with responsibility for them now increasingly to be found in business and technology ministries. One result of this has been a big change in how universities are perceived: from ivory towers, purveying a "liberal" education to a small elite, to centres of value creation and human capital formation. Coupled with the huge expansion in numbers going to universities in most countries, this has prompted a lot of thought into how to shift more costs from taxpayers onto the student. The rise of international rankings of universities has made people more aware of quality. For students and academics the university sector is increasingly seen in terms of a market, underpinned by a new organizational approach known as "new public management", which sees formerly public services increasingly as stand-alone businesses.[25]

Students approaching the end of their secondary schooling face a set of dilemmas about continuing in further education that is similar to those discussed earlier in the chapter. As before, HCT suggests they will weigh up the benefits of three or four more years of college in terms of how it embellishes the skills that improve their position in the job market. The UK government estimates that higher education adds £168,000 to the lifetime earnings of a male graduate and £252,000 to a woman's.[26] Added to the ledger will also be non-material benefits of greater self-confidence, improved social standing and the expectation of having a great time before knuckling down to a career. Set against these boons will be the downsides of living expenses, tuition costs and further time out of the labour market. Most consider it worthwhile, however, with the OECD estimating that 60 per cent of young people in rich countries now get some experience of higher education, compared with fewer than 40 per cent a mere two decades ago.[27]

This is undoubtedly a good thing. Aside from its contribution to the economy and advancing the learning society, mass education is good for social justice. Social justice is a key concern of educational policy-makers. Not only is it right ethically that an egalitarian society should make access to higher education as wide as possible, but doing so is also efficient, as it ensures countries are making best use of available talent. As long as the net returns from university remain positive – that the benefits exceed the cost within a reasonable space of time – a degree from a decent university can help poor students get a foot on the ladder of advancement. High enrolment rates indicate that university is now far from the preserve of a social elite and imply that at least some talented but poor students are finding their way to college.

The problem is that higher education is becoming very expensive as the numbers undergoing it soar, and so governments are wrestling with alternative ways to pay for it. The dilemma for policy-makers is that they have to balance several potentially conflicting goals: ensuring fair access; maintaining quality; and spreading the costs widely and fairly. More and more countries are following the United States and shifting the burden of paying for university courses from taxpayers onto the student. In the United Kingdom the government introduced tuition fees for public universities in the late 1990s, which are now among the highest in the developed world. Predictably, this provoked an outcry in the United Kingdom, and Australia, where they were also introduced. Tuition fees can seem paradoxical; after all, if we do not expect high school students to pay for their education then what justifies charging college students?

Nicholas Barr, an economist at the LSE who has advised a number of governments, points out some crucial differences that could make university fees justifiable.[28] First, a much larger share of the benefits of higher education are private

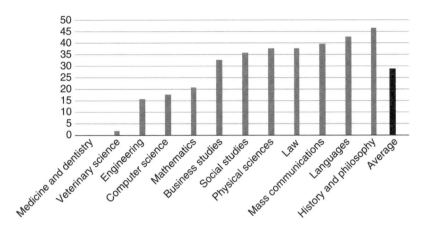

Figure 2.2 Percentage of UK graduates working in non-professional jobs by degree subject
Source: UK Higher Education Statistics Agency.

rather than public; in other words, they accrue preponderantly to the student. Graduates of higher education earn more than people who have completed only high school, with the gap ranging from 15 per cent in New Zealand to 119 per cent in Hungary.[29] Opponents of charging students tend to argue that education is a right and should be free. But Barr points out that we do not regard food as being free, even though it is more of a necessity. And there is a powerful equity argument to the effect that those who benefit from something should contribute to its costs. This is especially so in view of the fact that middle-class students continue to dominate higher education but free tuition would be paid for out of the taxes of all social classes. Fees also provide a powerful incentive to students to focus on their studies and finish their degrees on time,[30] although it may also reduce the attraction of less vocational subjects (see Figure 2.2).

The second reason why higher education is different from schools is that it is much more viable to organize it as a market. This can be beneficial, as markets in higher education force colleges to compete for students through varying their fees and the quality of the educational offer. Most of the market failures discussed earlier in the chapter that justify state provision of schooling cease to apply with universities because their "customers" are different. For a start, most students are mobile (over half those studying at the LSE are from outside the United Kingdom, for example), which is crucial in facilitating the consumer choice without which no market will function. They are also typically much better informed about the costs and benefits than school students or their parents, so they can make better decisions about whether it is worth attending. Numerous league tables are published to help them in this. Since 2015 the US Department of Education has published an online "College Scorecard", which lists earnings information for graduates at particular colleges alongside other important factors, such as cost and graduation rates.

A third reason is choice. People can choose to go to university or not, unlike primary and second schooling, which is largely compulsory, or other publicly funded services such as healthcare (for which you do not choose to require treatment for things such as appendicitis).

There are legitimate concerns, however, about high fees putting off poorer students, who might appreciate that there are career benefits to going to college but worry about the costs, especially if high fees are levied at the outset.[31] Students in the United States mostly pay their fees upfront, but reliance on fee income varies enormously, from about 90 per cent of revenue at private universities to only 20 per cent at public colleges.[32] Not surprisingly, private universities in the United States, which are often the gateway to good jobs, are much more socially exclusive despite generous bursaries on offer at richer places such as Harvard and Yale.

Barr's solution, which has been adopted by the United Kingdom and other countries, is to offer loans to cover fees and maintenance that have income-contingent repayments as a payroll deduction, a similar arrangement to social security contributions. In other words, the costs of getting a degree are back-loaded: there are no upfront charges and repayment begins only when the graduate's salary reaches a certain level. The United Kingdom's loans system finds favour with economists because it directly addresses the externality issue (countries benefit by having lots of graduates, but so do the graduates themselves) by splitting the cost between the taxpayer (students are borrowing from the government at a much lower rate than they could get from a bank) and the student. The system can also be manipulated to encourage enrolment on certain socially useful courses, such as engineering or teacher training.

Loans remain controversial, however, over fears they might conflict with the goal of widening participation. Students from well-off families graduate with lower debt than those with parents less able to pay off their loans for them. Data from the United Kingdom shows little impact so far on enrolment in higher education by working-class students,[33] although the effects could take time to show up, and the main impediment to broadening the social intake of universities is likely to be the lack of prior attainment already discussed. Alternatives to student loans could be a "graduate tax" or shifting the burden of paying for higher education more explicitly onto business, which arguably benefits from higher education as much as students do.

Universities are also themselves facing competition from upstart providers. What are known as MOOCs (massive open online courses) offer a huge range of cheap "micro-degrees" via the internet to students who wish to improve their skills but may not want to sign up for a three- or four-year degree. MOOCs are a classic disruptive technology challenging incumbents, and their cheerleaders hope they will shake up the higher education system and maybe even force universities to cut fees to compete. Such hopes seem misplaced, however. Many of the best-known MOOCs are actually offered by existing prestigious institutions, such as Harvard, the Massachusetts Institute of Technology (MIT) and Oxford, as complements to their regular course offerings, not replacements. Moreover, they suffer from extremely high dropout rates and appear most suited to a few technical subjects, such as coding, rather than replacing conventional degrees en masse.

What are the downsides to viewing higher education as a market? Varying the assumptions about the purpose of higher education sheds a different light on arguments about whether it is right to treat it as a chargeable commodity. Many academics cleave to the view that universities have multiple objectives, including providing a "liberal" education as well as human capital development. They argue that their function as places of learning are threatened and the culture impoverished by the relentless focus on maximizing efficiency. We are left with a final, sobering question about the marketization of universities. If higher education becomes intrinsically linked to economic advancement and ever-increasing numbers of young people are urged to get into debt to pay for it, what will happen if they cannot find rewarding work?

Universities have an additional rationale, besides providing a liberal education or acting as a skills production machine: to further the frontiers of human knowledge through basic research. The idea of research-led universities originated in Germany and was the brainchild of Wilhelm von Humboldt, a civil servant associated with the eponymous university in Berlin, which pioneered the "research degree", or PhD.

Universities are not the only organizations carrying out research, of course, but they tend to produce a lot of the basic scientific breakthroughs that other institutions may then adapt for other purposes, including developing commercial products. For example, researchers at the Cavendish Laboratory at the University of Cambridge split the atom, discovered subatomic particles and unravelled the structure of DNA. They won nearly 30 Nobel Prizes along the way and provided the scientific groundwork for numerous technologies in use today. Supporters of university-funded science argue that private laboratories or company R&D units would have been unlikely to undertake this sort of research because of its risky, speculative nature and lack of obvious commercial payoff. After all, most things fail, as the British economist Paul Ormerod has pointed out, making a lot of technological innovation a very risky proposition for a profit-seeking firm.[34] Universities face no such constraints, as this kind of work is part of their *raison d'être*. These discoveries, and others, have led to further breakthroughs in other universities and provide the technological basis for countless clever devices that improve our lives.

Such arguments underpin a "market failure" approach to technology and innovation. This holds that the positive "externalities" of research that benefit us all would be under-provided if left to the market. This problem arises because private firms with an eye on profitability will have short time horizons and so will be looking for discoveries that can be commercialized within a relatively short space of time. Even firms prepared to take a longer-term view will still want assurances that their efforts will produce a payoff at some point. They will also be worried about other firms "free-riding" to exploit their discoveries, although this can be averted to an extent by having a tough patent regime. These externalities provide a clear rationale for publicly funded universities to carry out basic research and develop "general-purpose" technologies – techniques that can be applied to a wide range of functions and are of benefit to the entire economy.

The trouble that universities often face is that they are great at coming up with bright ideas but not necessarily very proficient at developing these for practical use, including by the private sector. A few universities, such as Stanford in the United States, are good at this but the rest tend to want to focus on pure research. There may be a rationale for further institutions to be created – possibly, but not necessarily by the government – to spread the benefits of technological innovation by helping firms to commercialize breakthroughs and scale up production once a successful product has been brought to market. Mariana Mazzucato, an economist, argues that state-backed institutions such as Germany's Fraunhofer institutes or the United States' DARPA (Defence Advanced Research Projects Agency) can "crowd in" private investment once the state has laid the initial groundwork. Mazzucato points out that most of the key technologies of the iPhone, including GPS, the liquid crystal display – and, of course, the internet itself, were developed first by the US government.[35] Either way, there seems to be a lot of scope for fruitful collaboration over innovation, and universities play a big part in this.

Conclusion: what we have learnt about the place of education and training in the economy

- Education is hugely important for economic growth, and the richest societies tend to also be the best educated. A high general level of education also produces numerous spin-offs in terms of high social capital. Human capital theory explains why this is so: individuals with higher skills tend to be more productive at work, benefiting themselves, their employers and, presumably, the country.
- This is borne out by theories of economic growth, which ascribe an important role to education and skills owing to their importance in productivity and

innovation. But, if it is easy to see the benefits from education, it is harder to measure educational quality accurately and design policies to enhance it. It is not altogether clear which factors produce the best results.

- Governments in many countries are experimenting with their educational system by injecting an element of competition. There is also pressure to share the burden of paying for education by getting those who benefit from it to pay towards it. This marketization works better in universities than schools. There is similar pressure to provide non-academic routes into the workplace by encouraging vocational apprenticeships.

- Many governments are emphasizing the role of education in propagating the "knowledge economy", a concept that draws attention to the increasing technological sophistication of modern economies and their need for highly educated and skilled people to work in them. Universities, once bastions of liberal education, are increasingly being drawn into this as producers of skills and innovation.

Notes

1. For a good overview of the mountains of academic studies on all aspects of this, see M. Dickson & C. Harmon, "Economic returns to education: what we know, what we don't know, and where we are going – some brief pointers", *Economics of Education Review* 30:6 (2011), 1118–22.
2. For a similarly exhaustive survey of the non-material benefits of education, see L. Feinstein, D. Budge, J. Vorhaus & K. Duckworth, *The Social and Personal Benefits of Learning: A Summary of Key Research Findings* (London: Centre for Research on the Wider Benefits of Learning, 2008).
3. J. Vaizey, *The Economics of Education* (London: Faber & Faber, 1962).
4. OECD, *Education at a Glance 2016: OECD Indicators* (Paris: OECD Publishing, 2016).
5. M. Porter, *The Competitive Advantage of Nations* (London: Macmillan, 1990).
6. G. Becker, *Human Capital: A Theoretical and Empirical Analysis with Special Reference to Education* (Chicago: University of Chicago Press, 1964).
7. J. Riley, "Silver signals: twenty-five years of screening and signaling", *Journal of Economic Literature* 39:2 (2001), 432–78.
8. S. Bowles & H. Gintis, "The problem with human capital theory: a Marxian critique", *American Economic Review* 65:2 (1975), 74–82.
9. A. Sen, *The Idea of Justice* (London: Allen Lane, 2009).
10. R. Solow, "A contribution to the theory of economic growth", *Quarterly Journal of Economics* 70:1 (1957), 65–94.
11. P. Romer, "The origins of endogenous growth", *Journal of Economic Perspectives* 8:1 (1994), 3–22.
12. See www.pisa.oecd.org/pisa (accessed 1 December 2016).
13. E. Hanushek & D. Kimko, "Schooling, labour force quality, and the growth of nations", *American Economic Review* 90:5 (2000), 1184–208.
14. OECD, *The High Cost of Low Educational Performance: The Long-Run Economic Impact of Improving PISA Outcomes* (Paris: OECD Publishing, 2010).
15. OECD, *Education at a Glance 2010: OECD Indicators* (Paris: OECD Publishing, 2010).

16. E. Hanushek & L. Wößmann, *Education Quality and Economic Growth* (Washington, DC: World Bank, 2007).
17. K. Murphy, A. Shleifer & R. Vishny, "The allocation of talent: implications for growth", *Quarterly Journal of Economics* 10:2 (1991), 503–30.
18. E. Hanushek, "The economics of schooling: production and efficiency in public schools", *Journal of Economic Literature* 24:3 (1986), 1141–77.
19. S. Berger & M. Pilz, "Benefits of VET", in U. Hippach-Schneider & B. Toth (eds), *Germany: VET Research Report 2009*, 6–49 (Bonn: Bundesinstitut für Berufsbildung, 2009).
20. L. Gardiner & T. Wilson, *Hidden Talents: Skills Mismatch Analysis* (London: Centre for Economic and Social Inclusion, 2012).
21. C. Crouch, D. Finegold & M. Sako, *Are Skills the Answer? The Political Economy of Skill Creation in Advanced Industrial Countries* (Oxford: Oxford University Press, 1999).
22. Background paper, prepared for G20/OECD/EC conference "Quality apprenticeships for giving youth a better start in the labour market", Paris, 9 April 2014.
23. J. H. Newman, *The Idea of a University* [1852] (Charleston, NC: BiblioLife, 2009).
24. OECD, *Education at a Glance 2014: OECD Indicators* (Paris: OECD Publishing, 2014).
25. P. Santiago, K. Tremblay, E. Basri & E. Arnal, *Tertiary Education for the Knowledge Society*, vol. II, *Special Features: Equity, Innovation, Labour Market, Internationalisation* (Paris: OECD Publishing, 2008).
26. I. Walker & Y. Zhu, "The impact of university degrees on the lifecycle of earnings: some further analyses", Research Paper no. 112 (London: Department for Business, Innovation and Skills, 2013).
27. OECD, How are university students changing?, Education Indicators in Focus no. 15 (Paris: OECD Publishing, 2013).
28. N. Barr, "Higher education funding", *Oxford Review of Economic Policy* 20:2 (2004), 264–83.
29. OECD, *Highlights from Education at a Glance 2009* (Paris: OECD Publishing, 2009).
30. D. Johnstone, *Financing Higher Education: Cost-Sharing in International Perspective* (Rotterdam: Sense Publishers, 2006).
31. J. Williams, *Consuming Higher Education: Why Learning Can't Be Bought* (London: Bloomsbury, 2013).
32. See postsecondary institution statistics at National Center for Education Statistics, May 2016, https://nces.ed.gov (accessed 9 November 2016).
33. Universities and Colleges Admissions Service (UCAS), *End of Cycle Report 2014: UCAS Analysis and Research* (Cheltenham, UK: UCAS, 2014).
34. P. Ormerod, *Why Most Things Fail: Evolution, Extinction and Economics* (London: Faber & Faber, 2005).
35. M. Mazzucato, *The Entrepreneurial State: Debunking Private versus Public Sector Myths* (London: Anthem Press, 2013).

3
LET'S GET BUSY: WORK AND OCCUPATIONS

Work saves a man from three great evils: boredom, vice and need.
Voltaire

Key questions

- How does the labour market function and how are wages set?
- How does the work we do impact the wider economy?
- Can the government intervene to solve unemployment?
- What is the future of work?

Summary

Most of us spend most of our lives at work, and it is a crucial part of the economy. The labour we provide generates wealth for the wider economy and taxes for the government to spend on public services. But the world of work is complex and daunting, especially when first starting out. The range and quality of jobs available reflects many things: the structure and strength of the national and international economy; the health of particular business sectors; the present vibrancy and future plans of individual employers; and how each and every employee meshes with this – what they have to offer, in other words. Jobs also vary widely in terms of how secure they are, their hours and conditions, and the pay and other benefits on offer. What determines this, and, given the importance of work to society, should more be done to protect jobs and/or help the jobless back into employment? Meanwhile, the work we do and the wealth our labour creates drive the economy and generate the taxes to pay for the services we consume – health, welfare and defence, for example. But with an increasingly mobile and freelance workforce it can be difficult for governments to make sure highly paid individuals pay their fair share of tax. This chapter explains why the workplace is organized the way it is and how it is changing.

Main topics and theories covered

Theories of unemployment and labour markets; the political economy of skill formation; active labour market policies; the economics of job search; inequality and the labour market; the future of work.

3.1 Introduction: why work?

Apart from those of us lucky to be born wealthy enough to not have to work, or unlucky enough to be unable to work through some disability, nearly all of us are likely to encounter the labour market throughout a good portion of our existence. For a few people who are really driven, their job becomes the most important thing in their lives. For most others, it is more of a means to an end but still something that looms large in our minds because of the amount of time spent in the office or factory.

The focus on being in employment generates a view of people without work and in receipt of benefits as a drain on the state, requiring encouragement or perhaps coercion to get them to find a job. In reality, though, work and employment and the forces that generate these are partly outside the control of individuals and depend a lot on what else is going on in the economy.

As we saw in the previous chapter, individuals can make themselves as employable as possible through education and training, as well as, hopefully, being in possession of the kinds of personal attributes that employers value, such as showing up on time and being a good team player. But their chances of gaining and keeping employment also depend on impersonal economic forces that dictate the kind of jobs that employers choose to offer, where these are located and the terms on offer. And, in choosing whether or not to offer these jobs, employers respond in turn to their own expectations about what is going on in their particular market and the wider economy; will taking on more workers produce more sales to justify the extra expense? Obviously, therefore, there is a lot involved in getting and keeping a job.

This chapter tries to make sense of the forces involved in all of this, and how the world of work is changing. It starts off by explaining the place of work in the economy and why it is if such central importance. NCE does a good job of setting out the conditions under which labour markets will operate effectively.

It struggles with the fact that work is intensely political and invites government intervention in various ways, however. We will look at this too, and also examine the ways in which work is changing as a result of globalization and automation.

How work is changing

The main reason people work is to get paid, of course. But the sheer amount of time spent in the workplace means other things such as happiness, job satisfaction and the need for human contact are also important. All these things can be measured and modelled by economists. For example, researchers at Princeton University recently succeeded in putting a price on happiness: $75,000.[1] This was the annual salary at which people reported maximum satisfaction. Less than this and they felt deprived, although, curiously, earning more did not make them any happier. In the main, once an acceptable standard of living is achieved, job satisfaction increases in line with the skill involved in doing it and the prestige of the occupation; surgeons are far happier in their work than shelf stackers.

Economists have occasionally fretted that people work too hard and we should enjoy a shorter work week. Keynes saw a reduction in working time as a good way to achieve full employment and forecast that one day the working week would be just 15 hours, leaving more time for the "leisure society" that the cultured and artistic Keynes would have appreciated. John Stuart Mill advocated a "gospel of leisure" and looked forward to the day when technology would liberate people from the daily grind. Many economists predict that this might be about to come to pass, but a few pessimistically envisage a world divided by unequal access to work and the opportunities it brings. If this seems alarmist, just consider the massive changes in the world of work that have taken place over the past few hundred years.

First, shorter working hours. The number of hours people typically work has plummeted over the last two centuries. In the Netherlands, the working year was 3,285 hours in 1870, but only 1,347 hours in 2000.[2] Economic growth has tended to bring down working hours, but only to a certain point, after which cultural and political factors come into play. Pressure from trade unions and the political Left played a large part in winning more leisure time for working people. But the enormous increases in labour productivity made possible through automation and improving skills also played a key part. When employers were able to extract double or even triple the output from a given worker per hour they became a lot more amenable to cutting the working day, particularly when they realized that this would help to create a new class of consumers to enjoy their products.

Nowadays, 48 hours a week is seen as the safe limit, although it is estimated that one in five workers globally works more than this.

Second, the jobs have got a lot more pleasant. Factory jobs during the Industrial Revolution of the eighteenth and nineteenth centuries were even more diffi-cult and dangerous than the agricultural work they largely replaced. As Robert Gordon, an economic historian, has pointed out, a farmer who, 100 years ago, would have followed his horse and plough through a field in the baking heat now sits in an air-conditioned cabin in a combine harvester guided by GPS.[3] The number of people employed in dirty, manual jobs has sharply declined and those who remain have been transformed by better technology, automation and improved conditions.

Third, the variety of jobs has expanded massively. The two big shifts over the last couple of hundred years have been (a) the move from farming to fac-tory jobs, followed by (b) the slow decline of manufacturing as a share of GDP and employment in most Western countries and the shift to services. The loss of manufacturing jobs since the 1970s has been in response to productivity increases in industry, which meant fewer workers were required, as well as increasing competition from developing countries, which took most of the lower-paying, unskilled jobs. This deindustrialization was particularly severe in Europe, where a third of male industrial jobs had been lost by 2000. Service industries have replaced most, although not all, of these male jobs as well as providing employment for the large numbers of women who have entered the labour market.[4] A third shift now under way, explored later in this chapter, is arguably taking place as automation replaces many factory *and* services jobs. But, before we get to that, let us look at how economists explain work and the workplace.

The neoclassical view of work and employment

The study of work has tended to be a minority interest in mainstream economics, usually confined to a few subsections in economics textbooks.[5] NCE views work through the prism of a market, with labour treated as a special type of commod-ity alongside the other key inputs into production: land and capital. Sellers of labour (workers) and buyers (employers) are assumed to come together in a self-adjusting market that ensures that all who want a job can get one. Recently, how-ever, the persistence of high unemployment and skills shortages has renewed interest in employment and highlighted some problems with the NCE model.

For NCE, the main actors in the labour market are workers. We decide our-selves whether to work or not, how many hours to work and what pay we will accept, when to look for a new job, what skills to acquire along the way and when to retire. Work is modelled in NCE as a straight choice between two ways to spend our precious time: work and leisure. If we want to subsist, or, even better, have money left over to enable us to consume nice things, then we need to work. But when working we are obviously not at leisure, which is more fun. We may also have other commitments, such as doing childcare or housework. Other sources of income, such as welfare benefits, will also affect our taste for seeking work.

Box 3.1 Key terms

- *Reservation wage.* The lowest wage at which a worker will accept a particular job.
- *Opportunity cost.* An alternative that is given up when a choice is made.
- *Active labour market policies.* Using policy to increase employment opportunities – e.g. help in training, rather than leaving employment to the market.
- *Skill-biased technological change.* A shift in the structure of production that favours skilled over unskilled workers.

NCE allows that people are different. They possess their own individual *utility function*, reflecting how they approach these trade-offs. Some people are perhaps a bit work-shy, or, more technically (and perhaps kindly), we could say they place a relatively high value on their leisure time compared with the extra goods they could consume if they put in more hours at the office. Others are more industrious and/or place a higher value on the material things their wages can buy them, which leads them to want to do more work. Both face constraints in the form of the time they have available to them and the need to have access to necessities such as food, accommodation and money for bills.

In maximizing our utility we will calculate the work/leisure mix that suits us. This is embodied in what is called the "reservation wage", which is the minimum required to entice us into the labour market. If our reservation wage (the wage we expect to get) is more than the market wage (the wage that employers are prepared to offer) then we will not work. To put it another way, leisure has a specific "price", which is the income forgone from choosing not to work in favour of putting one's feet up or going hiking.

If the wage offered is sufficiently high, some individuals will even choose to work very long hours because the rewards will be high in terms of the extra material comfort this brings. The cost of this is, of course, much-reduced leisure time, which is why we increasingly see the phenomenon of "income-rich, time-poor" people, a trend first noticed by the Swedish economist and politician Staffan Burenstam Linder.[6] These are professionals who have enormous disposable incomes but little time to enjoy them. They include bankers, lawyers and doctors, at the very top of their professions, who have studied and worked hard to get there and command high salaries. In response to their predicament, service industries have sprung up in cities with clusters of these people, such as New York, San Francisco and London, to assist them in making the most of their truncated leisure time. These include butlers, nannies, concierge services and firms offering exotic "experience" vacations. Top earners also tend to sleep less than people on lower incomes, as they regard sleep beyond the biological minimum as an unproductive activity.

In terms of the work/leisure trade off, however, most people tend to be *satisficers* rather than *maximizers*. In other words, they will work enough to achieve a certain standard of living then, once this is achieved, the extra utility they get from another hour of work will cease to outweigh the disutility from giving up some leisure. Unless they receive a sharp rise in the wage rate they will be unwilling to put in yet more hours. Economists thus describe the typical individual in an average-paying job as having a *backward-bending supply curve* for his labour. The supply curve initially slopes upwards, as more pay encourages them to work for longer. But at a certain point the supply curve switches backwards as the worker reaches his target income and thereafter no matter how much the wage increases the worker will not want to work more.

People's appetite for work and their earning power are not fixed but vary over a lifetime. Earnings generally peak between the ages of 40 and 50, as accumulated experience makes us better at our jobs and we are still reasonably fresh and motivated. So it can make sense to "trade" leisure time in these years for extra earnings by working longer hours to make the most of the temporary wage premium. Later on in their careers, perhaps as they approach retirement, leisure is less "costly", and many older people choose to wind down gradually with a shorter working week or retire early.

Employees need employers

So much for individuals; what about the bigger picture? The labour supply curve for an entire industry will operate under different constraints as firms in the industry can continue raising wages to encourage more workers to enter the sector from outside. Thus, the labour supply curve for a whole industry, representing a group of workers, is a continuous straight line sloping upwards, reflecting the fact that employers can continue to bring in extra workers to the industry and the workforce can be boosted by outside factors such as immigration and the overall quality of the labour force.

So, if we are bringing employers into the picture, what about the "demand" for labour? Labour demand is a "derived" demand, in that employers do not hire people just for the sake of it but to help to produce a good or service that they can sell. Firms are therefore akin to a middleman between workers and consumers, and the terms on which they employ people will depend on how they mediate this exchange through their business activity. NCE argues that firms in the short run (when land or capital is fixed) hire workers up to the point at which the value added by the next worker they take on is at least equal to the cost of hiring him (in other words, when the wage equals the marginal revenue product of the worker).

This depends, in turn, on a range of other things to do with the market conditions the firm is facing and all the other costs it encounters in doing business besides the wage bill. These can be quite significant, and include things such as National Insurance contributions, training and healthcare benefits, as well as other overheads such as providing a desk and computer. Non-wage costs of employment account for over a quarter of the cost of a worker in EU countries, rising to a third in France.[7]

In the long run, employers have a lot more control over how they react to changing market conditions (in other words, they can change the shape and slope of their labour demand curve). For example, they could invest in new machinery, which would enable them to produce better products more cheaply. This would increase their need for skilled operators to work the machinery, as capital and skilled labour are "complements", in that an increase in the demand for one leads to an increase in demand for the other. On the other hand, capital and *un*skilled labour are "substitutes", as installing more machinery tends to be at the expense of a lot of unskilled workers, who thus lose their jobs, leaving behind just a few workers with the requisite skills to operate the machines. This explains the long-run tendency for employment to fall in industries prone to automation. Car manufacturing is a good example. Factories that might once have employed tens of thousands of people can now make do with a few hundred workers who spend a lot of their time tending the machines in "lights out" factories.

The decisions of company bosses about whether to bring in machines or human workers are complicated, however, and depend on the market conditions they face and the relative cost of the two main factors of production: labour and capital (machines). We see this clearly in the different ways countries respond to economic "shocks". For example, the labour markets of the United Kingdom and the United States are similar in many ways: they are both considered very "flexible", as the government imposes few restrictions on employer's ability to hire and fire. Yet they responded very differently to the shock of the "Great Recession" of 2007–2010 following the Lehman Brothers collapse.

In the United Kingdom, in the year or two of recovery after the recession's end, employment recovered strongly to reach a record high by 2013. This was at the cost of sharp falls in wages and productivity, however. This was probably to be expected; after all, roughly the same number of people were doing less work owing to the lower demand for their goods and services. The result was that their productivity suffered and they were paid less. One theory about the United Kingdom is that wages dropped so much in relation to the cost of capital that it became worthwhile to have more workers compared to machines, and so employers went on a hiring spree instead of investing in more capital. In the United States, by contrast, employers shed labour much rapidly, so that the workers who remained were more productive and commanded higher wages. This made it more attractive for employers to replace people with machines and US unemployment stayed higher for longer.[8]

Pay and rewards from work

Finally, why does the pay of different jobs vary so wildly? Why, for example, is being a movie or sports star so much more lucrative than working in a fast food restaurant, even though most people would be happy to put up with the wealth and fame to do these jobs? The answer is that wage rates vary according to the variable nature of each job and the diverse characteristics and talents of the workers who do them.

In some very dangerous occupations, such as deep-sea diving, employers have traditionally had to pay a wage premium to get people to do them. This is less the case now as robots are beginning to replace hazardous jobs and regulation is forcing employers to make them safer. In other jobs, it is very easy to find people to do them and so there is no wage premium at all. Fast food workers get paid little because these jobs require few qualifications or skills and so there is no shortage of people who could do them; the labour supply curve for these industries is said to be *elastic*, and the high staff turnover that results from the low wages and unstimulating nature of the work is not a problem as they are so easily replaced. Moreover, as the tasks involved are simple and repetitive they would also be quite easy to automate, and so the fact that the fast food industry offers rock-bottom wages is probably one reason why there are still lots of jobs for humans available there. The industry is also very competitive so holding down wages is a key strategy of management.

These arguments also apply to workers who may be highly educated but are at the start of their careers – for example, interns trying to gain a foothold in prestigious industries by working there for low or no pay. Human capital theory (explored in Chapter 2) implies that each job serves to develop your skills and

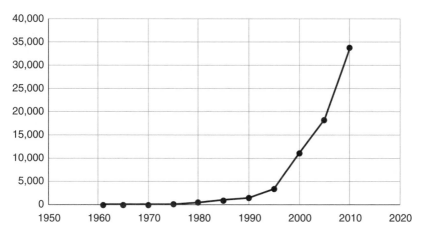

Figure 3.1 Weekly wages of footballers in English top division in pounds sterling
Source: Sporting Intelligence.

employability; it follows, however, that at the beginning of this process when you are young and inexperienced your value to your employer will be low or even negative. In fact, some employers in desirable industries reportedly think interns should pay *them* for the privilege of working there, as the experience and contacts gained by the interns are more valuable than any work they do.[9] More enlightened employers view internships as part of the recruitment process, as a means to spot and nurture talent.

In other jobs, the supply curve is generally a lot more *inelastic*, meaning that workers are harder to find and replace and so have to be paid better. Doctors are a good example. Their supply is inelastic because their lengthy and difficult training period limits the number of doctors available at any one time. Over time, however, it is possible to increase the number of people training in medicine or import trained doctors from abroad, so their pay is high but not stratospheric.[10] The market value of other workers may be greater still because of some unique talent they possess that happens to command a huge premium in their field. For example, a top La Liga footballer such as Ronaldo is worth untold millions of euros to his club, Real Madrid, because of his goals and marketability, so his pay is commensurately high – around €20 million a year. These astronomical wages do not result in a flood of people coming to play in top football leagues because the number of truly great players is extremely small; their supply curve is inelastic (the explosion in footballers' wages is shown in Figure 3.1).

But are these wage differentials fair? Mainstream economics tends to dodge these arguments, as it is primarily concerned with efficiency, not equity, and fairness is something best dealt with by elected politicians. Critics of high wages in football note the correspondingly high ticket prices for games, however, which price out many supporters on low incomes, and point out that a maximum wage operated in England until the 1960s without noticeably discouraging talented players into the game. In more everyday workplaces there is legislation and company policy to enforce fairness in wages, for example ensuring equal pay for men and women. The presence of trade unions may also blunt the impact of the market and dampen pay differentials between workers.

It seems fair to say, therefore, that markets are important in many aspects of our everyday lives, and this includes the world of work. But markets are embedded in a society replete with social tensions over wealth and one that is, furthermore, governed by politicians who respond to demands for fairness and equity. This will tend to produce a lot of distortions into the market, and it is to these that we turn next to consider.

3.2 Unemployment and the macroeconomics of labour markets

Labour markets are different from other markets in that workers are not passive objects, such as a car or tablecloth. This makes them more complex. A worker may intensify her efforts if she likes her job, respects or fears her boss or is paid a higher wage for better performance. Workers in some industries may organize to create or join trade unions, which may push up the wage of the whole firm or industry. And, ultimately, wages not saved are spent, so they form the basis of consumption and are an important source of the demand that keeps the economy going. What this means, therefore, is that the NCE view of labour markets explored in the first section gives only an incomplete picture of the world of work and employment and one laden with a lot of assumptions.

The main assumption is that an individual's job search take place in what is essentially a well-functioning market. For example, the job market is assumed to be transparent, as workers know about wages and job opportunities elsewhere in the economy, and employers can pick and choose among candidates to find the best one for the job. But we know from the economics of information that this is not particularly realistic. Around a third of jobs are not advertised but are filled through word of mouth, giving a huge advantage to insiders and placing new job seekers, such as young people leaving school or university, at a disadvantage.

Changing jobs or hiring new workers is also assumed to be relatively frictionless. Again, this is questionable. Although technology is making it easier to search for vacancies and apply online, an active job search can still be difficult and laborious. The OECD estimates that, during a given year, 20 to 30 per cent of workers leave their jobs. Most find new ones and are replaced in their old jobs, but this still means a lot of hiring and firing going on, and economists have recently begun pointing to the importance of rates of job creation and destruction in determining the level of employment in the economy. The 2010 Nobel Prize in economics was awarded for work in this area, specifically for highlighting the importance of policies that help firms and job candidates match up with each other.[11] The process can be a bit like dating: it takes time to get a good match, as jobs and the candidates for them vary in a number of ways. Information is scarce and possibly asymmetrical. The whole process takes time and commitment, and as a result the labour market is characterized by a certain amount of "frictional unemployment".

NCE also tends to assume that unemployment (wanting a job and not being able to find one) is voluntary and usually temporary. Well-functioning labour markets mean that workers are paid no more than is necessary to keep them in the job. Extra pay over and above this is considered a *rent*, and the attractiveness of this rent encourages other workers to arrive to compete for these jobs, causing wages to fall back to their competitive level. Thus, there is no involuntary unemployment in a perfectly competitive labour market as wages freely adjust to the demand for labour and all who want work can find it. In reality, though, labour markets tend to operate imperfectly and wages do not adjust freely to market conditions. Wages are "sticky" downwards, in that people are happy to accept a pay rise but will generally resist a cut as they will have become accustomed to a certain lifestyle. Unable to reduce costs in a downturn, employers may cut headcounts instead.

There may also be macroeconomic causes of high levels of involuntary unemployment. This was highlighted by Keynes during the Great Depression of the 1930s.[12] He argued that the high unemployment then being experienced in Europe and North America was attributable to deficient demand in the economy. Keynes' insight was that wages are not just a cost to employers; they also fund the consumption of goods and services in the economy. If firms cannot sell their products, for instance because no one has the purchasing power to buy them, then cutting wages as NCE suggests will cut demand further and so make the problem worse. The economy could become trapped in a situation in which a substantial proportion of the labour force were unable to find jobs and could not be "priced" into employment by cutting their wages. In other words, what perhaps made sense from an individual firm's point of view was disastrous when applied to the whole economy.

The Keynesian solution eventually adopted by governments was to supplement private with public demand by expanding the size of the public sector. Governments spent big on construction projects, including the New Deal in the United States, and encouraged firms to take on lots of workers. After the Second World War Keynesian policies continued, and were associated with full

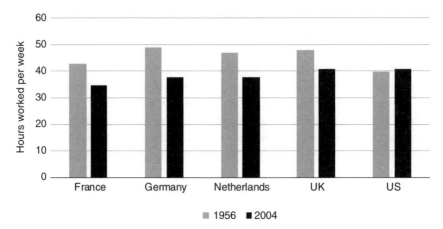

Figure 3.2 Changes in working hours
Source: Lee *et al.* See footnote 2 for full citation details.

employment and buoyant growth, although other factors were probably also at play. With debates about the best way to run a modern economy apparently over, a cosy political consensus emerged in the centre ground of politics around government-led solutions to economic problems in partnership with trade unions and business (unions helped to negotiate reductions in working hours in some countries: see Figure 3.2).

In the 1970s, however, for various reasons this approach seemed to stop working and unemployment began to rise again. Pumping up the level of demand, the classic Keynesian response, appeared to merely produce more inflation. NCE went on the counter-attack and attention turned in economics to other possible causes of joblessness. One of the main diagnoses for rising unemployment was that the economy had become over-regulated and labour markets too inflexible.

The 30-year period after the Second World War in Europe and North America had been marked by strong trade unions involved in macroeconomic policy-making through a system known as "corporatism" and increasing government regulation of employment. Many economists and politicians became concerned that this was storing up trouble by introducing too many rigidities into the economy and handing trade unions too much power. If so, these rigidities were well concealed, as Western countries prospered amid cheap energy prices and in the absence of competition from the developing world as they rebuilt after the war.[13]

Following the energy shocks induced by the Organization of the Petroleum Exporting Countries in the early 1970s, however, most Western economies began to run into trouble with unemployment and inflation, prompting a long period of economic and political turmoil that took decades to subside. Labour markets were at the eye of the storm in many countries as unemployment soared. In the United Kingdom and United States, the governments headed by Margaret Thatcher and Ronald Reagan, respectively, battled with trade unions over labour market and economic policies as they abandoned any commitment to full employment and rolled back the influence of the state over the regulation of work.[14] Much of continental Europe was more resistant to this liberalizing trend, however. The crunch point came in the mid-1990s, when the OECD began to blame European countries' poor jobs performance compared with that of the United States on excessive regulation and urged them to liberalize their labour markets to get people back into work.[15] The European Union took note, and by the late 1990s Europeans, too, were advocating flexible labour market policies.

Labour market flexibility

Whatever happened to "a job for life"? It has been largely replaced by "flexibility". Free-market-oriented economists worry a lot about barriers to labour market "flexibility" and the influence of trade unions. Flexibility refers to the ease with which employers can hire or fire workers (external flexibility) and adjust their pay and conditions (internal flexibility). A flexible labour market implies a minimum of government regulation or pressure, meaning that wages and conditions are set by market forces alone. In terms of efficiency, the advantage of this is that the managers of the firm have a lot of autonomy and can adjust quickly to changing market conditions, for example if they need to take on a lot of workers rapidly to meet a big order. Once the order is finished, however, the firm may want to lay most of these off. If regulation designed to protect workers' rights stops them from doing this then they might be discouraged from taking them on in the first place, and may turn down the order. Hence, measures to protect jobs may hinder their creation in the first place (Figure 3.3 shows the contrasting labour market performances of different countries during the Great Recession; note that macroeconomic factors as well as labour market structures influence unemployment rates).

Trade unions can provide a further source of rigidity in labour markets if they push up wages and hinder restructuring.[16] If enough workers can be persuaded to join a union then they can bargain with their employer collectively rather than individually. This naturally gives them much greater bargaining power, which they generally use to push for better pay and conditions. If strong enough, unions may operate a "closed shop" in the workplace, meaning that they effectively operate as a "monopoly" provider of labour. This makes the labour supply curve more

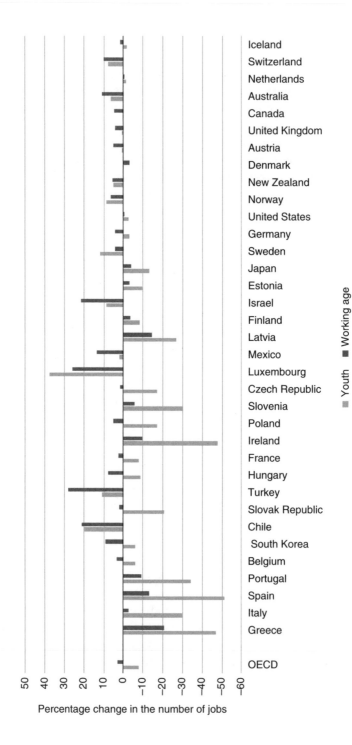

Figure 3.3 Changes in youth and adult employment, 2007–2015

inelastic than it otherwise would have been, reflecting the fact that non-union substitute workers will be hard to hire.

Is this always a problem? For sure, firms that thrive in very competitive, fast-moving business sectors are unquestionably advantaged by labour market flexibility. These may include all sorts of businesses, from cheap clothing manufacturers to hi-tech firms such as biotechnology companies and app developers. These typically operate in markets in which the barriers to entry to new firms are not particularly high and/or where the goods and services produced compete largely on price. They may also be very innovative, requiring the rapid recruitment of skilled workers on short-term contracts, perhaps poached from other companies. These industries have tended to be based in countries such as the United States, United Kingdom, Australia, Ireland and Canada, all of which score highly on indices of labour market flexibility and low on scores of employment protection. Indeed, it could be said that flexible labour markets constitute part of their comparative advantage. These "liberal-market" economies have also tended to have lower unemployment than more regulated countries and are better represented in some of the hi-tech industries of the future.[17]

But this system does not suit all employers in all countries. Two main consequences stem from very flexible labour markets that impact the strategies of firms and workers. The first, dealt with in more detail in Chapter 2, is that countries with very flexible labour markets tend to have trouble producing a lot of skilled workers suitable for work in high-quality manufacturing industries. The second consequence is that rapid staff turnover creates insecurity and stress among employees. It can result in poor relations between management and workers, which is probably the reason why governments in the United States and United Kingdom moved to crush trade unions in the 1980s, as these would otherwise raise hell. But even with weak unions the often conflictual industrial relations climate that ensues still leads to more frequent strikes and poorer worker motivation and loyalty.

In countries with more regulated labour markets, on the other hand, workers will be in a stronger position, because their jobs are protected by legislation and backed by strong unions. Free-market economists worry that workers will use this power to bid up wages and block company restructuring, but this need not be the case. Many countries in southern Europe are indeed afflicted with rigid labour markets that protect long-serving insiders at the expense of newcomers, especially the young, who are left on the outside. But in some north European countries, such as Sweden and Germany, workers are represented on company boards and widely consulted on corporate strategy, and this seems to encourage them to identify their interests with that of their employer as they have very good labour relations. Firms in these countries do well in industries reliant on production techniques that require long-term commitment from technically skilled workers, such as high-quality cars and luxury items.[18]

None of this is to say that either flexible or more "coordinated" labour markets are necessarily better, merely that they are suited to different economies. It is really horses for courses.

3.3 Labour market policies

In light of some of the problems with the NCE view of labour markets highlighted above, most economists now accept that some degree of state involvement can be beneficial in maximizing employment opportunities and equipping workers for the labour market. The biggest area of state involvement (dealt with in Chapter 2) is probably education and training, for which the state can act to ensure the adequate provision of skills. Section 3.2 above also described situations in which governments can act to stimulate the overall level of demand in the macroeconomy, which may help to create jobs (although potentially at the cost of also stoking inflation and enlarging the deficit).

But there are numerous other indirect ways in which governments can influence the labour market. It should first of all be borne in mind that the public sector tends to be a major employer in its own right in most rich democracies. The proportion of the labour force working for the state ranges from about 15 per cent in the United Kingdom to around 30 per cent in the Nordic countries.[19] Asian countries tend to have much smaller public sectors, as does the United States. For instance, only 8 per cent of Japanese work for the state. As well as the government bureaucracy itself, publicly run services such as police, schools, social services and healthcare (when state operated) place large numbers of people onto the public payroll.

Public sector pay tends to be slightly lower than in the private sector (adjusted for the fact that public sector workers tend to be slightly better educated), but they usually enjoy a superior set of benefits, including earlier retirement on more generous pensions and shorter hours. Choosing to work for the state in many ways therefore involves a trade-off between a set of monetary factors (lower pay) and non-monetary factors (better job security and, for some, a sense of public duty).

A common pattern is for people in some occupations, such as nursing or the civil service, to begin their careers in the public sector, benefiting from the training they receive there, before moving into the private sector for further opportunities. The public sector therefore has quite an important influence on the quality of the overall labour force and can be a good source of trained workers to compensate, if necessary, for a lack of private training provision. It may also be an important tool of regional economic policy. For instance, governments can move public sector organizations to deprived regions to bring jobs and stimulate the local economy, as the United Kingdom's public broadcaster, the BBC, did when it moved a number of programmes out of London to Manchester in the hope of fostering a cluster of media companies there.

The size of the public sector workforce and supply of government jobs can be an important tool of social and macroeconomic policy itself. For example, Sweden responded to the decline in manufacturing employment in the 1990s by deliberately creating a large number of public sector jobs rather than expanding the share of often low-wage services jobs, as happened in the United Kingdom and United States. Many of these jobs have been in caring professions, which has expanded opportunities for women to enter the labour market, giving Sweden one of the highest female labour participation rates in the world.

The state can also intervene more directly at the micro level through what are known as active labour market policies (ALMPs). In the European Union, maximizing employment has become an important goal, but, particularly since the advent of the single currency, countries in the Eurozone lack the macroeconomic tools to achieve this. ALMPs are a combination of training, tightened eligibility for unemployment benefits, subsidized employment and pro-employment welfare policies that are designed to encourage people back into work.[20] Anyone unemployed in an EU country is therefore likely to be offered a range of carrots and sticks to get them into work. Although the European Union has formulated the European employment strategy to foster best practice, the details of these policies are left up to individual countries. One of the most effective (and often copied) is the Danish "flexicurity" model, which mixes a generous, Continental-style system of unemployment benefits with easy, Anglo-Saxon-style rules on hiring and firing. This reconciles workers' desire for security with employers' desire for flexibility.

Minimum wages and anti-discrimination

One of the areas in which the state has become directly embroiled in labour markets is in the imposition of minimum wages in many countries. Minimum wages have been instituted in a number of countries over fears that low wages contribute to poverty. One of the first things the centre-left New Labour government of Tony Blair did when it took office in the United Kingdom in 1997 was to introduce a national minimum wage, to be set in consultation with business and unions. In this it was initially opposed by the Conservatives, and yet in 2015 the Conservative government proposed a "National Living Wage" at an even higher rate. After years of opposition from trade unions, Germany opted for a minimum wage in 2013 in a belated response to unification with the East two decades earlier, which had opened up its labour markets to low-paid workers. This had caused a crash in wages and forced the government to top these up with benefits. Statutory minimum wages are now in place in all EU members bar Austria, Cyprus, Denmark, Finland, Italy and Sweden. The US Federal government also sets a minimum wage, and the level can be raised further by state or local government.

Economists are divided about the effects of minimum wages. NCE theory argues that, as the demand curve for labour slopes downwards, raising its price decreases demand for workers and so causes unemployment. But research in the fast food industry in the United States in the 1990s showed that the downward slope of the D curve is quite gentle, implying a small cost in jobs.[21] By closing off for employers the "low road" approach to wages and skills a minimum wage might even force them to invest more in their workforce. The United Kingdom saw unemployment fall and stay very low after it introduced its minimum wage. If fears over minimum wages causing unemployment have been exaggerated, however, it also looks as if their contribution to tackling in-work poverty is minimal. Studies of their impact found that it mainly benefits workers in better-off households who may be doing a part-time job to earn a bit of extra money, such as teenagers in affluent families saving money for college.

Families also complicate people's participation in the labour market, and this can provide another rationale for government to step in. Having a family is costly in a variety of ways, but one of the main expenses is that at least one parent (at the moment usually the mother) has to drop out of work to raise the child. This means forgoing at least some income (maternity pay or benefits may replace some, but probably not all, of this) as well as losing seniority at work. This may reinforce other discriminatory factors, meaning that mothers in demanding professions find it difficult to progress through the "glass ceiling" to claim the top jobs. The "opportunity cost" of having children varies according to the family's position in the labour market. Children will be "cheap" when the loss of income or status from one family member quitting work is low or if, as in agricultural societies, they can later on be put to work. Conversely, kids are "expensive" when the time and cost of looking after them is relatively high, perhaps because the expectation is that they will be expensively educated and entertained. This is one reason why fertility rates among educated professionals in most countries are low and falling.

Governments in rich, Western countries (less so in more traditional Asia and Latin America) have therefore come under pressure to act to ensure women are not disadvantaged at work by having a family. Legislation can outlaw overt discrimination, but policy-makers have generally found that encouraging men to take equal responsibility for childcare is more effective and can be fostered by putting paternity leave on a par with maternity leave and heavily subsidizing childcare.

3.4 The future of work: offshoring, the "winner takes all" society and automation

The world of work is changing rapidly and is seemingly full of contradictions. Unemployment in many countries is high, but there are shortages of workers with the right skills. Globalization and technological change are disrupting labour markets in rich countries, yet opportunities for skilled and ambitious people have never been greater. What is happening? Broadly, there are three main trends now disrupting established patterns in work and employment. We can label these as follows: offshoring; the "winner takes all" society; and automation.[22]

Globalization and offshoring

Changes to the organization of global production networks have had a profound effect on the kinds of jobs available, as well as their conditions and prospects. The word "globalization" is used a lot to describe a general move towards increasing international openness to trade and capital movements. But what really made globalization possible from the 1980s onwards were improvements in transport and information technology (IT). These allowed manufacturers to decompose different stages of the production of a good into complex "value chains" spread across the globe, with each stage comprising different bits of the process and located in different places.[23]

Chapter 9 explores these in more detail, but the important point here is that labour costs have once again started to become an important factor in production decisions after decades of strong trade unions in rich countries taking wages out of competition. Plummeting international freight costs as a result of containerization means it is no longer necessary for producers to be sited close to their market. In fact, they can be sited almost anywhere, so firms have been moving jobs overseas to developing countries in search of cheap, willing workers in a process known as "offshoring". Even the mere threat of doing this has been enough to keep the lid on wages on rich countries.

Most manufacturing jobs requiring basic skills have long since been offshored. Now increasing numbers of services jobs are following them. This process started with call centres operating telephone helplines and has spread increasingly to back-office functions for legal, commercial and medical businesses. Now more high-end design and marketing positions are following them. The logic of outsourcing puts relentless pressure on workers in developed countries to constantly upskill or face redundancy.

Proponents of globalization, such as the *Financial Times* journalist Martin Wolf, acknowledge its disruptive effect on low-wage sectors in developed countries but argue that the costs are outweighed by the benefits from greater economic specialization that globalization represents.[24] By shedding low-wage, low-skill jobs, rich countries can divert people and resources to more productive activities.

This makes sense from a theoretical point of view, but doubts are creeping in as to whether it is actually happening this way. Almost all job creation in the United States in recent years has taken place in sectors that are not exposed to foreign competition, according to the 2001 Nobel-Prize-winning economist Michael Spence. The sector of the economy that can be traded overseas (most manufacturing, some service industries), which accounted for more than 34 million jobs in 1990, grew by a negligible 600,000 jobs between 1990 and 2008 compared with 10 million additional jobs in non-traded government and healthcare. Competition from low-wage economies such as China was to blame, according to Spence.[25] Those jobs that remain are increasingly reserved for highly skilled knowledge workers, as these are things that people in developing nations cannot yet do.

Of course, as developing countries become richer and more middle-class they may start to lose some of their cost advantages. Some Western firms have begun pulling production facilities back to their home countries as it dawns on them that cheap labour is not all it is cracked up to be. There are also suspicions that offshoring is as much about exploiting tax competition between countries as low labour costs. A mere 5 per cent of the cost of an iPhone is accounted for by labour costs, for example. Although everyone benefits from cheap consumer goods, people also want the chance to be productively employed in order that they can afford to buy them. We probably should not get overexcited about the potential for "reshoring" jobs back to the West, however, as those who return are likely to be highly skilled but few in number.[26]

"Winner takes all" labour markets

One important effect of globalization has been to reduce income inequality *between* countries, while increasing it *within* them. More trade and investment has made most of the world richer. But at a national level it also weakens the ability of trade unions to maintain good wages and hands advantages to the owners of capital and those with mobile skills who can exploit the new opportunities.

The result has been stark increase in inequality within rich countries, caused largely by stagnant or slow-rising wages for most workers and enormous rises at the top. Joseph Stiglitz argues that, over the last few decades in the United States, those with low wages (whom he actually classes as being in the bottom 90 per cent) have seen growth of only 15 per cent in their incomes. Those in the top 1 per cent have seen growth of almost 150 per cent, and the top 0.1 per cent of more than 300 per cent.[27] Countries in supposedly more egalitarian Europe have also seen sharp rises in inequality.

One cause of this may have been the emergence of what Robert Frank and Philip Cook have called the "winner-take-all" society.[28] These are societies in which small variations in performance make huge differences to rewards, and their emergence helps to explain why incomes at the top have risen dramatically. Previously, wages were based mainly on absolute performance: what you got out was roughly equivalent to what you put in. Rewards now are often based on relative performance, with the top echelon of performers in a particular field cornering the lion's share of the rewards.

This has long been the norm in entertainment and sports; the top half-dozen "bankable" movie stars command multi-million salaries, but the sums drop off dramatically outside this charmed circle. It is also now increasingly familiar in business and is particularly salient in technology fields, as the economics of the industry tends to hand out huge "first-mover" advantage to those firms, and their owners, that lead the way. Consider how Amazon dominates internet shopping with few serious rivals, or how Uber is taking over electronic ride hailing. In many consumer markets there is less and less room available for second best. The market leading device or app may be only marginally better than its closest competitor but this small edge may be more than enough to enable it to dominate, and the entrepreneurs and developers behind it will reap most of the rewards.

Moreover, the concentration of wealth among entrepreneurs and owners of successful businesses may continue and even accelerate because of the tendency of the value of capital to increase more rapidly than GDP, which is the thesis of Thomas Piketty, a French economist who caused a stir in 2014 with his book *Capital in the Twenty-First Century*.[29] The importance of ownership rather than labour in determining wealth could help explain why so many of the super-rich "0.1 per centers" are founder-owners of businesses, especially technology firms, rather than salaried professionals or even top-performing artists. They have leapt ahead in the wealth stakes and are far in front of even highly paid people such as bankers and plastic surgeons, who form part of the "mere" 1 per cent as opposed to the mega-wealthy.

Of course, a ruthless market for talent probably benefits society if it helps to throw up the next Taylor Swift or Zinedine Zidane. There is an argument also for adding the likes of Jeff Bezos (founder of Amazon) and Bill Gates (Microsoft) to that list, as they create products of considerable value to consumers. But the "winner takes all" scenario is less persuasive in explaining pay explosions else-where, for instance in finance, blue chip businesses and the professions. The pay of CEOs, for example, has increased from 20 times the average worker in their company in 1965 to more than 300 times today.[30] Top lawyers, financiers and consultants, while not qualifying for membership of the 0.1 per cent, have reaped similarly outsize rewards.

The justification for high executive pay is based on a set of management theo-ries (often promoted by CEOs themselves) that emphasize the huge importance of "leadership" qualities of CEOs. The contribution to a company's profits of a highly effective boss will massively outweigh the extra cost of hiring her, as no matter how large her salary package it is still a fraction of the operating expenses of the company as a whole.[31] Paying 20 per cent above the market rate for an outstanding leader, say $12 million a year, will be well worth it to a $10 billion company if having this corporate star on board raises performance – an extra 5 per cent of after-tax profits, for example: a mere $2 million in extra pay for an extra $500 million of profit.

The main problem with this argument is that, in practice, it is very difficult to link pay to results. Is the performance of a CEO accurately reflected in her com-pany's share price? Not necessarily. It may be a result of unexpectedly favourable market conditions, or difficult decisions taken by her predecessor that are only now bearing fruit. Worse, linking executive remuneration too tightly to share price performance may encourage her to pursue reckless expansion for the sake of a temporary lift in share prices. One way that big firms have boosted their share price is through aggressive cost-cutting, including cutting headcounts and holding down wages.

A further source of disquiet is that the business models of some technology firms relies on the increasing casualization of their workforces, further fuelling inequality. The taxi firm Uber is a case in point, helping to give rise to the so-called "gig economy" of casual, freelance workers with little of the benefits or job security available to permanent employees on contracts. Uber drivers are not employed by the firm but are self-employed and work from job to job with no guaranteed number of hours. Free-market economists argue that such perks interfere with the operation of labour markets and point out that no one is forced to work for these firms. But independent work in the gig economy may not be entirely voluntary and could reflect a dearth of jobs in the regular economy. Definitional problems make it hard to gauge the size of the gig economy but one US government estimate puts it at 8 per cent of the workforce.[32] Workers in this sector are also younger and less educated and earn considerably less than work-ers in the regular economy.

Automation

The third trend in labour markets is potentially the most far-reaching. It is the growing extent of automation as human functions are increasingly taken over by cheaper and more methodical machines. Most observers agree we are undergoing a period of rapid technological change. In most previous eras when this has been happening, new industries and jobs have emerged to replace dying old ones. But there is no necessary reason why the two processes have to work together in lockstep. Some economists worry that this era of change is different in that old jobs might be lost at a much more rapid pace than they are replaced, assuming they are replaced at all. The "age of the machines" could entail the end of work as we know it.

The extent to which it is possible to replace a job entirely with a machine varies greatly. Most people do a job that is possible to automate to some extent. Even otherwise highly skilled jobs probably involve some tasks, such as handling data or typing e-mails setting out important information, that it would be possible usefully to automate. Skilled manufacturing work and the majority of service jobs that involve creativity or dealing with the public are still, for the moment, best done by humans. Even some ostensibly very simple jobs that nevertheless require visual recognition of complex patterns, such as tidying a messy desk, are still well beyond current machine capability. But for many jobs this point in time has already arrived. Most agricultural work is now performed by machines, and many factories similarly automate very repetitive or heavy operations.

The economic rationale for automation is usually a combination of cost (even expensive machines work out cheaper than humans over a period of time, particularly with high batch numbers) and precision (machines do not make mistakes, get bored or go on strike). Even if the business case for automation is not immediately compelling, many companies will embark on this process regardless on the assumption that their competitors will probably be doing the same.

Automation has actually been going on for a long time, since before the Industrial Revolution, in fact, although it is most usually associated with increased use of computing in offices since the 1950s and factory robots from the 1980s. But many analysts believe it has reached a tipping point and is now accelerating as we begin increasingly to exploit what is often called the "knowledge economy". The UK government describes this as "one in which the generation and exploitation of knowledge has come to play the predominant part in the creation of wealth. It is not simply about pushing back the frontiers of knowledge; it is also about the most effective use and exploitation of all types of knowledge in all manner of economic activity."[33]

Application of the knowledge economy can be seen in an increase in the use of big data and deployment of increasingly "smart" IT to solve complex and unpredictable work-based problems. As a result, automation is now moving out of the factory to encroach into many service-sector jobs. The key development here is that improvement in the computer processing power that lies behind automation has reached a sufficient level of sophistication to allow machines to take on a number of jobs once thought to be the exclusive purview of humans.

In 2004 Frank Levy and Richard Murnane published an explosive study in which they split tasks between information-processing and rule-following tasks, which machines were good at, and pattern recognition tasks, which they are bad at.[34] This distinction is dissolving rapidly. For example, it would have been assumed that driving a car would have been one of the tasks suitable for humans only. But Google's driverless car has been given the all-clear for commercial trials and looks set to make inroads into occupational sectors such as taxi drivers and truckers by the early 2020s, entailing major job losses. An additional implication is that driverless cars can be easily shared, so we will need many fewer of them and certainly not the tens of millions of cars manufactured every year: bad news for mass car makers and their workers.

Many other service jobs could follow; for example, a lot of work examining medical and legal documents can now be done by computer. Ominously for developing countries, these are the kinds of jobs they have only recently succeeded in poaching from developed countries, and yet they could be among the first service jobs to be taken over by the new breed of intelligent machines. Arguably a key development is that artificial intelligence programmes are now increasingly able to mimic – albeit imperfectly as yet – human thought processes rather than simply crunching through vast quantities of data to try to produce the same result.[35] This is the difference between grinding down grand masters at chess through computational brute force and a much more subtle programme such as the Go-playing Deep Mind, which really does "think" for itself. The advent of these tools allows employers to automate a much wider tranche of service-sector jobs embodying a wider set of skills.

Automation and the knowledge economy therefore look set to have an impact on what is known as "technological unemployment", or unemployment caused by improvements in technology running ahead of the ability of the economy to absorb it.[36] Jobs vulnerable to such skill-biased technical change (SBTC) include swathes of reasonably well-paid but semi-skilled ones held by middle-class workers (see Table 3.1). The conventional assumption, based on an upward-sloping industry cost curve for labour, has been that demand would increase for the most highly skilled jobs and fall for the lowest-paid least skilled jobs, as these are the cheapest to replace. But this has not really happened. Instead, it has tended to be

Table 3.1 Jobs most and least at risk of automation

Least at risk
  Recreational therapists
  Supervisors of mechanics, installers, repairers
  Emergency managing directors
  Mental health and substance abuse social workers
  Audiologists

Most at risk
  Telemarketers
  Title examiners, abstractors and researchers
  Mathematical technicians
  Insurance underwriters
  Watch repairers

Source: Oxford Martin School.

middle-skill jobs embodying a middle range of skills that have been disappearing in greatest numbers in recent years, with high- and low-skilled jobs seeing increases – a phenomenon known as the "hollowing out" of the labour force, which is also fuelling inequality. This has even been linked to political turmoil in Europe and North America as centrist, middle-class parties representing these workers become torn between protecting workers whose jobs are threatened through inward-looking policies and cultivating younger "knowledge workers" who want change.

Analysts of SBTC are divided over how profoundly it is changing labour markets for the worse. "Techno-optimists" accuse the doomsayers of "Luddite" tendencies and point out that technological change produces productivity improvements that generate increases in wealth that fuel the job-creating machine that is the economy. Schumpeterian "creative destruction", acting this time through the knowledge economy, will clear out old, defunct industries and replace them with shiny new ones. For example, the smartphone industry is only around a decade old yet is already worth $400 billion.[37] In short, they challenge the "techno-pessimists" to prove that something really is different this time. The pessimists point out that for most of the last 200 years technology has boosted productivity, but that this relationship has broken down recently, with job growth increasingly decoupling from both. Facebook's acquisition of WhatsApp in 2014 would seem to illustrate this. The social media giant paid $19 billion – the market valuation of Sony – for an upstart messaging app with only 55 employees. With value being increasingly concentrated among small groups of highly skilled technology workers, where does this leave the rest of us?

In truth, all three of these big trends are probably reinforcing each other in ways that are making life very uncomfortable for policy-makers in rich countries. Changes to the nature of the key factors of production – labour and capital – are undoubtedly taking place. The lucky and the talented will probably thrive in this new work environment, but many more are in for a struggle.

Conclusion: what we have learnt

- The world of work has changed enormously over the last two centuries in response to economic development – the switch from farming to manufacturing, and latterly to services – as well as social and political changes, such as the growth and decline of trade unions and female empowerment. It is now changing again as globalization and automation alter the way business is done.
- Mainstream economics builds on notions of demand and supply for labour to explain how jobs are created and who does them. It can also provide a realistic, though not complete, picture of how labour markets operate in the aggregate.
- Government also plays a major role in the labour market. It can act to stimulate demand in the economy and boost employment when countries are stuck in recession and the market is unable to self-right. It also plays a more passive role in regulating employment conditions and, in many countries, setting a statutory minimum wage.
- Economists believe labour markets will be changed profoundly by automating many tasks now done by humans, but are unsure of the effect on the economy and society, with optimists focusing on the benefits of this for productivity and pessimists forecasting mass unemployment.

Notes

1. D. Kahneman & A. Deaton, "High income improves evaluation of life but not emotional well-being", *Proceedings of the National Academy of Sciences of the United States of America* 107:38 (2010), 16489–93.
2. S. Lee, D. McCann & J. Messenger, *Working Time around the World: Trends in Working Hours, Laws and Policies in a Global Comparative Perspective* (Abingdon, UK: Routledge, 2007).
3. R. Gordon, *The Rise and Fall of American Growth: The US Standard of Living since the Civil War* (Princeton, NJ: Princeton University Press, 2016).
4. G. Andrew, *Capitalism Unleashed: Finance, Globalization and Welfare* (Oxford: Oxford University Press, 2006).
5. The two mainstream economics textbooks that focus on labour markets are T. Boeri & J. van Ours, *The Economics of Imperfect Labor Markets* (Princeton, NJ: Princeton University Press, 2008); and G. Borjas, *Labor Economics*, 6th edn (New York: McGraw Hill, 2012).
6. S. Linder, *The Harried Leisure Class* (New York: Columbia University Press, 1971).

7. See "Wages and labour costs", Eurostat, http://ec.europa.eu/eurostat/statistics-explained/index.php/Wages_and_labour_costs (accessed 28 September 2017).
8. J. Pessoa & J. Van Reenen, "The UK productivity puzzle: does the answer lie in wage flexibility?", *Economic Journal* 124 (2014), 433–52.
9. R. Perlin, *Intern Nation: How to Earn Nothing and Learn Little in the Brave New Economy* (London: Verso, 2011).
10. P. Cramp, *Labour Markets: The Economics of Work and Leisure*, 5th edn (Stocksfield, UK: Anforme, 2011).
11. C. Pissarides & D. Mortensen, "New developments in models of search in the labour market", Discussion Paper no. 2053 (London: Centre for Economic Policy Research, 1999).
12. J. M. Keynes, *The General Theory of Employment, Interest and Money* [1936] (Whitefish, MT: Kessinger Publishing, 2010).
13. B. Eichengreen, *The European Economy since 1945: Coordinated Capitalism and Beyond* (Princeton, NJ: Princeton University Press, 2007).
14. Perhaps the most concise and influential intellectual statement of the free market counter-revolution of the 1970s is Milton and Rose Friedman's *Free to Choose: A Personal Statement* (New York: Harcourt, 1980).
15. OECD, "The OECD jobs study: facts, analysis, strategies", 1994, www.oecd.org/els/emp/1941679.pdf (accessed 13 July 2016).
16. A. Rees, *The Economics of Trade Unions*, 3rd edn (Chicago: University of Chicago Press, 1989).
17. P. Hall & D. Soskice, *Varieties of Capitalism: The Institutional Foundations of Comparative Advantage* (Oxford: Oxford University Press, 2011).
18. S. Vitols, "German industrial policy: an overview", Discussion Paper no. FSI 96–321 (Berlin: Wissenschaftszentrum Berlin für Sozialforschung, 1996).
19. OECD, *Government at a Glance 2015* (Paris: OECD Publishing, 2015), 84–6.
20. D. Card, J. Kluve & A. Weber, "Active labor market policy evaluations: a meta-analysis", *Economic Journal* 120 (2010), 452–77.
21. D. Card & A. Krueger, "Minimum wages and employment: a case study of the fast food industry in New Jersey and Pennsylvania", Working Paper no. 4509 (Cambridge, MA: NBER, 1993).
22. For a good overview of the way labour markets are changing, see R. Donkin, *The Future of Work* (Basingstoke, UK: Palgrave Macmillan, 2010).
23. G. Gereffi, J. Humphrey & T. Sturgeon, "The governance of global value chains", *Review of International Political Economy* 12:1 (2005), 78–104.
24. M. Wolf, *Why Globalization Works* (New Haven, CT: Yale University Press, 2004).
25. M. Spence, "The impact of globalization on income and employment", *Foreign Affairs* 90:4 (2011), 28–41.
26. R. Avent, *The Wealth of Humans: Work, Power and Status in the Twenty-First Century* (London: Penguin Books, 2016).
27. J. Stiglitz, *The Price of Inequality* (London: Penguin Books, 2013).
28. R. Frank & P. Cook, *The Winner-Take-All Society: Why the Few at the Top Get So Much More than the Rest of Us* (London: Penguin Books, 1996).
29. T. Piketty, *Capital in the Twenty-First Century* (Cambridge, MA: Harvard University Press, 2014).
30. L. Mishel & A. Davis, Top CEOs make 300 times more than typical workers: pay growth surpasses stock gains and wage growth of top 0.1 percent, Issue Brief no. 399 (Washington, DC: Economic Policy Institute, 2015).
31. G. Mankiw, "Defending the one percent", *Journal of Economic Perspectives* 27:3 (2013), 21–4.
32. US Government Accountability Office, "Contingent workforce: size, characteristics, earnings, and benefits", 20 April 2015, available at www.gao.gov/assets/670/669766.pdf (accessed 15 July 2016).

33. Department for Trade and Industry, *Our Competitive Future: Building the Knowledge-Driven Economy* (London: Stationery Office, 1988).
34. F. Levy & R. Murnane, *The New Division of Labor: How Computers Are Creating the Next Job Market* (Princeton, NJ: Princeton University Press, 2005).
35. M. Ford, *Rise of the Robots: Technology and the Threat of Mass Unemployment* (Oxford: Oneworld, 2015).
36. E. Brynjolfsson & A. McAfee, *The Second Machine Age: Work, Progress and Prosperity in a Time of Brilliant Technologies* (New York: Norton, 2016).
37. *Forbes* estimate, 2015.

4

GET WELL SOON: HEALTH AND HEALTHCARE

He who has health has hope; and he who has hope has everything.
Thomas Carlyle

Key questions

- Who should pay for and/or provide healthcare: the public or private sector?
- Why are healthcare costs rising, and are they containable?
- Is there one "best" way of organizing healthcare systems?
- How can we ensure that healthcare is equitable, affordable and effective?

Summary

Healthcare systems vary widely across countries, but individuals everywhere face versions of the same set of choices: whether to pay for, or get their employer to pay for, a good personal healthcare package, or to fall back on the state. People face dilemmas over how much to put aside for unknown future health risks, however, and how to offset the costs of doing this against more immediate demands on their time and money. Governments can always step in to provide collective, public solutions but given that health is a massive, global business with vast economies of scale should more of a role be handed to the private sector? And, if so, how should big pharmaceutical and medical companies that operate across borders be regulated? Ultimately, with ageing populations in advanced economies putting a massive strain on resources, individuals may need to take more responsibility if societies are to avoid having to ration ever more expensive healthcare.

Main topics and theories covered

Health economics and arguments for public intervention; why national health-care systems differ; markets in healthcare; longevity and public health; the role of big drug companies and private medicine.

4.1 Healthcare and risk pooling

This chapter is about the role of healthcare systems in keeping us healthy and happy. The contribution of economics to this might not be immediately obvious. Surely, meeting our healthcare needs is a simple matter of building enough hospitals, stocking them with enough equipment and drugs and letting the medical professionals get on with the job?

As can be imagined, though, the reality is a lot more complicated than that. For a start, it is quite hard even to define "health" in terms useful to an economist or policy-maker. The founding documents of the World Health Organization denote health as being "a state of complete physical, mental, and social well-being and not merely the absence of disease or infirmity".[1] A nice, encompassing definition perhaps, but not really a cast-iron guide to building a system for achieving this goal.

Underlying most policy dilemmas in healthcare, ultimately, is the issue of resources. Spending on health varies enormously across the globe. As might be expected, the richest countries spend the most, reflecting the fact that healthcare is what is known in economics as a "superior good": the wealthier you get, the more of it you want; after all, what is the point of money if you do not have the good health to enable you to enjoy it? Americans spend the most, $9,145 per person annually, compared with $61 in India.[2] But, in line with predictions, poorer countries are catching up rapidly as their economies develop; Chinese spending is projected to hit $1 trillion by 2020.[3]

What exactly is all this money being spent on? Healthcare systems can probably be said to have three main roles. The first of these is pretty obvious: to heal the sick. The second tries to obviate the need for the first by keeping people healthy to begin with. The third recognizes that this is very difficult – humans are fragile beings who inevitably need care at various points in their lives – and so tries to protect them from the financial catastrophe resulting from unexpected medical bills.

Individuals themselves obviously have primary responsibility for their own health and well-being, and this can also extend to close relatives, especially children and elderly parents. But we all have a wider interest in a healthcare system that enables us to live surrounded by a population of happy, healthy people rather than impoverished, disgruntled invalids.[4] History suggests that public policy – diet, economic growth and political conditions, as well as the development of healthcare systems themselves – have all combined to produce a massive uptick in longevity. Life expectancy in Europe was just over 40 years for men and women in 1900, the same as a chimpanzee, but by 2008 it had risen to around 65 for men and 74 for women.[5]

The sheer complexity of healthcare suggests some sort of role for government, either in providing care directly, or at least getting involved in regulation and the training of medical professionals. The actual delivery of healthcare varies widely, though; from largely state-provided national health services to countries where private hospitals have the leading role. The development of new drugs and technology is generally left to private companies, but there is also great variation in how individuals can choose their own treatment, as opposed to leaving it up to doctors or regulators.

Ultimately, however, the various structures and arrangements are merely different means of producing the same good: better health. The knottiest problems in health policy by far arise from the fact that health*care* is very expensive and there is almost unlimited demand for it. Economics therefore has an important role to play in examining the inevitable trade-offs that arise. The rest of this chapter deals with how we should think about "health" in economic terms; how to organize "healthcare"; how to contain the vast costs; and the role of the private sector.

The basic economics of health and healthcare

Let us start by laying out what constitutes a healthcare "system". The foundations of national systems are family doctors, who are often the gatekeepers to specialized care and usually the initial and most regular point of contact for patients. The other key building blocks of the healthcare edifice are hospitals, for emergency and clinical needs, and nursing homes, for elderly people requiring long-term care (LTC). Behind the scenes are some other big players. These include national regulatory authorities, which dictate how care is regulated and prioritized, and the big drug and technology firms, which develop new treatments. Finally, insurance companies in many countries provide medical cover for people in exchange for regular payments.

Thus, in most systems, there is a complex mix of market and state provision and funding, with individuals either paying indirectly for their healthcare through taxation so it is free at the point of delivery (such as the United Kingdom's National Health Service: NHS) or directly out of pocket or via their health insurance policy (most of the rest of the world).

> **Box 4.1 Key terms**
>
> - *Derived demand.* A demand for a commodity or service that relates to (is "derived" from) the demand for something else.
> - *Resource input–goods output model.* Analysis of the connections between the producing and consuming segments of an economic system.
> - *"Big pharma".* Large, global biotechnology firms with big R&D budgets responsible for a large share of new drug development.

Lionel Robbins' dictum, that economics is about satisfying chosen ends with scarce means, is particularly relevant here because there is almost limitless demand for good health, which is contributing to spiralling costs. If you get sick, you understandably want the very best treatment available, and medical professionals at the sharp end of the system – the doctors and nurses treating you – will want this too. It is probably why they went into medicine in the first place. But hospital accountants – the managers of healthcare systems in charge of budgets – have to balance this aim with the limited resources available. Any one allocation of scarce healthcare involves opportunity costs, in that devoting resources to treat patient A means less for patient B.

Economics helps us approach healthcare from the perspective of both equity and efficiency in order to find the system that best manages these trade-offs. Efficiency is obviously important here, for the reasons of cost containment outlined above. But almost every healthcare system in the world includes equity as an important objective as well. Note that equity here does not mean equality, as this would imply that everyone has equal demands on healthcare resources regardless of medical circumstances. Instead, most systems regulate access according to need – how sick you are, in other words.

The next step is to reconcile "need" with the resource constraints that are a feature of all healthcare systems. The subdiscipline of "health economics" has evolved as a means to uncover evidence about the value of specific interventions and the impact of policies or practices. Should preventing obesity or treating heart disease be a priority, for example? How much should be spent on costly "wonder drugs" that may prolong life for only a short time in terminally ill people?

Health economics is grounded in welfare economics (see Chapter 8), which is itself steeped in the NCE assumption about individuals generally knowing what is in their own best interests and acting upon their choices in a market setting. But, as with welfare issues, health economists acknowledge myriad information problems surrounding choice in healthcare that generally render pure market solutions unviable, requiring at least some involvement by regulators and governments. Behavioural economists also contribute a lot to the field of health economics by reminding us that individuals may not be rational or consistent and sometimes make poor decisions, particularly when sick. Both sets of issues – limited information and irrationality – may also justify a considerable amount of state provision. Let us not forget, though, that public healthcare is itself prone to "government failure": waste, bureaucracy, limited choice and regulatory "capture".

What is healthcare, and who should get it?

As with other branches of economics, health economics models the medical system by looking at the demand and supply of healthcare. In general, healthcare is viewed in economics as a "consumption commodity", as consuming it makes people feel better. Viewed in this way, as a good, healthcare can be treated as something that is manufactured and brought to market. It therefore involves producers (doctors) as well as consumers (patients).

Let us start with the demand side: patients. In common with general goods markets, healthcare concerns something that is desired by people who may be willing to pay more in taxes or insurance premiums to get more of it. As already mentioned, healthcare resources are scarce relative to demand, so the price of healthcare rises as demand for it increases. Suppliers of healthcare respond to this rise in prices, as well as other, non-financial, incentives such as regulation, to improve quality or shift resources around in response to changing demand. On the other hand, healthcare is also subject to diminishing returns, in that its utility decreases after a certain point as more is consumed: a health check-up every year or two feels prudent, but one every week probably makes me a hypochondriac.

This might seem like an argument for delivering all healthcare privately through the market; but that is not at all the case, for there are also a lot of ways in which healthcare is special, making it very unwise to treat it like any other market.[6] For a start, the relationship between people's health and their demand for health*care* is not one to one. In fact, a range of factors determine how healthy people are, such as their own lifestyle and genetics. Health is also less tangible than other goods, and so cannot be passed around to others like a book (although some infectious diseases can). It is also important to note that demand for healthcare is a derived demand: we want it because it produces some other benefit. When cancer sufferers undergo chemotherapy it is in the hope of being free from cancer, not because they enjoy the treatment. In a way, individuals "produce" their own health through their own attitudes and through interaction with the healthcare authorities.

For most goods and services the benefits accrue exclusively to the individual consuming it. But some healthcare services involve externalities; they affect people who are not paying for it. These can be good externalities (getting a flu shot so I will not infect my work colleagues) or bad ones (passive smoking from my cigarette habit). Either way, externalities are difficult to put a price on, which distorts the market and may need to be corrected by the government. Policy-makers can do this by subsidizing flu vaccinations or taxing cigarettes.

Health is also characterized by great uncertainty.[7] We can guess the grocery shopping we need to do next week but a broken leg or pneumonia is hard to predict. This all makes it difficult for doctors and administrators to tell how much demand there will be for healthcare services. They also cannot be sure how patients will respond to treatment – if, and how quickly, they will get better. Medical sciences and diagnostics are making big strides in analysing risk factors (for example, studying the influence of genetics and lifestyle on health) but injury and illness are still intrinsically unpredictable, and this vastly complicates the already difficult business of planning where best to direct scarce resources. In other words, the complicated nature of healthcare *demand* severely complicates the business of *supplying* it. Let us look in more detail at how this is done.

Your good health: leave it to the market?

Economics offers two perspectives on supply-side factors in healthcare – how it is delivered, in other words. One is known as the "resource input–goods output model", which simply relates costs to results. This approach looks at things such as economies of scale (are a few big hospitals better than lots of smaller ones?), productivity (how many extra operations can a hospital provide if it hires an extra nurse?) and factor substitution (does replacing one dentist with two dental hygienists benefit patients?). An alternative approach focuses on market structure, particularly in relation to private healthcare: how many firms are there in the market and how competitive is it?

What else influences supply? The physician is obviously central to how healthcare is delivered. Doctors make life or death decisions about treatment and are the patient's main point of contact with the system. Health economists sometimes worry about this because of information asymmetries, meaning that doctors know so much more than patients. This arises because most patients who are not doctors themselves are rationally uninformed about medical matters – which tends to be why they seek medical advice. In fact, one of the core services that doctors supply to their patients is, arguably, information about their maladies and expert suggestions for courses of treatment.

Such information asymmetries can prevent markets in healthcare working properly, however. In normal markets, people are usually willing to pay a higher price for a better service, and competition will eliminate providers that offer poor value for money. But all this depends on consumers (patients) having access to good information about care quality and cost, as well as the existence of alternative healthcare providers who might offer something better. In the absence of this, a poor quality of care could result or doctors could over-prescribe treatment to increase the income of their practice. Patients may also have problems interpreting what they are told (bounded rationality) and resist acting on medical advice (quitting smoking, even when bluntly told it is killing them, known as bounded willpower), making their treatment less effective.

These issues probably explain why medical doctors are one of the most highly regulated groups of professionals around. As well as undergoing long and intensely competitive training, on qualifying they have to take the Hippocratic oath, obliging them to meet rigorous ethical standards. Failure to abide by this oath can mean dismissal. Doctors keep themselves up to date with the latest medical advances and new treatments by reading peer-reviewed journals and enroll in continuing education. But, ultimately, the medical system depends a great deal on trust. I have to trust that my doctor knows what she is talking about and has my best interests at heart.

Finally, healthcare systems are also hugely political. Consider the contrasting attitudes of the United States and United Kingdom to private medicine.[8] Both are market-oriented economies comfortable with presumptions of individual choice in most matters. Yet they have utterly different attitudes as to who should provide healthcare services. In the United Kingdom, the National Health Service is the jewel in the crown of the welfare state, and private involvement is generally met with hostility. It is the opposite in the United States, where any interference in the market is derided as un-American socialism. Politics is not everything, but it helps to explain why healthcare systems in rich countries are organized so differently, and we turn to this next.

4.2 Public or private: how are healthcare systems organized?

Look around the developed world and you will see a wide range of healthcare systems. They differ principally over how care is delivered (whether it is mainly by the public sector, voluntary bodies or private companies), and how it is paid for (indirectly by taxpayers, or directly by individuals taking out insurance or paying out of their own pockets). Economists divide healthcare systems into three main types:[9]

(a) "NHS" systems (publicly funded and publicly delivered);
(b) "market systems" (privately funded and privately delivered);
(c) "social insurance systems" (a mix of public and private funding and delivery).

The classic example of the first type is probably the United Kingdom's National Health Service. As the name implies, the NHS is a universal, taxpayer-funded system managed by the state. Sweden has the same model, and both countries also allow some private hospitals for those prepared to pay for using them. Access to specialists is by referral only, with doctors in local surgeries performing a "gatekeeper" function. They are on a salary rather than getting their income from fees, removing a major incentive for them to oversupply treatment. The NHS is hugely popular – indeed, it was a centrepiece of the opening ceremony of the London Olympic Games in 2012 – possibly because being taxpayer-funded means it is free at the point of delivery, so you do not need to bring your wallet with you to the hospital.

Many people assume that the United States is organized in exactly the opposite fashion (privately funded and delivered), and the US system is undoubtedly governed more by market forces than elsewhere. Doctors' surgeries and hospitals essentially operate as self-employed entrepreneurs offering services on a fee basis paid by patients or their insurance company. Most hospitals are owned either by private, not-for-profit or government operators; the exact mix varies across states. But the United States is actually a long way from being a pure market system. While the private sector has a proportionately much bigger role than in other countries, almost half the funding still comes from the government (see Figure 4.1). In fact, public health spending in the United States takes up a larger share of GDP (almost 8 per cent in 2012) than social democratic Sweden.[10] The reason for the large public component is that the government funds two care programmes for vulnerable groups who might otherwise be condemned to lacklustre coverage: the old (Medicare) and the poor (Medicaid).

Even so, around 90 per cent of Americans have private health insurance, with about 55 per cent of this from workplace schemes.[11] People pay monthly premiums to ensure they will be covered when they need to be seen by a doctor or undergo treatment. Medicare and Medicaid clients may go to private hospitals, where their medical bills are paid from federal government funds. Insurance providers generally have thousands of fee-paying clients, which puts them in a good position to be able to negotiate competitive fees with providers. Thus, care is generally provided only by doctors and hospitals within the network, and patients seeking treatment elsewhere will have to pay extra for it. Insurance providers will usually cover only services considered necessary by the doctors with whom they deal, and often will not cover services that they consider "elective".

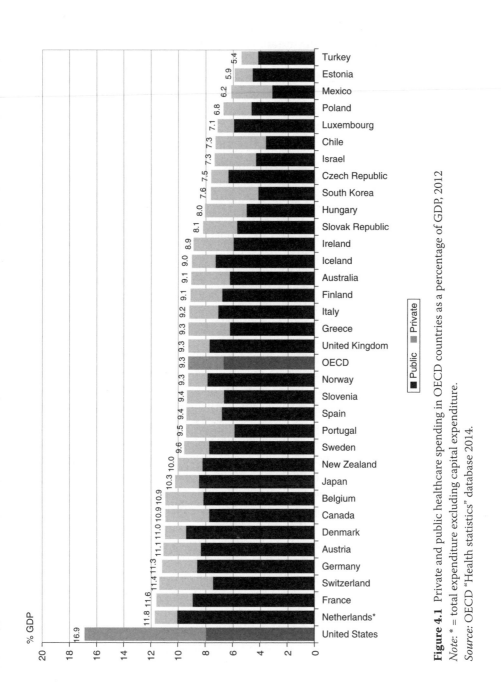

Figure 4.1 Private and public healthcare spending in OECD countries as a percentage of GDP, 2012

Note: * = total expenditure excluding capital expenditure.

Source: OECD "Health statistics" database 2014.

The third main type is the "social insurance" systems prevalent in continental Europe. Care is provided either in hospitals owned by regional governments, non-profit organizations or private firms, or by doctors in local practices. The system is funded through a mix of regional, industry-based or occupational insurance schemes. In social insurance systems, healthcare is in the hands of hospitals, which may be owned by local government, non-profit organizations or private firms and are funded by occupational schemes, often subsidized by the government. Canada arguably constitutes a fourth "type", with public funding for healthcare that is largely delivered through the private sector.

There are advantages and disadvantages with all these systems. Taxpayer-funded NHS-style systems are popular among patients as they do not have to take out insurance or pay upfront. As "universal" systems, they are also not prone to gaps in coverage for under-insured groups, although, in practice, care quality is far from uniform. The lack of competition among medical providers for a long time tended to restrict patient choice: you went to see your local GP, who sent you on for further treatment, and you had little say in the matter. The NHS's monolithic, bureaucratic structure can also be inefficient and inflexible. The overall amount of care available varies according to the inclination of central government to pay for it and so tends to be rationed whenever public finances are tight.

NHS reformers have tried to introduce an element of competition in the belief that market forces can eliminate rigidities and make the system responsive to patient demands. In the 1990s the government ceased being both funder and provider of services and encouraged hospitals to opt out of local authority control and compete for business from groups of doctors, who were given more responsibility over commissioning. Such "quasi-markets" have made healthcare providers more cost-conscious and responsive to patients, but probably not by very much, as they still lack the clear profit motive deemed necessary for a true market to operate.[12] Swedish reforms have been less about market forces and more about decentralization to get doctors to respond to local needs.

The insurance-based schemes found in the United States and continental Europe face a different set of problems. In principle, buying insurance for unexpected events (falling ill, in this case) is a good mechanism for individuals to spread the cost of potentially large medical bills if the government will not take on this responsibility for them. Without the dead hand of government, free-market arguments go, the system will be more efficient and closer to the needs of the patient. A wide mix of healthcare providers (private, state-run, not-for-profit, etc.) may also help in this regard by increasing competition.

But there are a number of market failures in health insurance systems that means things do not work out as planned. Market failure here can produce a situation in which the extra cost of an additional treatment exceeds the extra benefit of this to the patient. The doctor may still be incentivized to prescribe more treatment even though it is no longer cost-effective, however. This may inflate healthcare spending and reduce efficiency. As with the doctor–patient relationship discussed earlier, information asymmetries are the source of a lot of market failures. In this instance though, it is the client (the potential patient taking out insurance) who knows more than the insurance provider about her own lifestyle and health.

The main market failure here is known as "adverse selection". It is a problem for all insurance markets, as they require a diverse group of clients for the costs to be manageable. This client group is known as a "risk pool", and ideally comprises low-risk individuals, who pay premiums but are unlikely to claim, alongside those of higher risk, whom they effectively subsidize (see Chapter 8 for more on social insurance markets). But this risk pool may be difficult to achieve in practice. If insurers set premiums at a level that allows them to break even, the insurance is an attractive prospect for high-risk individuals (those likely to get ill and make a claim) but an unattractive one for those who are low risk (fit, healthy people). The low risks quit and leave the insurers with the high risks, whom they have to charge very high premiums to break even, leaving most people uninsured. This makes it difficult for the insurance company to make money from the business unless it charges high premiums.

Continental social insurance systems deal with this either by making insurance semi-compulsory or by subsidizing alternative provision for the under-insured. Universal systems obviously do not suffer from this problem at all, as all taxpayers are under the umbrella of the system and if they want to opt out the only way to do this is to go private. But private insurance systems such as in the United States have tended to end up with a large group of high-risk people who remain uninsured.

Another problem is moral hazard, as patients are typically insulated from rising healthcare costs. This arises when the insured person can covertly affect the insurance provider's liability. Having insurance that covers my risk of illness means I may become less risk-averse and adopt an unhealthy lifestyle, such as drinking and eating too much. There are several ways around this for insurers. One is to levy an extra charge on top of the insurance premiums on some treatments, which helps to make people think twice about their health and lifestyle. Another is simply to ration treatment, or to monitor the consumption of healthcare services and withhold insurance coverage for some treatments.

A further problem with health insurance is the "third-party payment problem". Insurance companies are the third party here, as they sit between the patient (you or me) and the provider (the doctor or hospital) and so have no way of preventing the other two parties from inflating costs. In this situation, doctors may tend to over-prescribe care as they are not themselves bearing its cost; it is the insurance company paying out. Doctors may also be unsure about which treatment will actually work and so may try several. Patients, who are paying for this only indirectly through their premiums, will usually concur in their eagerness to get better. And they are under-informed about medicine anyway, so who are they to argue with their doctor?

Box 4.2 The Affordable Care Act ("Obamacare")

Market failures in the US healthcare system have led to an explosion in costs, with the United States spending a higher proportion of GDP on healthcare (17 per cent) than any other nation in return for merely average outcomes, and with significant parts of the population left without cover. One solution to this was health maintenance organizations (HMOs) – new structures that merged doctors with insurance companies. Members of such schemes would pay direct to the HMO, whose administrators arranged their care while keeping an eye on expenses. HMOs helped to cut costs but did nothing to tackle the gaps in coverage, with around 20 per cent of the US population remaining uninsured.

President Obama's Democratic administration proposed a more radical solution, the Affordable Care Act (ACA), which was enacted in 2010 after a long fight with Congress. The ACA effectively strengthened existing healthcare markets and created a new market for the uninsured. US healthcare moved towards European models with a new legal expectation of health insurance for all US citizens. The ACA tried to make healthcare more affordable by expanding Medicaid and subsidizing poorer households through tax credits. Insurance companies were also banned from cancelling policies and excluding people with pre-existing conditions (helping to overcome the problem of adverse selection).

The plan was only a partial success. Although it halved the number of uninsured people and helped to keep a lid on costs, many people with existing policies complained about rising premiums, and the incoming president in 2017, Donald Trump, has pledged to reverse the ACA.

The third-party payment problem is thus a sure way to inflate costs, as the incentives operate to encourage too much healthcare rather than too little. It is probably one reason why the US healthcare system in particular is so expensive relative to its performance on indicators such as life expectancy and the prevalence of chronic conditions such as type 2 diabetes. Researchers find that Americans have relatively few hospital admissions and doctor visits, but make greater use of expensive technologies such as MRI machines. In general, health-care prices are notably higher in the United States than other countries.[13]

US regulators have tried various ruses to solve these problems, including set-ting up independent bodies to mediate costs and pricings. President Obama tried to reform the whole system to broaden coverage, with mixed results (see Box 4.2 on "Obamacare"). Another possible intervention is for governments to act to bear down directly on costs. For example, Canada regulates the prices of patented drugs and in some cases imposes a cost ceiling. Universal healthcare systems as in the United Kingdom also grapple with surging costs, but because the NHS is centralized it has a greater range of tools available to put a ceiling on cost increases through rationing. For example, in 1999 the UK government set up the National Institute for Health and Care Excellence (NICE), which advises on the most cost-efficient medication and clinical guidelines for care. But NICE comes in for a lot of political flak over this, and it never looks good when new drugs are being denied to cancer patients to save the government money. Ultimately, the NHS is subject to many of the same cost pressures as other systems face, as these are largely outside its control. The next section looks at some of these.

4.3 Why is health spending rising so rapidly?

Is the rise in healthcare spending affordable? Only governments and voters can really answer this question. Spending on medical services is certainly high, and rising, but it is hardly unmanageable. OECD countries on average spend around 9 per cent of their GDP on health, although this varies wildly from 7 per cent in Luxembourg to 17 per cent in the United States.[14] Nevertheless, on cur-rent trends, the demand for healthcare services is outstripping supply, which is showing up in rising cost pressures. In general, healthcare is a superior good: as income rises, demand for good healthcare rises too. But there are also a number of specific factors driving demand beyond this.

First, populations are ageing. The median age in the European Union has increased by four years since 2001, so that half the population is now aged 42 or over. There is also a particularly large population of "baby boomers", who were born between 1946 and 1964 and are now nearing retirement. By 2060 mean life expectancy is expected to increase by 8.5 years to 84.5 years for men, and by 6.9 years to 89 years for women. The rise in the number of "very old" people, aged 80 and over, will be particularly pronounced.

Ageing populations have two potential implications for the affordability of healthcare. They mean an increase in the dependency ratio, with fewer working people supporting retirees through their taxes (assuming retirement ages fail to keep pace: see Chapter 8 on welfare for a discussion of this). This puts pressure on all areas of government spending, not just healthcare; healthcare is a particularly large portion of spending in most countries, however, so it is heavily affected. In addition, older people tend to consume more healthcare. As we age, we accumulate more ailments as our bodies wear out and we begin to be afflicted by chronic conditions.

Opinions differ, though, on the significance of this factor. Some analysts pessimistically believe that, while medical progress will continue to increase the number of years people will live, much of these will be spent in costly ill health and disability.[15] This is based on the assumption that improvements in healthcare and healthy behaviour over the course of the last hundred years or so mean that humans are already close to their "natural" life expectancy and efforts to push the envelope further will be unproductive. Others are more optimistic, believing there is no reason why increased longevity should not be balanced by better control of chronic illnesses, as has already happened with heart disease and many cancers.[16]

In fact, the majority of analysts find that ageing is only likely to moderately increase spending on acute care. The really big impact will be on long-term and social care, which is less expensive per unit.[17] Nevertheless, although most long-term care for older people is still provided for free by family members, its cost is beginning to impact public health budgets in a big way: it is expected to double to 2.3 per cent of GDP in the European Union by 2060, for example. Various forms of dementia, such as Alzheimer's, cost the United States a quarter of a trillion dollars in 2010, according to a RAND study.[18] In the absence of a cure, these numbers are set to spiral further as more people live long enough to develop the disease and require care in a nursing home if their families cannot cope. The overall impact will therefore depend on how increasing incidences of dementia interact with public policy – in other words, how much governments are prepared to spend to support families and other carers.

Obesity is potentially an even more serious problem than dementia, as it leads to conditions that require acute care – heart disease, strokes and type 2 diabetes – and are therefore more expensive to treat. Globally, more than 2.1 billion people – around a third of the world's population – are overweight or obese, and this is two and a half times the number who are malnourished. Treating obesity already accounts for 16.5 per cent of all US healthcare spending and is forecast to rise significantly.[19]

The second important factor is the cost of medical technology, which is rising at a much faster rate than general inflation: 8.75 per cent compared with 3.2 per cent in 2015.[20] The impact of technology on health budgets ultimately depends on what the technology is for: if it treats symptoms of a disease (as with type 2 diabetes) then it is cost-increasing; but if it prevents or cures diseases (as with coronary angiography) then it is cost-reducing. Unfortunately for hospital accountants, it seems that the former is true and technological improvements are contributing significantly to spending growth – accounting for around half the increase, according to some studies.[21] The cost of drugs is also rising steeply, with 12 of the 13 newly approved cancer drugs in 2012 costing more than $100,000 a year per patient.[22] Fashions are also changing, and the availability of new types of healthcare may create its own demand. Having a baby at home costs the NHS much less than delivering it in hospital. In 1960 one in three babies was delivered at home; the proportion is now about one in 50.

An acute and growing problem is that longevity is driving up the number of people requiring long-term care. LTC of elderly and infirm people is usually provided through a partnership between their relatives and medical providers, either public or private. At first glance, LTC might not seem too much of a problem for government accountants, as it is a much cheaper and more low-tech form of treatment than, say, accident and emergency services, and the burden is shared with the old person's family. But its impact is already significant and set to increase. There are around 6.5 million informal carers in the United Kingdom, many of whom are older than 65 years themselves, providing care that would cost taxpayers £165 billion a year if their services were assumed by the state.[23]

Alzheimer's is a major driver of this. In the United States in 2012 an estimated 15 million dementia caregivers provided 17.5 billion hours of unpaid care.[24] There is a major opportunity cost here, as carers normally have to withdraw from the workforce, which they find difficult to rejoin later.[25] Carers are particularly likely to be women, even when workplace leave policies are gender-neutral, as they are typically paid less than men, which makes for a smaller income loss to the family.

Valuing a human life

A controversial issue underlying approaches to paying for healthcare is how to value a human life. This might sound callous, but pricing lives is a key step in working out how best to preserve them. Doctors attending serious emergencies, or on the battlefield, routinely prioritize cases (known as "triage"). Less dramatically, much of the complexity of health systems involves decisions about allocating scarce resources to competing ends – prenatal care versus emergency services, for example – so it helps to be able to see whether treatments are cost-effective or not.

Since we can easily know the marginal cost of an extra treatment, if we can also estimate the value of the life it may save then we can judge whether the extra investment makes sense financially. So-called "death economists" (probably the most dismal part of the dismal science) produce a measure of this called "value of a statistical life" (VSL). VSL can be used to model the efficiency of various public policy interventions – not just healthcare, but also road safety measures and environmental protection. Using VSL, the adoption of a medical procedure is considered justified if its cost is lower than the value of the number of years of life it saves.

But are all years of a person's life equal? Not necessarily, particularly if the extra years bought by the treatment are miserable. So, a further refinement to the calculations is probably necessary, the "quality-adjusted life year" (QALY), which may give extra weight to years spent in good health.

Naturally, this leads to complex ethical conundrums. Should a young child's life be worth more than an elderly person's? The child has longer potentially to live, but the older person may have acquired useful skills that it would be costly to replicate. Should we also adjust the value of a life according to the efforts that individuals expend to prolonging it? Some doctors argue that heavy smokers and alcoholics should go to the back of the queue for treatment as their own lifestyle choices raise the cost of making them better compared with others.

The converse argument is that these substances are addictive and the solution lies in advertising their impact on health rather than restricting treatment. The problem, of course, is that pricing a human life, although not completely subjective, can still vary wildly depending on the assumptions you make. A benchmark widely used by insurance companies is that a worthwhile treatment must guarantee one year of good-quality life for $50,000 or less.[26] Other studies put this higher, at $129,000.[27]

4.4 Business and the globalization of healthcare

Health is increasingly an international concern. Globalization and international travel and migration are opening up the world to the risk of global pandemics. Emerging diseases such as Ebola and bird flu are worrying international bodies such as the WHO and the United-States-based Centers for Disease Control and Prevention. Less dramatic, but equally serious, is the spread of "rich world" diseases such as type 2 diabetes in developing countries. This was once confined to the populations of Europe and North America, where fat-rich diets and sedentary lifestyles were prevalent; yet rising living standards outside the West mean it is almost everyone's problem now. The current number of people with type 2 diabetes globally is 387 million, and that number is expected to increase to 592 million by 2035.[28] Yet China and India already have the largest number of sufferers in the world, at more than 96 million and 66 million, respectively.

Historically, developed countries led globalization in healthcare by pushing drugs and services into developing countries that lacked domestic healthcare industries. Now, as with consumer products, it is more of a two-way street. Developing countries with fast-improving healthcare sectors as well as low labour costs are benefiting from "offshoring" by Western healthcare firms, which are relocating services such as medical diagnostics and drug testing to low-cost countries. For example, if you go for a chest X-ray at your local hospital, the chances are that the data will be scanned and sent to India for analysis, with the results e-mailed back to your doctor. Medical research, as well as numerous back-office functions, is also being outsourced. Such practices help to contain costs, although they are accompanied by worries about credentialling and quality control.

Economic integration in healthcare is led by private companies, rather than governments. The growth of private-sector involvement in health systems and economies of scale in medical research mean it is becoming an increasingly important global *business*. This worries some on the political Left, who fear the "corporatization" of medicine. Others are more relaxed, pointing to the cost savings that accrue from exploiting globalized medicine.

Private companies are particularly dominant in drug development. The basic economic model here is that companies innovate and governments pay for whatever they come up with. Drug development has been described as sifting through tens of thousands of molecules to find the single one that has a clinical use. As can be imagined, it is an expensive and rather hit-and-miss affair, requiring huge resources and considerable patience. The research and testing phase of a new medicine can easily take five years, followed by another five just to complete initial development. Completing trials and gaining certification with regulators such as the United States' Food and Drug Administration (FDA), before commercializing the drug and bringing it to market, can easily add another ten years to the process, making 20 in all.

And only a few drugs are a commercial success. Just two in ten approved medicines produce revenues that exceed average R&D costs.[29] Development is getting ever more expensive, with the cost of bringing a single new drug to market more than doubling in the last ten years, to $2.9 billion.[30] Figure 4.2 shows that, although the total number of drug approvals is holding steady, these are proving increasingly expensive for their developers to achieve.

One reason for this is that regulators are becoming much more demanding. Prior to the 1970s a drug had merely to be safe and effective to be approved. Now it needs to show clear advantages over drugs that are already available. Shifting healthcare priorities driven by longevity are also adding to the expense. There has been a pronounced increase in drug trials in therapeutic areas that have potentially higher sales, such as chronic and degenerative diseases, but carry a

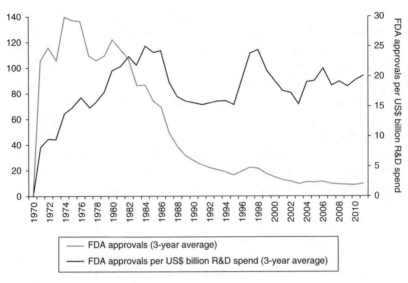

Figure 4.2 Annual FDA pharmaceutical approvals per US dollar billion R&D spend, 1970–2010
Note: Indexed to the 2008 US dollar.
Source: OECD, various.

greater risk of failure.[31] This is driving drug firms to get bigger through mergers, which make some of them very powerful in the process. The increasing power and concentration of "big pharma", coupled with a greater sense that health and well-being are now global, not national, problems, are leading some commentators to conclude that drug research is an international public good that is far too important to be left up to the market.

Critics of big pharma therefore worry that too much market power is being concentrated in a small number of major drug firms. With most drug research being concentrated among these companies, who answer to their shareholders, not patients, they effectively set their own research agenda and can focus their efforts on what is most profitable. Some commentators worry that the changing economics of the industry is seeing R&D focused increasingly on "lifestyle" and "convenience" drugs that are driven by rich-world problems, such as the expensive but so far fruitless cure for baldness.[32] The small number of new drugs that do have therapeutic benefits are increasingly too expensive to be affordable.

Consider this example of conflict over drug development and procurement. A few years ago a new drug, Sovaldi, was approved to cure hepatitis C, which attacks the liver and can also lead to cancer. Sovaldi is extremely effective and works on a wide range of patients. But it is also very expensive, costing around $1,000 a day for all 12 weeks of treatment. Gilead, Sovaldi's manufacturer, points to research and development costs that must be recouped. This presents the health authorities with a dilemma. The drug is clearly effective in curing large numbers of hepatitis C sufferers, so there are major public health benefits. But the opportunity cost of paying for courses of Sovaldi means (a) there are is less money available for treating other conditions and (b) there may be ethical issues if access to the drug is restricted only to those who can bear some or all of the cost of it privately.

Cannot governments simply regulate to bring down prices? Drug markets are very complex, and countries with different healthcare regimes face varying constraints. For example, one reason why Americans seem to pay a higher price for drugs than other countries is that Medicare and Medicaid are barred from using their dominant positions as purchasers of healthcare to barter down prices. In other countries such as Germany, however, the insurance companies are free to negotiate and can use their buying power to drive a harder bargain.

Drugs are also marketed differently. In the United States they are marketed directly to patients, who are told to ask their doctor about getting hold of them. But in the United Kingdom many medicines are available only through prescription, leaving doctors in charge of purchasing. Defenders of America's free-market arrangements argue that it is the potentially large profits from a successful drug that incentivize companies to develop new ones. If these profits are curtailed, the risk–reward calculation will be altered and they could respond by cutting R&D budgets or focusing their energies on less risky drug categories. Ultimately, healthcare authorities have to try to balance the needs of private drug companies to make a profit, in a business characterized by great uncertainty and huge upfront costs, against the wider public interest: the need to get the best drugs to patients without busting their budgets.

Nevertheless, other critics of big pharma argue that the way this trade-off is presented is too simplistic. While Sovaldi is undeniably effective, critics of "big pharma" accuse drug companies of creating entirely new markets irrespective of clinical need. A well-known example is Prozac, a drug that treats depression. Prozac and its extended family is one of the most profitable drugs of all time, reaching annual sales of over $1 billion within just a couple of years of its launch in the mid-1990s. The drug has been energetically marketed to doctors to boost sales and cover the costs of development, but it has been criticized for its side effects.[33] Prozac's manufacturers dispute these claims, but the controversy illustrates how money and health policy have become intertwined.[34]

Other analysts have also warned of "regulatory capture". This occurs when big companies get too close to the regulators who are supposed to be supervising them. It allegedly means they can get away with sharp practices, such as overcharging or neglecting certain groups of patients. A report to the UK parliament in 2005 cited numerous complaints that, because of the size and importance of drug companies, their influence permeated governments, regulators and researchers, skewing priorities. The MPs were unable to say how harmful this was, however, or propose a new way of regulating the industry to align its incentives more closely with the needs of patients.[35]

Drug companies have also come under attack over patents and the alacrity with which they pursue violations of these. Patents protect the intellectual property rights of companies doing R&D. Nevertheless, rows over the licensing of generic drugs to fight serious diseases such as HIV have led to battles between drug companies and developing countries such as South Africa, which tried to import cheap copies of patented drugs to fight the illness. The negative publicity terrified the industry and it backed down. In fact, as developing countries get wealthier and their people begin to suffer more from rich-world diseases such as type 2 diabetes, there may be more scope for drug firms to vary their prices – charging Africans less than Europeans, while still staying profitable.

What of the future? Many analysts believe that advances in genetics research mean that medicine will be increasingly personalized in future. It will be difficult to continue to develop "blockbuster" drugs that serve large markets. Instead, care will be tailored to your individual genetic make-up. This holds out the exciting prospect of more effective drugs and treatments, but will it be too costly for widespread use?

As this chapter has argued, cost control looms large in the economics of healthcare because of the potentially limitless demand from people for long and healthy lifespans. As with other areas of economic life, markets provide some much-needed dynamism, particularly in drug development, but they are replete with failures and can usefully be supplemented with socialized arrangements. Economists have a big role to play in managing the numerous trade-offs involved in developing structures to ensure we can all get and stay well without bankrupting ourselves.

Conclusion: what we have learnt about the role of healthcare in the economy

• There is potentially almost unlimited demand for healthcare, but limited means. A lot of healthcare policy is therefore about maximizing efficiency while not ignoring equity concerns, such as ensuring that all people get access to the care they need.
• The healthcare industry is prone to a number of "market failures", which blunt the effectiveness of purely market solutions in healthcare and imply the need for some government involvement (the exact extent of this is more often than not dictated by politics). These market failures include information problems (your doctor knowing more than you; you knowing more than your insurance provider); adverse selection (bad risks driving out good risks, making

insurance-based risk pooling unviable); and behavioural issues to do with bounded rationality and will-power (individuals not doing what is in their own best interest).

• Costs in healthcare are exploding. Reasons for this include an ageing population demanding more healthcare; the increase in chronic lifestyle diseases such as type 2 diabetes; and the rising price of drugs and technologies. There is no reason to suppose that healthcare systems are becoming unaffordable though, and the "right" level of spending is in any event a political, not economic, decision.

• Health and healthcare are increasingly global concerns. All countries are now vulnerable to disease, and so solutions should be reached globally. Global healthcare markets are also giving rise to global drug companies, and the power of "big pharma" is a concern for some.

Notes

1. WHO, "Constitution of the World Health Organization", in *Basic Documents*, 48th edn, 1–20 (Geneva: WHO Press, 2014).
2. Deloitte Touche Tohmatsu life sciences and health care (LSHC) industry group analysis of the WHO's "Global health expenditure" database.
3. Bloomberg News, "China healthcare spending may hit $1 trillion by 2020", 29 August 2012.
4. N. Daniels, "Justice, health and healthcare", *American Journal of Bioethics* 1:2 (2001), 2–16.
5. J. Mackenbach & C. Looman, "Life expectancy and national income in Europe, 1900–2008: an update of Preston's analysis", *International Journal of Epidemiology* 42:4 (2013), 1100–10.
6. M. Grossman, "On the concept of health capital and the demand for health", *Journal of Political Economy* 80:2 (1972), 223–55.
7. K. Arrow, "Uncertainty and the welfare economics of medical care", *American Economic Review* 53:5 (1963), 941–73.
8. This example is used by Nicholas Barr in his LSE lectures on the political economy of welfare states.
9. R. Freeman & H. Rothgang, "Health", in F. Castles, S. Leibfried, J. Lewis, H. Obinger & C. Pierson (eds), *The Oxford Handbook of the Welfare State*, 367–77 (Oxford: Oxford University Press, 2010).
10. D. Himmelstein & S. Woolhandler, "The current and projected taxpayer shares of US health costs", *American Journal of Public Health* 106:3 (2016), 449–52.
11. J. Barnett & M. Vornovitsky, *Health Insurance Coverage in the United States: 2015* (Washington, DC: US Government Printing Office, 2016).
12. J. Le Grand, *The Other Invisible Hand: Delivering Public Services through Choice and Competition* (Princeton, NJ: Princeton University Press, 2007); and J. Le Grand, "Quasi-markets and social policy", *Economic Journal* 101 (1991), 1256–67.
13. D. Squires & C. Anderson, US healthcare from a global perspective: spending, use of services, prices and health in 13 countries, Issue Brief (New York: Commonwealth Fund, 2015).
14. OECD, "Health statistics 2016" database.
15. E. Gruenberg, "The failures of success", *Milbank Memorial Fund Quarterly* 55:1 (1977), 3–24.

16. K. Manton, "Changing concepts of morbidity and mortality in the elderly population", *Milbank Memorial Fund Quarterly* 60:2 (1982), 183–244.
17. M. Townsend, "Evidence review: the impact of an ageing population on end of life care costs", Discussion Paper no. 2912 (London: Personal Social Services Research Unit, LSE, 2016).
18. RAND, "Monetary cost of dementia in the United States", *New England Journal of Medicine* 368:14 (2013), 1326–34.
19. J. Cawley & C. Meyerhoefer, "The medical care costs of obesity: an instrumental variables approach", Working Paper no. 16467 (Cambridge, MA: NBER, 2010).
20. Aon Hewitt, *2016 Global Medical Trend Rates* (London: Aon Hewitt, 2015).
21. P. Willeme & M. Dumont, "Machines that go 'ping': medical technology and health expenditures in OECD countries", *Health Economics* 24:8 (2015), 1027–41.
22. D. Light & H. Kantajian, "Market spiral pricing of cancer drugs", *Cancer* 119:22 (2013), 3900–902.
23. L. Buckner & S. Yeandle, *Valuing Carers 2015: The Rising Value of Carers' Support* (London: Carers UK, 2015).
24. Alzheimer's Association, *2013 Alzheimer's Disease Facts and Figures* (Chicago: Alzheimer's Association, 2013).
25. M. Lilly, A. Laporte & P. Coyte, "Labor market work and home care's unpaid caregivers: a systematic review of labor force participation rates, predictors of labor market withdrawal, and hours of work", *Milbank Quarterly* 85:4 (2007), 641–90.
26. For a good survey of these kinds of studies, see M. Weinstein, "Spending health care dollars wisely: can cost-effectiveness analysis help?", Paper no. 13 (Syracuse, NY: Maxwell School Center for Policy Research, 2005).
27. K. Kingsbury, "The value of a human life: $129,000", *Time*, 20 May 2008.
28. International Diabetes Federation.
29. Pharmaceutical Research and Manufacturers of America, *Biopharmaceuticals in Perspective: Spring 2016* (Washington, DC: Pharmaceutical Research and Manufacturers of America, 2016).
30. R. Mullin, "Cost to develop new pharmaceutical drug now exceeds $2.5bn", *Chemical and Engineering News*, 24 November 2014.
31. F. Pammolli, L. Magazzini & M. Riccaboni, "The productivity crisis in pharmaceutical R&D", *Nature Reviews Drug Discovery* 10:6 (2016), 428–38.
32. J. Law, *Big Pharma: Exposing the Global Healthcare Agenda* (New York: Carroll & Graf, 2006).
33. E. Wurtzel, *Prozac Nation: Young and Depressed in America* (London: Quartet Books, 1995).
34. For a discussion of the research on this, see A. Das, "Pharmaceutical industry and the market: the case of Prozac and other antidepressants", *Asian Journal of Psychiatry* 4:1 (2010), 14–18.
35. House of Commons Health Committee, *The Influence of the Pharmaceutical Industry: Fourth Report of Session 2004–05*, 2 vols (London: Stationery Office, 2005).

5

MAKING THE WORLD GO AROUND: MONEY, BANKING AND PERSONAL FINANCE

Anyone who lives within their means suffers from a lack of imagination.
Oscar Wilde

Key questions

- What is money and saving, and why is money so useful?
- What is the role of banks in the financial system?
- Is it ever possible to prevent financial crashes, or is instability the price to be paid for a vibrant financial sector?
- What is the future of money and banking?

Summary

The banking and personal finance industry can do a useful job in smoothing out consumption patterns over people's lifetimes: lending to them when they are young and cash-poor, but with most of their working life ahead of them; helping them save for family, house buying and retirement when they are older and earning at their peak; insuring against risks and misfortunes along the way; and, finally, paying out through pensions and annuities when they quit work to spend more time in the garden. Businesses also need credit to grow, and in order to employ people to generate income and savings. Balancing out the demands of these groups and their various needs, across the whole country is a big and complex business, begetting an enormous financial services industry. The flow of credit has to be managed and regulated through complex regulation alongside other tools, such as interest rates. Stabilizing these financial activities is a headache for the authorities, and sometimes – as in the financial crisis of 2007–2010 – things go horribly wrong.

Key topics and theories covered

Money, savings and investments – the banking system and the role of central banks; the economic role of debt and credit; theories of investment; stock markets and booms and bust; interest rates; Bitcoin and new forms of money and saving.

5.1 Introduction

This chapter deals with something close to many people's hearts: money (and saving). Money is central to economics because spending it greases the wheels of commerce and consumption. Saving our income instead of spending it can finance investment in the practices and technologies that fuel wealth creation. Both activities also entail the creation of financial institutions, such as banks, that help us manage this. But banks can potentially inject instability into the financial system though their ability to create new purchasing power in the form of credit. Managing the financial system that provides the lifeblood of modern economies is therefore one of the most urgent tasks of governments and regulators, a job further complicated by the advent of revolutionary new technology that is transforming how we use and view money.

Before getting to all this, let us start by examining money itself. What is it and why is it so useful? To most people, money is simply cash. Economics, on the other hand, views it in a slightly wider sense, as the portion of your income that is transformed into a medium acceptable as a means of payment for goods or services rendered, or repaying debts. Economic textbooks generally see money as having three specific functions: a convenient means of exchange; a unit of account; and a store of value.[1]

The first two functions are fairly intuitive and easy to grasp. If we did not have money we could maybe barter instead for the things we want but we could not provide for ourselves. If I had chickens and you had bread, we could swap them to add a bit of variety to our diet. Barter would work fine in simple societies with only a small number of things worth trading and in which most exchanges probably take place between people who know each other. But bartering is clunky and inefficient and is not a lot of use in complex commercial systems, as it lacks two useful qualities: "transferability" and "divisibility".

Transferability refers to situations when you want something your potential trading partner has, but you have nothing they want. So you have to find a third party who will trade what you have for something else that you can then trade with the first person in order to make the exchange work. Divisibility is to do with the ease with which tradeable goods can be broken down into smaller units of value. A bag of rice can be easily divided, but a mule is more difficult. So, if the bag of rice is worth less than the mule, the bargain will not take place.

Money solves these two problems by acting as an easily exchangeable ready reckoner. I can convert my goods into cash in the necessary denominations by selling them and exchange the right amount of cash for other goods that I want. The transaction costs of goods exchange are thus massively reduced, and money has been a huge spur to economic development through increased trade.

It is probably worth noting at this point, however, that the origins of money are contested. The conventional view of money as conveniently emerging from below to replace barter is contested by heterodox economists as well as anthropologists, who find little evidence of barter in primitive societies but plenty of indications that they had rudimentary currencies. A more rounded view of the development of money may therefore be one that views it as representing more abstract obligations between creditworthy individuals, rather than simply revolving around the exchange of physical items per se – be they coins or bags of rice.[2] It probably also required some kind of governmental authority to establish it.[3]

Money and liquidity

These debates notwithstanding, once money was established it initially had to be something that was valuable in itself but relatively easy to measure, store and transport, so traders were happy to take it as payment standing in for the goods they wanted to exchange. Gold fitted the bill nicely, and gold coins served for a long time as official currencies in many countries. But gold was in limited supply, so it began to be replaced by so-called "fiat" money, notes and metal coins, which, though largely worthless themselves, had the backing of a central authority. A lot of early banknotes included the promise to pay the bearer in gold if he wished. But this proviso has long been dropped, as the amount of cash in circulation now vastly exceeds the amount of gold held by the authorities.

The contemporary monetary system thus depends almost entirely on continued public trust. Money not backed by gold, or something similarly precious, works only to the extent that we believe in it and are prepared to accept it as payment for something we produce that we can later exchange for something else of value to us. Without this trust, the financial system is in deep trouble. Many historians believe that the collapse of public confidence in the financial system owing to hyperinflation in Weimar Germany in the 1920s paved the way for the Nazis to overthrow democracy a few years later.[4]

Cash is also inconvenient, however, particularly for large transactions; you would need armfuls of the stuff to pay for a car. So a more recent development in payment was personal cheques (actually, the successor to medieval bills of exchange) and debit cards. Both of these have the advantage of allowing easy, cashless exchange. Cheques are slow, however, as they need to be cleared by the payments system. Their use is rapidly receding as they are replaced by electronic debit cards, which do much the same thing but a lot more quickly. The wallets and purses of most people will probably contain debit and *credit* cards. Credit cards seem like identical pieces of plastic to debit cards but in fact are a very different proposition, as they involve a promise to settle a transaction in the future, rather than at the moment when goods are exchanged (as with cash, cheques and debit cards). Credit cards are thus a short-term liability, a form of borrowing, as well as a means of settling payments.

Money also has a third function: as a store of value. In other words, it can be saved. Saving can be thought of as deferred consumption, in that you save that part of your income not held in cash immediately available for buying things. NCE models saving in the most stripped-down way possible by imagining Robinson Crusoe alone on his island. He has to decide how many of the bananas he picked today to put aside to eat when he is spending time building his raft; a one-person, one-good economy with perfect information, in other words. Working out how many bananas to eat or save is thus a matter of subjectively trading off between consumption now and consumption in the future, given his desire to invest in raft building in order to escape back to civilization.

In the real world, of course, there is incomplete information, which means uncertainty about the future. Keynes was the first to notice that this uncertainty creates additional reasons for saving.[5] Saving is not just the intention to consume later but also entails taking a view on what is going to happen in the future: the sofa you want but cannot afford might come down in price; your gas bill may double; or you might be dead but still want to care for your surviving family.

Money saved does not have to always be held in cash, as the financial services industry offers different levels of "liquidity" to savers. Liquidity is all about immediacy: how easily savings can be transformed back into cash if needed in a hurry. An instant savings account is very liquid, stocks and shares less so, and property is very illiquid. Keynes identified three levels of liquidity that might be wanted by savers: (a) for everyday transactions (say, when you are being paid monthly but you need money for food and rent in between pay cheques); (b) a precautionary motive (the desire for a bit of security in the face of unforeseen expenses); and (c) what he called a "speculative" motive (using your money to generate more money in the form of investments).

An individual's liquidity preference determines the savings vehicle chosen. A deposit account with a high street bank will probably be a good choice for Keynes' first two motives – day-to-day expenses and money for a rainy day. And it will probably even pay you a little bit of *interest* on your money. Interest is a payment from the bank to you for allowing them to hold your money. Nobody gets rich by keeping money in a bank account, however. In exchange for high liquidity (being able to get hold of your money quickly if you want to go out for dinner, or the washing machine breaks down) the interest rate will probably be fairly low. If it is less than the inflation rate (which is effectively the rate at which liquid savings lose their value) then the *real* value of your savings will go down. Hence the attraction of putting your savings to work.

Speculating and accumulating

Keynes was particularly interested in the investment motive for saving (he was a successful investor himself). Keynes stated that only investment generates the employment and income out of which people can save, although he also noted that investment does not entirely depend on savings as banks are able to generate more credit than they have savings deposits. Investment can be either in real assets, such as houses or fine art, or financial assets. Outside the banking system and its often miserly rates of interest, the best way of earning a decent return from your money is probably through investing in financial markets, as these strike a balance between high returns while still offering some liquidity (buying and selling property is time-consuming and has high transaction costs, for example, while the market for fine art is probably best left to the experts).[6]

There are two main types of financial investment widely available: bonds; and stocks and shares. Bonds are effectively an IOU. Bonds are also known as fixed-income investments, as, in return for a lump sum, they are a contract specifying that the holder will be paid a fixed nominal yield on the face value of the bond (which is typically different from the market value, hence yields go up and down). There are different kinds of bonds as financial engineering is constantly generating new ideas, but the main ones are issued by legal entities, such as private companies or public authorities – central or local government. Sometimes they are tied to big civil engineering projects, known as "project bonds", or to finance a company's expansion. Once issued, bonds can also be traded on secondary markets. They are therefore pretty safe, as your payment schedule is an official contract enforceable by law so long as the issuer of the bond does not go bust. Even then, bondholders are usually near the head of the queue to be paid out of the remaining assets. Government bonds, especially those issued by rich, stable countries, are particularly safe, although the income stream is likely to be smaller to reflect this extra security.

Stocks are different. They are shares, or fractions of ownership, in companies that have been publicly "listed" on the stock exchange, which is a marketplace for raising capital and trading shares among private investors. Stocks offer investors two potential types of return: dividends and capital gain. The first is a payment to shareholders out of profits, offered once or twice a year at the discretion of the company's management. The payment of dividends is connected to the company's ability to reinvest excess cash flow and its future growth prospects. Unlike bonds, though, this payment is not guaranteed. If the company does well and makes a profit it will generally offer some of this back to shareholders in the form of dividends. It is in the interests of the firm's managers to keep shareholders happy by paying dividends as they are free to sell their shares any time they like.

"Shareholder capitalism" is therefore one way of aligning the interests of firms' owners (shareholders) with their managers (the CEO and board of directors). Companies paying high dividends tend to be large "blue chip" firms with an established market position and loyal customers, and so they suit investors with a moderate to low tolerance for risk and a desire for a regular income stream, such as pensioners.

Box 5.1 Key terms

- *Quantitative easing (QE)*. An unconventional form of monetary policy whereby the central bank creates new money to buy government bonds or other financial assets, increasing the money supply and easing credit conditions.
- *Leverage*. Borrowing to buy financial assets.
- *Lender of last resort*. A central bank can lend to financial institutions such as banks that get into trouble, in the interests of stabilizing the financial system.
- *Liquidity*. The preference for holding cash, the most "liquid" of all assets.

Investors looking for something a bit racier will favour shares offering capital growth. A growing company in a flourishing market with the prospect of high future profits will be an exciting prospect for investors and so demand for its shares will therefore be high, causing the share price to rise. Investors looking for capital growth often target new companies in areas such as technology, or the shares of companies serving "emerging markets" – developing economies with high economic growth rates, such as India or Vietnam.

Although successful investing is ultimately about the price you buy in at and sell at, both types of shareholding strategies tend to be inherently more risky than holding bonds. There is no guarantee of dividend payments nor that that exciting app developer will live up to its potential, or even necessarily survive for very long. Bondholders know they can take the cash and walk away at the end of the term, but the only way out for a share owner is to sell to someone else. Stock markets are volatile and so there is always a chance you might have to sell at a loss: the Japanese stock market lost three-quarters of its value in a crash at the end of the 1980s and has never recovered. And, if a firm goes bust, shareholders are towards the back of the queue to get their money back after other creditors have been paid off. It is for this reason that some classes of shareholders get voting rights at annual company meetings, giving them a say in how the company is run.

Financial advisers often recommend that inexperienced investors spread their investment risk widely by not tying up all their savings in just one company's shares. Individuals can buy "funds" comprising shares in several companies, picked by a professional manager who knows the market and charges a fee for his expertise. These funds may have a particular theme, such as risky emerging markets for the adventurous, or, for the more cautious, income funds consisting of established firms paying regular dividends.

But even professional investment managers suffer from the information asymmetry afflicting all lenders and investors. This stems from the fact that firms' professional managers always know more about the underlying state of the business than their owners. Moreover, their incentives may diverge. Analytically, this is known as the "principal–agent problem", and it occurs when, lacking due restraints, the "agent" (the firm's managers) runs the business to suit his own ends in ways that may be contrary to the interests of the "principal" (the firm's owners). For example, managers may divert company profits to spend on private jets and high pay for themselves. Or they may pursue risky and unwise short-termist strategies to bump up the share price and increase the value of their stock options.[7]

To tackle the information gap, publicly listed firms are obliged to publish detailed information in annual reports and quarterly earnings forecasts. These offer, at best, an incomplete picture, however. Moreover, given the need for investors to minimize risk by owning a wide portfolio of shares, there may be a free rider problem with regard to owners keeping tabs on firms' managers. If you own only a small portion of a firms' shares, say 5 per cent, why should you go to all the effort of keeping executives on the straight and narrow while others do nothing? This may explain why some companies are badly managed despite the stratospheric pay of their executives; no one sees it as her job to monitor them.

One solution, particularly for bond investors, is to use credit rating agencies. These centralize the costly business of credit analysis for a fee, providing investors with a detailed report of the creditworthiness of the company. Their reliability hinges on their reputation for impartiality and thus having no ulterior motives when making assessments. This reputation is not always deserved. Some credit agencies got too close to the financial companies they were rating and issued glowing reports on them and their products even as they were hurtling towards insolvency.

Borrowing and start-ups

There is another way of financing consumption, besides paying for things out of your current income or savings or out of the proceeds from the income-generating investments you have made with your savings, and that is to borrow. Borrowers, who can be individuals or businesses, can go to a financial institution such as a bank to ask for a loan. But how do banks decide who to lend to?

Being a successful lender is all about managing risk. Lenders lend money out in the hope that they will get it back (this is called the principal of the loan), plus something to compensate them for the risk of this not happening (this is called the interest). Together, these comprise the repayment schedule. Managing the risk of default (not getting your money back) is therefore incredibly important to financial institutions. There is no reliable mathematical formula to value the risk of this, so banks follow certain procedures to try to estimate it. They try to come up with a risk profile for borrowers by looking at their credit and work history, or company accounts and profit forecasts in the case of businesses. Bankers drawing up credit reports often refer to the "five 'C's of credit": character, capacity, capital, collateral and coverage (which is an insurance policy against the death or disability of a key person).[8]

Mortgage companies, which are either banks or dedicated mortgage providers, go through similar calculations when deciding whether, and how much, to lend on a property purchase (see Chapter 6). They will also factor in the value of the house that their customer is intending to buy to prevent her overpaying and leaving herself vulnerable to default if her personal circumstances change, such as losing her job. The lending risk with mortgages is larger (although the house itself can be used as security), and is also spread over a much longer period of time than a simple, everyday loan. It will also include the possibility that the value of the house the mortgage company is lending on will go down over time, leaving the borrower in "negative equity" and at greater risk of default.

Businesses also use loans to finance their operations but have additional means of accessing funds. Fledgling business "start-ups" can have a particular problem in getting finance as they may have a sound business model (good products or ideas) but no current profits to reinvest. From a conventional lender's point of view, they also have no track record to analyse and no history of making profits or paying dividends; hence the risk of default is possibly high, but very difficult to calculate. What a start-up can do, however, is offer a share of projected future earnings to entice lenders or investors. It can issue debt and sign over to lenders some voting rights over company policy through covenants, and pledge any assets as collateral.

Even so, a lot of conventional lenders are wary of start-ups. Thanks to technology, however, but also possibly disillusionment with the conservatism of traditional banks, there are now myriad other ways of financing a business start-up. For example, venture capital (VC) firms are often happy to back start-ups, as these may be in fast-growing sectors such as biotech and software, offering the potential for fast growth and a lucrative exit from the business further down the line. Apple, Google and Intel all started off with support from venture capital. VC firms will normally take seats on the company's board, both to monitor their investment and to provide expertise. Fewer than 1 per cent of start-ups actually succeed in raising venture capital, however, the rest resorting to the "three 'F's": friends, families and fools – networking, in other words. Most entrepreneurs actually start off working for other companies, where they build up expertise and connections before striking out on their own.

And, if networking is not their forte, future tycoons can always try "crowdfunding". The internet allows start-up entrepreneurs to talk to thousands of potential investors. In return for small amounts of funding they may receive an interest payment on their capital or an equity stake, which could soar in value if the company is a success. The first crowdfunded project is thought to have been in 1997 when the rock band Marillion needed to raise cash to fund its next tour and turned to the internet to raise $60,000 to tour the United States. Whatever the business – software or soft rock – start-ups now have a wider choice of funding than ever before.

5.2 Banking and the financial system

Mainstream economics views the banking and financial system as serving as a "middleman" between lenders and borrowers. There are agents with surplus funds who are prepared to lend, and others with a deficit of funds who want to borrow. But how do they find each other without a great deal of effort? And how can they be sure the other party is trustworthy? You need a centralized system to bring them together. You need institutions that reduce otherwise large transaction costs by bridging the information gap between potential lenders and borrowers. You need financial intermediaries. You need a banking sector.

Banks perform several functions that benefit individuals and the economy. The first and most obvious is providing a safe place to store your savings. But there is more to a bank than its vault, so the second service, as described above, is providing credit intermediation by acting as middlemen between borrowers and savers. Borrowers and savers often have different time horizons, however,

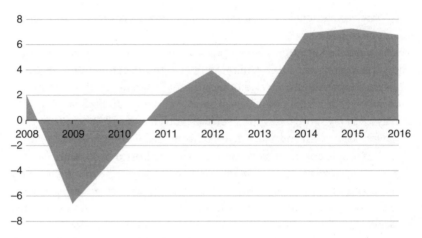

Figure 5.1 US commercial bank lending, percentage change year on year, 2008–2016
Source: US Federal Reserve.

so the third service that banks perform is what is known as maturity transformation: turning short-term deposits from customers who want security with liquidity into longer-term loans that are needed for things such as buying houses. Fourth, they offer a convenient clearing and payment system for their customers. Finally, they are effective institutions for managing the risks associated with all these activities. Banks can spread risks by having a broad spread of customers and developing effective means of overcoming the information asymmetries (basically, "How can I trust this person to pay me back the loan?") that bedevil lending.

But this view of banks and the financial sector as passive middlemen is a bit one-dimensional, as it ignores their critical role in creating "leverage". Leverage is the term for when banks borrow to acquire additional assets. They actively create debt instruments to finance credit that generates assets, on the basis of which they can borrow again to acquire more assets. And so it goes on… Highly leveraged banks, whose borrowings were large multiples of their assets, were a key feature of the financial crisis, as they were vulnerable when panicked customers tried to liquidate their deposits and found that they could not, producing a bank run (see Figure 5.1).

The key thing to note about banking is that it is a profit-driven business, with mostly privately owned banks operating in a competitive market. Banks make a profit (known as their margin) from the difference between what they pay for liabilities (their own borrowings) and what they earn on assets (loans). So there is a game going on here. Lenders want to maximize the profit from lending their surplus money and borrowers want to minimize the cost of borrowing money to cover their funding deficit. This equilibrium process takes place in the market through what is known as "price discovery": in a competitive lending market rational, self-maximizing individuals and others can compare the interest rates offered for both lending and borrowing in order to find the best deal.

There are two main types of banking: commercial and investment banking. Commercial banks mostly concern themselves with deposit taking and lending and so their clients are usually individuals or smaller, private businesses that may not have access to the stock market. Investment banks have a different role. They do not take deposits but raise the funds they need on financial markets, and their customers are usually larger firms, governments or other financial institutions. Individuals tend to encounter investment banks only if they are very, very rich; many provide private banking for "high net worth" individuals. Investment banks are usually split between a "buy" side, which offers services to clients such as issuing debt and advising on mergers and acquisitions, and a "sell" side, which buys and sells financial products for a profit on behalf of clients or the bank itself, known as "proprietary trading".

There are also an increasing number of non-bank financial institutions (NBFIs) providing financial services. These are part of the financial system and operate a bit like banks (making loans, providing financial services and otherwise facilitating the financial system). As they do not have a banking licence, however, they are not allowed to take deposits from the public. NBFIs include insurance firms, venture capitalists, currency exchanges, some microloan organizations and pawn shops.

Watching over it all: the role of central banks

At the apex of the financial system sit central banks. The central bank is the banker's bank, and each country has one (members of the European single currency have national central banks that answer to the European Central Bank). Their exact responsibilities vary, but in most countries they oversee the payments system, manage foreign exchange reserves and the convertibility of domestic money in other currencies, set interest rates and manage the money supply and, ideally, act as a "lender of last resort" to commercial banks that get into trouble.

Central banking was arguably invented by the Dutch in 1609 with the foundation of the Bank of Amsterdam. Its original role was to maintain a stable system of coinage required to run the Netherlands' fast-developing trading system.[9] It did this very effectively, so the idea spread; first to the Riksbank of Sweden in 1668, then the Bank of England, founded in 1694 and the oldest central bank in continual existence. The Federal Reserve, the United States' central bank, came later in 1914 and was a response to several earlier banking crises. The arrival of "the Fed" brought to an end the era when private banks printed their own currency.

Managing the nation's money has remained a core responsibility of central banks ever since then and they retain their monopoly right to print cash. Cash is only a relatively small part of the overall amount of money in circulation, however. Most money – 97 per cent in the United Kingdom, for example – is created through bank lending and is therefore outside the direct control of central banks.[10] The problem with the view of banks as mere intermediaries, lending out the money that is deposited with them by their customers, is that banks make far more loans than are covered by deposits, subject to doing so profitably and any restrictions on lending imposed by regulators. This creates a conflict of interest, as commercial banks are in competition with each other for lending business and may become lax in managing the risks of default. Spread across the entire banking sector, these risks may become "systemic" and threaten the stability of the entire financial system.[11]

Central banks therefore have a key role in managing and regulating the banking system. They can exert direct control over commercial banks in several ways. The central bank can settle debts between commercial banks and it also sets the "reserve requirement", which is the amount of capital that has to be held by banks. Lowering this requirement allows them to lend more; raising it has the opposite effect.

Central banks also determine the interest rate, which is a charge for borrowing money. When individuals think about central banks (if they do at all) it is normally because of their interest-rate-setting function, as changes to interest rates affect the returns on their savings accounts and the cost of their mortgage payments. But central banks do not actually set these directly. What they do is to regulate what it costs commercial banks to access money from the central bank. This is possible because commercial banks maintain a current account with their central bank and can borrow money from it in the short term at the rate it sets, which is known as the "base rate" in the United Kingdom and the "federal funds rate" in the United States. Raising this rate makes it more expensive for banks to get money to lend, and they pass this extra cost on to their customers. More expensive lending by the banks cuts the demand for loans and mortgages, and reduces the amount of money in circulation. Lowering the rate obviously does the opposite.

Thus, the base rate and the market rate are not exactly the same. The two normally track each other quite closely, because of the need for banks to make a profit on their lending in a competitive market. But during the financial crisis banks were short of liquidity and much keener to attract savings than they were to lend. So even when, as in the United Kingdom, base rates were 0.5 per cent, banks were lending money out at 4 or 5 per cent. The artificially high cost of borrowing caused a "credit crunch", which was a major factor in the following deep recession, as it tipped a lot of firms that were already in trouble into bankruptcy.

Interest rates and the supply of money

Since interest rates affect the cost of lending they also determine the amount of money in circulation around the economy, as higher rates cause people to seek fewer loans, and loans are mostly made with newly created money. "Monetarist" economists therefore claim the money supply is the main variable affecting the rate of inflation. If you have too much money chasing too few goods its value must fall, they argue, so influencing the money supply is the only reliable means to control the price level.[12]

While other economists doubt the tight link between the money supply and the inflation rate, price stability remains a central concern for policy-makers, as high inflation rates can be a sign that the economy is overheating. Most of the world's central banks, such as the European Central Bank, the Bank of England and the Bank of Canada, have a specific mission to keep inflation within a low, narrow band, usually around 2 per cent. The Fed also follows an inflation target, although its mandate includes stabilizing the US economy as well, which is generally interpreted as securing a steady, positive growth rate of GDP.

In order for central banks to control inflation effectively, policy-makers have deemed that it is necessary for them to be operationally independent – free from political interference, in other words. This insight owes to "rational expectations" theory, which holds that the public and international investors need to know that monetary policy is not being "politicized". Otherwise, central banks might be pushed by politicians to keep interest rates low to boost the economy before elections. If people see through this they will anticipate higher inflation and adjust their spending accordingly, nullifying the impact of the rate change.

But some argue that central banks have become politicized in other ways, particularly when they have resorted to "quantitative easing" to keep the economy growing. Many banks resorted to QE to combat the Great Recession, including the Bank of England, the Fed and latterly the ECB. QE involves the central bank creating money to buy government securities via what are called "open market operations". To buy these securities the central bank has to create new money, which increases the money supply and thereby eases credit conditions. QE was seen as a last resort to combat depression after the financial crisis, but it has been criticized for fuelling a stock market bubble rather than benefiting the wider economy. At some point the securities purchased by the central banks will have to be sold again as QE unwinds, and no one is sure what the effect will be.

5.3 Financial regulation and the crisis

Banks are probably at the top of most people's list of culprits for the financial crisis. Their reckless lending and poor risk management saw a number of them fail and then have to be rescued by governments, at enormous public expense. Although most of the direct costs of the bailouts have since been recouped (as opposed to the lasting damage caused by the credit crunch and deep recession), the unedifying spectacle of rich bankers being saved from their own follies while other industries were allowed to go to the wall caused enormous public anger. The crisis has been exhaustively covered,[13] so this section focuses on a couple of the themes that animate this chapter: can banking be regulated to ensure the crisis is not repeated, or are crashes an unavoidable part of capitalism?

Mainstream economics sees the finance industry as existing largely to serve the "real" economy of physical goods and non-financial services. The job of regulators, therefore, is mainly to ensure stability in the financial system so that any mishaps there do not spill over into other areas of the economy. They are supposed to stand apart from the industry they are regulating; the financial sector is a significant generator of wealth and taxes, however, making it a powerful lobbyist, and bankers and regulators regularly swap jobs. The authorities therefore face relentless pressure from banks to keep regulation as light as possible.[14] Economic theory provides few guidelines on the "correct" amount of regulation, however. Prior to the crisis the protocol was largely to let banks do their own risk management, as they had "skin in the game".

Economists were aware of previous banking crashes but thought these were part of the background "noise" of capitalism and inflicted no lasting harm on the economy. The scale and shock of the banking collapses of 2007–2010 have shown this to be complacent and put the spotlight on the long period of financial deregulation that preceded the crisis. The 1990s and 2000s had been a period of high growth and relative economic stability. It looked obvious that free-market capitalism had triumphed over socialism, and so regulators, particularly in the United States and United Kingdom, eased back on their responsibilities to regulate.[15]

In 1999 the US repealed the Glass–Steagall Act, which had been put in place in 1933 following the Wall Street Crash. Glass–Steagall had drawn a line between the activities of commercial banks, which were barred from trading in securities, and investment banks, which were forbidden from taking deposits. The idea was to prevent a failing investment bank dragging down its commercial banking arm, causing panic and a bank run among its retail customers that would spill over into the real economy. Traditionally, commercial banks have been seen as a lot less risky than investment banks, as their profits are linked to borrowing and lending conditions in the real economy, rather than volatile financial markets.

The demise of Glass–Steagall brought an end to this firewall, as many commercial banks, under pressure from shareholders bored with the staid returns from retail lending, began to dabble in riskier investment banking activities.

The growth of investment banking in the 1980s and 1990s had led to the creation of a huge derivatives market – worth almost $600 trillion in December 2007, eight times the value of the real economy – and the fusion of the banking and insurance industries. Banks had thought that by bundling together, or "collateralizing", default risks from property loans they could share and hence neutralize them. But these risks were grossly underestimated, and the system merely ensured that once the crisis blew up it quickly infected the real economy by destabilizing consumers' savings and destroying confidence. A "shadow banking system" of hedge funds had also grown up to avoid regulation. Hedge funds relied on leverage (borrowing) with a very small capital cushion to make profits, further increasing the risk of contagion while monopolizing the rewards for their investors.

The proximate cause of the financial crisis was the collapse of several major banks and insurance companies between 2007 and 2009. This was triggered by huge losses incurred on lending on "sub-prime" US real estate, which became acute after US house prices slumped in early 2006. Under-regulated banks and hedge funds had bet the farm that house prices would rise, not fall. The interconnected structure of the global financial industry ensured that this national event had international repercussions. Disaster ensued. How did we get to this?

Explaining the crash

Most analysts of the crisis agree that banks were under-regulated and complacent about the risks they faced, while policy-makers failed to intervene until it was too late.[16] One explanation for this blind spot is ideas. Although economists and officials generally resist the suggestion that they are influenced by ideology, rather than facts or experience, the truth is that they are highly susceptible to intellectual fashion.

Underlying the belief that finance could be left largely to market forces with minimal supervision was an influential set of ideas known as "efficient markets theory" (EMT).[17] EMT states that financial products, such as shares, are always correctly priced, so there is never any need for intervention in financial markets. This is based on the belief that markets are efficient and relay information instantly to buyers and sellers, which is immediately reflected in the price of the asset. Although the future is risky these risks are probabilistically measurable, so only unpredictable shocks will cause asset prices to deviate from their true, intrinsic value. Nevertheless, these shocks are incredibly rare. Underlying this belief was an increasing trend towards the idea that all economic concepts must be quantifiable: if they can be expressed as a number or equation then all associated risks and rewards will thereby be measurable and controllable.

Policy-makers, including central bankers, believed in EMT and its underlying assumptions about the superiority of markets and the difficulties of intervention by the authorities. Alan Greenspan, the Fed chairman from 1987 to 2006, argued that no one could possibly know what a sensible level of borrowing was and saw the role of central bankers as being not to try to prick asset bubbles but merely to deal with the aftermath.[18] Other proponents of EMT allowed that bubbles might occur but insisted that financial markets operate effectively in allocating capital and dealing with risk in the long run.[19] Such was the hold of EMT that, even when Long-Term Capital Management, a US hedge fund, collapsed in 1998 after taking a number of extreme positions its risk models said were perfectly safe, the regulators refused to change course.

EMT has been made to look complacent by the recent crisis. It also appears to reflect a broader misunderstanding of the particular nature of financial risk. Prior to the crisis all bank risk management models were based on assumptions informed by EMT. These models estimated the likelihoods of various events based on a standard Gaussian bell curve, implying that risks are scattered around a normal distribution with thin tails – i.e. that the chance of anything going badly wrong was vanishingly small. Financial risk models based on bell curve probability estimations grossly underplayed the danger of a disastrous crash, however, partly because they borrowed statistical concepts from the general insurance market, which deals with one-off natural disasters such as earthquakes.

Banks assumed that natural and financial disasters could be predicted and insured for in the same way if they diversified their asset bases so as to reduce and contain the impact of risks, which would thereby affect only one type of asset. But this assumption was incorrect, as financial risks cannot be made independent of each other because of the interconnection of the financial system and its reliance on leverage. Finance, in other words, is "systemically" risky in ways the natural world is not.

Nassim Nicholas Taleb, an author and former trader, argues that economics, unlike natural science, is dominated by rare but extreme events ("black swans") that are not captured properly by standard bank risk models. Thus, when banks talked of risk (which was measurable), what they were really describing was uncertainty (which was not).[20] George Soros, the Hungarian financier, has refined this idea slightly with his concept of "reflexivity", to explain why the risk of crashes is magnified in supposedly self-correcting financial systems. Soros argues that mistaken opinions about market positions tend to reinforce each other because of herd instincts affecting traders. Prices can stay too high or low for too long because of this.[21]

Soros's views are similar to those of behavioural economists, who view financial instability as symptoms of a form of irrational behaviour by consumers and traders. According to Robert Shiller, whose book *Irrational Exuberance* was published just before the hi-tech stock bubble burst in 2000, this manifests itself in overconfidence and anchoring – whereby people base expectations about uncertain events on familiar but unreliable tenets of knowledge.[22] These critiques were aired after the event. But a number of prominent economists had been sounding warnings for many decades of the dangers of crashes, and we turn to these next.

Theories of financial cycles

If financial institutions such as banks are unable to safely manage risks, why are we not faced with continual instability in the financial system? One answer is: because economic change follows long cycles, during which credit bubbles may emerge unnoticed until it is too late. A number of theories try to explain this that lie outside the mainstream economic theory of self-correcting markets.

The first of these was developed by the Vienna University economist and founder of the "Austrian school" of economics, Ludwig von Mises. Von Mises blamed crashes on extreme investment swings driven by changes in interest rates and the politicization of monetary policy.[23] Politicians tend to want to keep rates low to boost employment while they are in office, triggering a boom during which investment is artificially stimulated and flows into projects with marginal returns, such as housing. When this pushes interest rates above their natural level the eventual result is a credit contraction followed by bust. Markets eventually rebalance but not before a lot of people have lost their jobs and vast amounts of capital been wasted. Von Mises and his followers said the solution to this is free markets with monetary policy taken out of the hands of politicians and overseen by independent central banks. Independent central banks were powerless to prevent the crash of 2008, however.

Keynes and his followers also focused on swings in investment but came to the opposite conclusion to the Austrians. Economic cycles could be explained by swings in investment arising from changes in business sentiment and profit expectations. Optimism produces high investment, but this could become excessive and lead to a downturn. The cycle was not symmetrical, however, as the economy could get stuck in a vicious circle of low confidence, largely because of the risk aversion of financiers following crises or recessions that required the intervention of the government. The G20 governments concluded this in April 2009 when they agreed to boost credit to avoid a slump, although the Europeans

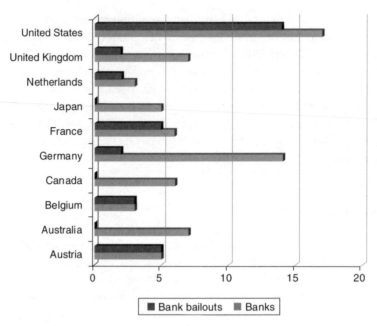

Figure 5.2 Numbers of bank bailouts by country
Source: Bank for International Settlements.

changed tack soon afterwards to embark on austerity programmes of public spending cuts, which critics argue deepened the downturn unnecessarily.[24]

But what about the disturbing possibility that gyrations in financial markets are largely outside the control of policy-makers, even if they recognize them? One economist whose reputation was significantly (albeit posthumously) enhanced by the crisis was Hyman Minsky. Minsky's "financial instability hypothesis" was ignored by mainstream economists until the crash of 2008, which it had correctly predicted. Minsky's argument was that long periods of stability prompt banks to continually innovate to seek new areas of business and find new justifications for taking on risk. But the unwinding of these risky positions at the end of the credit cycle occurs abruptly and unpredictably, not gradually, as free-market theorists predict, with chaotic results (see Figure 5.2).[25]

Minsky identified three stages of financial booms. In the early stage, of cautious hedge finance, lenders have to meet interest costs and be able to cover the principal of the loan; in the second stage they abandon this risk-averse posture and pursue riskier investments that cover the interest only; the third and final stage is a Ponzi scheme, whereby loans are advanced to people who cannot even meet the interest payments. The US housing boom required many borrowers to rely on a rise in the price of the asset they were holding to stay solvent, but the fall in house prices from 2006 led to widespread panic as lenders got nervous and called in some loans. Struggling to meet repayments, some indebted borrowers liquidated other assets at a discount, causing a general fall in asset values.

Minsky's writings on financial cycles also fitted into an earlier Marxian approach to growth and instability. Sensing their moment after a couple of decades in the shadows, Marxist economists have used the crisis to sharpen their critiques of capitalism by claiming that excessive, dangerous financial speculation does not represent a warping of capitalism but is intrinsic to capitalism's divorce of the ownership of capital from its management.[26] In spite of this divorce finance remains parasitical on the real economy because of its ability to generate money independently of the production process. This is dangerous, as it enhances the tendency within capitalism to *over*estimate the wealth-making potential of the real economy. Once this becomes clear, as happens during crises when house prices or overblown profit forecasts come back down to earth, individuals and firms attempt to convert their financial assets back into cash and find themselves empty-handed.[27] A financial crash is the result.

What all these theories have in common is that they reject the idea that economies can function by relying on markets alone for their regulation. They point to long-run cycles that govern economic progress and determine how funds for investment are allocated. The Austrian school apart, all also emphasize the key role of confidence and sentiment in economic life, as well as the fact that investors and businesses may have short time horizons and limited information. Aside from the Marxists, who see capitalism as doomed to fail, they imply the desirability of government intervention to stabilize what is often a decidedly unstable economy. Yet central bankers, such as Mervyn King, who was governor of the Bank of England during the crisis, ultimately concede that both sides – banks as well as their regulators – are prone to 'unavoidable mistakes made by people struggling to cope with an unknowable future'.[28]

5.4 The future of finance and the end of cash?

Like a lot of the things covered in this book, money and finance are being transformed by technology. The financial services industry is arguably ripe for disruption, as so much of it revolves around the costly and cumbersome intermediation of banks between borrowers and lenders. Technology is intervening to make the process of accessing finance simpler and cheaper, although not necessarily safer. The application of technology to financial services has a name, "fintech", and it is leading to new forms of banking and insurance and even, possibly, the end of money as we know it.

Fintech is a fast-growing sector in the often staid banking business; the value of global fintech investment grew by 75 per cent between 2014 and 2015, to $22 billion, and its advance shows no sign of halting.[29] There are, basically, two kinds of fintech companies: those directly challenging financial institutions; and those that collaborate with them to improve how they operate. Conventional banks are still the favoured place to store money, so at the moment fintechs tend to focus on streamlining particular bits of the transaction chain. Handling electronic payments was the obvious starting point for fintech companies, as it is an easy thing to automate. PayPal began this way, and the company is now worth around $50 billion, but new arrivals on the scene are moving into handling ingoing and outgoing payments from tablets and smartphones. By some estimates, banks stand to lose up to a third of their existing lending business to fintech as their more tech-savvy customers exploit the lower cost and greater convenience.[30]

Fintech is significant for several reasons. It dramatically reduces transaction costs between borrowers and lenders and so makes accessing finance cheaper and more convenient. Fintechs do away with costly physical branches and rely on algorithms and crunching data to manage risk. Fintechs are also less exposed to the downside risks of maturity mismatches. Conventional banks operate by taking short-term liabilities and converting them into assets with longer maturities. Competition and higher fixed costs mean they have had to grow their loan books in order to increase their margins, which increases their risk. As most fintechs are currently mere intermediaries, matching lenders and borrowers directly over the internet, the increases in their profit margins comes from the relative safety of simply doing this more efficiently.

To date, fintech has mostly been seen in banking and securitization, but it also has a potential role in insurance. Instead of the conventional, risk-pooling approach requiring large numbers of diverse customers, fintech insurance companies can individually monitor customers' biometric data through wearable devices and reward those with good habits with lower premiums. Some may dislike the idea of being judged by a machine and a line of code, but neutral algorithms help do away with human prejudice. Italian banks charge female owners of small businesses more than male ones, for example.[31]

Even so, fintech worries some commentators, who see it as the latest incarnation of the unregulated "shadow banking sector" that turbocharged the lending binge that led up to the financial crisis. Fintech lenders certainly seem keen to fill niches in the credit market, including for those who would struggle to get loans from conventional banks. One fintech firm, Lending Club, advertises personal loans of up to $40,000 available in a few days.[32] This activity is clearly moving on from basic financial intermediation into outright credit expansion.

Another notable development in fintech is the emergence of "virtual" currencies. These are electronically administered currencies ranging from simple IOUs of issuers, such as airline miles, to more sophisticated exchanges backed by gold. The most up-to-date versions use peer-to-peer technologies to create their own method of payment and unit of account and so sidestep conventional monetary systems entirely. The most sophisticated of these are known as cryptocurrencies, which use advanced cryptography technology to secure transactions. There are a number of cryptocurrencies in use with names such as Dash, Monero and Ethereum, but by far the best known is Bitcoin, founded in 2009 by a mysterious figure named Satoshi Yakamoto. Bitcoin is an entirely decentralized currency that makes use of "blockchain" technology to generate Bitcoins on computers in the network and maintain a ledger of holdings. As payments and transactions are made through the system, participants are rewarded for processing these with newly minted Bitcoins. The number of Bitcoins in circulation at any one time is strictly controlled, and transactions are "pseudo-anonymous" – that is, they are recorded but users can still conceal their real identity.

But are Bitcoins actually money? Recall the essential properties of money discussed at the start of the chapter: as a medium of exchange; store of value; and independent method of account. To Bitcoin's fans, it is certainly very useful as a medium of exchange. Bitcoins can be swapped for goods and services, or traded for money in other currencies. The low transaction costs involved in using Bitcoin make it a particularly popular way of settling international transactions. But it still has a very long way to go before it can be considered a true currency with widespread appeal. There are estimated to be globally around 5.8 million users of the half-dozen or so cryptocurrencies in use, which together have a market value of $25 billion – a threefold growth on 2016.[33] But this is still infinitesimal compared with the $1.2 trillion in circulation on even a very narrow definition of the United States' monetary base.

As a store of value, cryptocurrencies also suffer from extreme volatility. Gyrations in Bitcoin's value are much more rapid and violent than those of most national currencies, which represent the liabilities of sovereign states. And they do not really represent a separate unit of account either, as their value reflects their convertibility into the local currency at that currency's exchange rate.[34] Bitcoin's anonymity also makes it a favourite of organized criminals, which may one day prompt a crackdown.

Many still argue, though, that cryptocurrencies represent the future of finance. Their key feature is the lack of a central authority, which is both a strength and a weakness. Critics blame the absence of regulation and lack of transparency in virtual currencies for problems over user protection. Regulators point out that Bitcoin is backed by no state and is therefore explicitly legal tender in no country. Its use amounts to a private contract between individuals that might have status within the Bitcoin universe but is not enforceable by conventional law.[35] Users are therefore vulnerable to scams. Unlike a credit card, if anything goes wrong with your transaction it cannot be reversed.

Advocates accept these drawbacks but argue that better safeguards will come as cryptocurrencies establish themselves. They point out that most financial assets today exist merely as digital records within clearing institutions that answer to a central bank. But there is no necessity for this centralized structure, and the blockchain technology behind cryptocurrencies allows these layers of control to be bypassed, something that probably appeals to the libertarian instincts of fintech entrepreneurs.[36] If this happens, coupled with the ambitions of other fintech firms to digitize banking entirely, could we soon see the end of cash entirely?

The end of cash?

Cash has been on the way out for a while, as it is being superseded by other forms of payments. But the idea that we can do away with it entirely is being strongly resisted by central banks, concerned about losing their "seignorage" rights. Seignorage is the profit on printing a currency, and it allows central banks to be self-financing, helping to guarantee their independence. As we saw in section 5.2, central bank independence plays an important part in regulating banks and maintaining trust in the value of the currency, so they are not things we should dispense with lightly. In addition, it is not clear how going cashless would work initially. Any country that unilaterally abolished its currency might simply find its population using another currency, euros or US dollars, for example.

Nevertheless, the opponents of cash are gathering momentum. Banks in Norway and Sweden have lobbied their governments to accelerate moves towards a cashless society, and a number have already ceased dealing in cash at their branches. Denmark has changed the law so that shops and restaurants are no longer legally obliged to accept cash payment.[37] The ECB is pushing hard for a European Payments Area, which will introduce common standards for electronic payments in the European Union.

Aside from the lower transaction costs involved in making payments electronically, rather than lugging around pockets full of notes and coins, another argument for a cashless society is that the anonymity of cash makes life easy for criminals. Without cash, criminals would have to use banks, exposing them to detection. A cashless society would therefore reduce street muggings and organized crime alike. A good way to start would be to eliminate high-denomination bills. Crooks can easily fit $1 million in $100 bills into a briefcase, as the cash weighs just 22lbs. But in $20 bills the same amount of money would weigh 110lbs and fill four briefcases – too much for one courier to handle.[38] The European Union has already phased out its €500 note but the United States has yet to follow suit with the $100 bill.

Some economists also argue that suppressing cash makes it easier for central banks to boost economic growth by pushing interest rates into negative territory. In theory, negative rates make saving costly compared with spending, but when cash is available people will simply withdraw their savings in the form of cash and keep it under the bed.[39] Of course, there are also civil liberties arguments to consider. Many dislike the idea of electronic payment arrangements, even systems such as Bitcoin, because their anonymity and lack of transparency make it hard to tell who is behind them. Getting rid of cash might make it easier for governments or corporations to monitor electronic transactions. Some, no doubt, just like the feel of a roll of tenners in their hand. It may therefore be too soon to write the obituary of notes and coins just yet.

Conclusion: what we have learnt

* Money is incredibly useful in easing the exchange of goods and services. In an uncertain world where we cannot know the future, income can also be saved for a rainy day, or put to good use as investment to generate more money.
* An entire financial system has grown up to manage all this, with banks at its heart. Banking is inherently risky, though, since one of its principal functions is to borrow short and lend long, which can lead to a crisis of "liquidity" if people all suddenly want their money back. Regulators, especially central banks, have emerged to control the system and try to manage these systemic risks. Central banks have also taken on other, macroeconomic, tasks such as controlling inflation.
* Central banks and regulators were unable to stop the financial crisis, however. Even if they had sought to regulate banking risks more closely, the inherent uncertainty in finance might not have prevented the shock, and may not do so again in future.
* Technology is being applied to money and banking. Fintech is making finance easier and cheaper for everyone with an internet connection, and is even leading to the emergence of new "virtual" currencies – and maybe even, one day, the end of money as we know it.

Notes

1. F. Mishkin, *The Economics of Money, Banking, and Financial Markets*, 11th edn (London: Pearson, 2016).
2. F. Martin, *Money: The Unauthorised Biography* (Doubleday Canada, 2014).
3. C. Desan, *Making Money: Coin, Currency and the Coming of Capitalism* (Oxford: Oxford University Press, 2015).

4. A. Fergusson, *When Money Dies: The Nightmare of the Weimar Hyperinflation* (London: Collins, 1975).

5. J. M. Keynes, *The General Theory of Employment, Interest and Money* [1936] (Whitefish, MT: Kessinger Publishing, 2010).

6. For a good introduction to investing written by an economist for non-financial experts, see J. Kay, *The Long and the Short of It: Finance and Investment for Normally Intelligent People Who Are Not in the Industry* (London: Erasmus Press, 2009).

7. L. Babchuk & J. Fried, *Pay without Performance: The Unfulfilled Promise of Executive Compensation* (Cambridge, MA: Harvard University Press, 2004).

8. J. Tirole, *The Theory of Corporate Finance* (Princeton, NJ: Princeton University Press, 2010).

9. S. Quinn & W. Roberds, "The big problem of large bills: the Bank of Amsterdam and the origins of central banking", Working Paper no. 2005–16 (Atlanta: Federal Reserve Bank of Atlanta, 2005).

10. M. McLeay, A. Radia & R. Thomas, "Money creation in the modern economy", *Bank of England Quarterly Bulletin* 54:1 (2014), 1–13.

11. A. Faure, *Central Banking and Monetary Policy: An Introduction* (Bookboon, 2013).

12. M. Friedman & A. Schwartz, *A Monetary History of the United States, 1867–1960* (Princeton, NJ: Princeton University Press, 1963).

13. A contemporary account of the crisis, but still one of the best, is C. Morris, *The Trillion Dollar Meltdown: Easy Money, High Rollers, and the Great Credit Crash* (New York: Public Affairs, 2008).

14. J. Hacker & P. Pierson, *Winner-Take-All Politics: How Washington Made the Rich Richer – and Turned Its Back on the Middle Class* (New York: Simon & Schuster, 2010).

15. M. Sherman, "A short history of financial deregulation in the United States" (Washington, DC: Center for Economic Policy Research, 2009).

16. For an excellent, critical and very readable insider's account (by a former US Treasury secretary), see T. Geithner, *Stress Test: Reflections on Financial Crises* (New York: Crown, 2014).

17. E. Fama, "Efficient capital markets: a review of theory and empirical work", *Journal of Finance* 25:2 (1970), 383–417.

18. A. Greenspan, *The Age of Turbulence: Adventures in a New World* (London: Penguin Books, 2007).

19. B. Malkiel, *A Random Walk down Wall Street: The Time-Tested Strategy for Successful Investing* (New York: Norton, 1973).

20. N. N. Taleb, *The Black Swan and the Impact of the Highly Improbable* (London: Penguin Books, 2008).

21. G. Soros, *The New Paradigm for Financial Markets: The Credit Crisis of 2008 and What It Means* (New York: Public Affairs, 2008).

22. R. Shiller, *Irrational Exuberance* (Princeton, NJ: Princeton University Press, 2000).

23. L. von Mises, *The Theory of Money and Credit* (London: Cape, 1912).

24. M. Blyth, *Austerity: The History of a Dangerous Idea* (Oxford: Oxford University Press, 2015).

25. H. Minsky, *Stabilizing an Unstable Economy* (New York: McGraw-Hill, 2008).

26. J. Sklansky, "Marxism in the age of financial crises: why conventional economics can't explain the great recession", *New Labor Forum* 21:3 (2012), 49–56.

27. S. Shuklian, "Marx on credit, interest and financial instability", *Review of Social Economy* 49:2 (1991), 196–217.

28. M. King, *The End of Alchemy: Money, Banking and the Future of the Global Economy* (London: Abacus, 2016), 12.

29. Accenture, *Fintech and the Evolving Landscape: Landing Points for the Industry* (Dublin: Accenture, 2016).

30. D. Drummer, A. Jerenz, P. Siebelt & M. Thaten, "Fintech – challenges and opportunity: how digitization is transforming the financial sector" (New York: McKinsey, 2016).

31. *The Economist*, "The fintech revolution", *The Economist*, 9 May 2015.
32. J. Maxfield, "Lessons for fintech from the history of banking", *Fox Business*, 8 February 2017.
33. G. Hileman & M. Rauchs, *Global Cryptocurrency Benchmarking Study* (Cambridge: Cambridge Centre for Alternative Finance, Judge Business School, 2017).
34. D. Yermack, "Is Bitcoin a real currency? An economic appraisal", Working Paper no. 19747 (Cambridge, MA: NBER, 2013).
35. European Central Bank, *Virtual Currency Schemes: A Further Analysis* (Frankfurt: European Central Bank, 2015).
36. S. Rosov, "Beyond Bitcoin: crypto-currencies are only the beginning", *CFA Institute Magazine*, 26:1 (2015), 37.
37. B. Antenore, "The end of cash money?", European Institute, 4 February 2016, www.euro-peaninstitute.org/~european/index.php/ei-blog/276-february-2016/2127-the-end-of-cash-money-2–4 (accessed 14 May 2017).
38. P. Sands, "Making it harder for the bad guys: the case for eliminating high denomination notes", Working Paper no. 52 (Cambridge, MA: Mossavar-Rahmani Center for Business and Government, John F. Kennedy School of Government, 2016).
39. K. Rogoff, *The Curse of Cash* (Princeton, NJ: Princeton University Press, 2016).

6

HOME SWEET HOME: THE HOUSING MARKET

Home is not where you live, but where they understand you.
Christian Morgenstern

Key questions

- Why do house prices keep on rising, and is this good or bad for individuals and the wider economy?
- What determines whether individuals can get onto the housing ladder or whether they have to rent?
- What is the place of the construction and mortgage lending industry in the economy?
- How does housing contribute to financial crises and cycles of boom and bust?

Summary

For those lucky enough to afford one, a house is the most expensive thing they ever buy, and entails assuming the biggest debt they ever take on. Having got on the housing ladder, homeowners stand to gain from rising house prices. Tight planning laws and limits on credit push prices up still further. Governments rake in a lot of taxes from housing transactions and so encourage this situation to continue. The trouble is, housing forms a huge part of the stock of wealth of society, and periodic gyrations in the market therefore have a massive effect on the economy; the recent financial crisis had its origins in reckless mortgage lending, and central banks have often had to hike interest rates to choke off previous housing booms, triggering recessions. It is no wonder we keep seeing booms and busts with this crazy situation. This chapter examines housing and the impact it has on lifestyles and the wider economy itself.

Key theories and topics covered

Demand and supply of housing; housing as privatized welfare; planning laws and restrictions; housing and construction in the wider economy; new forms of homeownership.

6.1 Economics of the housing market

Housing has always been a critical part of the economy and is central to most people's lives. It is not merely a place to live but also, for those who take the plunge and buy their own home, a massively important asset. Housing is probably the only major type of wealth holding that a majority of people have access to in their lives. It is easily the biggest thing they ever buy, entailing taking out the biggest loan they will ever manage, and, if all goes well, it can provide them with a significant asset that they can realize in their old age and possibly pass on to their children in the form of an inheritance.

Yet over the last decade housing has tended to make the headlines for all the wrong reasons. Many Western countries experienced a rampant housing boom during the latter part of the 1990s and first half of the 2000s. The bust that followed its bursting nearly brought down the global financial system and helped stoke the financial and Eurozone crises. Housing has often been rather peripheral in mainstream economics, however, particularly microeconomics. The market for homes has generally been assumed to operate like any other type of goods market, albeit with a few quirks and eccentricities. When housing has been taken seriously it has usually been over its impact on macroeconomic cycles.[1] The authors of a major recent study of housing economics that attempts to correct this imbalance complain that no Nobel Prize has yet been awarded for research on how the housing market works.[2]

This seems a bit of an oversight, given the size of the housing market and recent trends. According to Savills, a global estate agent, the total housing stock was worth $162 trillion in 2015, with over a fifth of that in North America alone.[3] In 1945 the average UK house cost just £1,000 and even by 1973 it was worth only £10,000. But by 1999 this had shot up to £75,000, and four years later in 2003 it had doubled to £150,000.[4] The boom was widespread. By one estimate, prices rose at an annual average rate between 1997 and 2005 of 75 per cent in the United States; 160 per cent in the United Kingdom; 130 per cent in Australia; and 185 per cent in Ireland. And, lest anyone think the boom was restricted to the 'Anglo-Saxon' nations, noted for their love of property speculation and overdeveloped financial services industries, Spain (145 per cent) and Sweden (80 per cent) also saw destructive housing bubbles.[5] Only a few countries, such as Germany, where most people are renters, were spared from this mania.

Clearly, then, housing is far from a regular market operating according to normal economic laws of supply and demand. Numerous other things are bound up in our insatiable desire to own property. Politics, speculation and high finance are all embroiled in housing. This chapter examines some of these factors and their place in the economy. It begins by examining what makes the housing market behave as it does, then explores how housing affects, and is affected by, social and political pressures. The final part of the chapter looks at new forms of owning and managing property that could possibly help to end the destructive cycle of boom and bust.

The demand for housing

The bulk of the housing stock is built and sold by the private sector, either as new builds or second-hand homes purchased by families or investors. Property can be owned outright (usually financed through a type of long-term loan called a mortgage), rented or co-owned by individuals and associations. In the United Kingdom and a few other countries there are also various forms of ownership, with property either being owned outright (freehold) or leased from the owner of the land. Most countries also have a sizeable public, or "social housing", sector in which the government, or quasi-public bodies, builds and rents out homes to mainly low-income occupiers. The size of this sector range from almost a third of all homes in the Netherlands to fewer than 10 per cent in Germany, Ireland and Spain.[6]

Probably the number one thing that people want to know about housing is why a market that is so systemically important experiences such damaging and seemingly irrational gyrations. One minute, prices are going through the roof and people are paying silly money to get a foothold in otherwise scary areas of town; the next, mortgage brokers are going bust and realtors are sitting on unsold, half-completed ghost towns. What is going on? Why is the housing market so strange? The answer is that housing is subject to certain constraints that make it behave differently from other markets. As we have already seen, in economics the price of a good is generally determined by demand and supply. Houses conform to this rule to some extent but the housing *market* is full of quirks, which make it unpredictable. It is distinctive in two key ways. First, an increase in the price of a house often leads to an *increase* – not a decrease – in demand for it. Second, the supply of houses is relatively fixed, certainly in the short term but sometimes the long term too, so that any rise in price may not lead to many more houses coming on to the market in response. Supply constraints stoke further price rises and have been implicated in damaging housing booms and a general lack of affordability in many countries.

These features of the housing market are persistent and have vexed policy-makers and buyers alike. So let us look at what is causing it. One reason that housing demand seems at times to defy gravity is that housing is both a consumption *and* an investment good. In other words, although it is usually something we want to buy to consume (by living in it), it has also come to be perceived as a solid investment as well. Rather a good investment, come to that. If you had bought wisely, or even unwisely, in many Western countries in the 1990s and hung on to it you would now own an asset that has appreciated in value possibly several times over – a fact not lost on others trying to clamber onto the housing ladder in subsequent years.

But what explains the seemingly masochistic willingness of people to pay high prices for a pile of bricks? In a "normal" market, talking about a mainly consumption good, if the price of the good rises then people on a fixed amount of income would probably simply switch to some other form of consumption; they would buy something else of value to them, or save the money instead. This helps to keep the lid on prices, because demand evaporates if prices get crazy. But if something appears to have exciting investment potential then buyers may interpret rising property prices as clear proof that housing is a one-way bet and will pile into the market in order not to miss out.

Robert Shiller, a Yale economist who has looked closely at housing's impact on the economy, has observed that over the long term house prices actually track quite closely the overall rate of inflation.[7] But there are two caveats. First, house prices are much more volatile, so at certain points in time they rise quite rapidly. Second, housing is usually heavily leveraged, so home ownership in a rising market can be immensely profitable. For many families lucky enough to buy at the right time, it is the best investment they ever make. A deposit of 20 per cent means that a price increase of just 3 per cent produces a 15 per cent increase in the homeowner's equity. In rising property markets, the investment motive eventually squeezes out the consumption factor (the idea of a house as simply something to live in), and we have a market with seemingly inexorably rising prices that may edge towards bubble territory. Leverage works both ways, however. A 20 per cent fall in prices, not unknown during severe recessions, would wipe out all your equity. Moreover, equity takes time to build. The way home loans are structured, most repayments in the early years of the mortgage go on interest and make little impact on the principal. People losing their home during this period will be left with nothing. This might be enough to put some people off, especially first-time buyers.

Naturally, there are other factors at play in determining the demand for housing that make the market difficult to predict. Most house buyers finance their purchase with a mortgage, which is a long-term loan with repayments pegged to interest rates. Changes in rates therefore have a big impact on monthly mortgage payments, which has a major knock-on effect on consumer spending, since mortgages are typically a large proportion of an individual's monthly outgoings. Many studies therefore correlate house price increases with rising disposable incomes: as our income rises we can afford larger mortgage payments. Indeed, economists describe houses as having a "high income elasticity of demand"; as people's income rises they will want to consume proportionately more of it. Reaching a certain earnings threshold often makes people want to switch from renting to buying, or existing owners to trade up to a bigger home.

The availability and affordability of finance also plays a big part. Banks have the ability to "create" wealth every time they make a new loan. During the 2000s boom they quadrupled the amount of money available for housing so there was a lot more money chasing roughly the same amount of property, leading to a huge price spike (more on this in section 6.3).

Finally, macro factors to do with population size and demographics are also important. A rising population, possibly fuelled by immigration or a high birth rate, will increase the overall demand for housing. The age structure of the population also has an effect. Young families will want big homes with nice gardens, preferably in suburbia so the parents can get to work. But many European countries and Japan have ageing populations and are seeing increasing demand for smaller dwellings in quieter areas. Rising divorce rates fuel a clamour for small flats and apartments in cities. If the market does not keep pace with changing tastes it can lead to bottlenecks and price spikes.

Not in my backyard: planning laws and housing supply

The other way in which housing markets work differently, which also contributes to rising prices, is that the supply of housing is either fixed or somewhat inelastic, particularly in the short term. In other words, house builders are often unable or unwilling to push more houses into circulation, even in the face of a palpable rise in demand, and so the price of those already on the market shoots up. By the time builders have responded to an explosion in prices the boom may already be over and they could end up with unsold dwellings, further depressing prices. This was a particular feature of the aftermath of Ireland's recent house-building boom, and these risks tend to make builders cautious.

As part of its copious research into the causes of the housing bubble and financial crisis in different countries, the OECD has concluded that the responsiveness of supply determines the extent to which surges in housing demand translate into higher prices.[8] Bottlenecks in new housing construction play a big part in price spikes, in other words. The OECD found that housing supply tends to be relatively flexible in North America, outside the big coastal cities, where there is plenty of space and a competitive building industry. On the other hand, it is also quite flexible in the Nordic countries, but more unresponsive in other north European nations with similar population densities, suggesting that other factors may be at play.

There are several reasons why supply can be rigid. Building houses requires sourcing construction materials and acquiring the skilled labour to assemble them, entailing complex logistics, which can go wrong. But volume builders who have been in the business a while generally know what they are doing and this is rarely a major constraint. The other key input is land, however, and this is something that can have political and social sensitivities entirely unconnected to the market. Although the supply of land is ultimately fixed, in most countries there still appears to be plenty of it ripe for development. The United Kingdom might seem a crowded little island but by some estimates only about 2.5 per cent of it has actually been built on.[9]

The key thing to remember, though, is that not all land is of equal value to developers. Because of transport costs involved in getting to work and the need for local amenities, people tend to like to live clustered together in towns and cities, and this puts a particular premium on land in urban areas available for development. And, although city dwellers are normally happy to put up with higher residential densities (more neighbours and smaller flats), there are limits to this once a certain threshold is passed – when your neighbours can see into your bedroom, for example. So, once ensconced in their neighbourhoods, residents generally lobby planners in local government to limit the number of new dwellings, and this imposes a cap on supply while at the same time there may be no let-up in demand.

Box 6.1 Who are the homeowners?

Analyses of OECD data by Dan Andrews and Aida Caldera Sánchez[10] suggest that homeownership varies by the following factors.

- Age: in the United States, a head of household aged 45 to 64 years is 37 percentage points more likely to be a homeowner than where the head is aged 20 to 24 years. In Germany, the same household type is 54 percentage points more likely to be a homeowner than younger counterparts.
- Family size: the probability of homeownership is much lower for single-headed households, particularly if they have children. This is probably

a result of financial constraints; if you are a single parent it is difficult to afford a mortgage as well.

• Income: the probability of homeownership rises in line with real house-hold disposable income.

• Education: although tertiary (university) education tends to be positively associated with homeownership, this varies by country, with a particularly strong relationship in the United Kingdom but a weaker one in continental Europe.

• Nationality and ethnicity: the probability of homeownership is generally lower for immigrant households – particularly in Italy and Luxembourg – and also minority households and those not proficient in the official language of the country. In the United States, African Americans and Hispanic Americans are over 15 percentage points less likely to be home-owners than other Americans.

Much the same thing happens in rural areas, where political pressure from well-organized voter-residents forces planners to step in to regulate the use of land. Those attracted to country living enjoy having idyllic farmland on their doorstep but often draw the line at human neighbours too close by. Accordingly, distortions abound, because planners are obliged by local politics to attach differing values to particular land uses to reflect local needs and concerns. For example, the value of residential land around expensive, hi-tech Cambridge, in the United Kingdom, is around 300 times that of nearby farming land, almost entirely because of local and national planning restrictions designed to restrict development.[11] Postwar UK planners enacted a "green belt" around London and other big cities to prevent urban sprawl. It achieves this, but at the cost of pumping up prices in surrounding towns and suburbs, as well as London itself.

House building is a competitive industry and so, other things being equal, the price of a house ought to not be much more than the cost of building it. Any sizeable price mark-up should therefore be a clear indication of artificial barriers to new construction, and, to no one's great surprise, property prices in Manhattan in New York City are typically two or three times higher than construction costs.[12] Land use restrictions are the natural explanation for this gap. For most of its history New York was able to keep the lid on prices by expanding supply, with blocks of low-rise apartments demolished to make way for denser buildings as land owners were generally free to cash in on their property by adding extra floors to buildings. But from the 1970s onwards residents got organized and became adept at lobbying and protesting against new developments. The city authorities began to slap restrictions on further building and enacted regulations to limit development. At the same time there was political pressure at the bottom end of the social scale to cap rent rises. These protected the tenancies of the lucky few in rent-controlled apartment buildings but at the cost of further discouraging new development. Cities in California also saw a boom in house prices, but this was caused by erratic zoning regulations and tax policies that encouraged city authorities to favour retail over housing development.[13]

Compare this with another American city where a lot of people come to make their fortune: Las Vegas. The desert city saw its population triple between 1980 and 2000 but real median houses price barely budged as there were few supply restrictions. Analysts have observed large, long-run differences in average house price appreciation across metropolitan areas over the past 50 years, which can be explained by an inelastic supply of land in some unique locations combined with an increasing number of high-income households fuelling demand. The evidence is most visible in popular, expensive cities, where many people desire to live but increasingly only the rich can afford to dwell.

Numerous studies have documented the rise of such "superstar cities", such as New York, London and San Francisco.[14] Here, wealthy families who want to live in prestige locations simply outbid lower-income families, who are forced to flee the city, no doubt adding further to the snob appeal. Housing in these superstar cities thus becomes a luxury good for which people are prepared to pay a sizeable premium. Cities are also highly attractive to entrepreneurial people with bright ideas, argues Edward Glaeser, a prominent urban economist. They cluster in urban areas in order to exchange ideas and learn from one another.[15] With the San Francisco area being a magnet for highly paid technology workers, and New York and London for finance professionals, rich buyers can generally blow their lower-income competition out of the water when it comes to bidding for apartments.

Of course, the downside for those who get to live in super-cities is that all this ratchets up the cost of living, as everything simply becomes more expensive. By one 2009 estimate, a $60,000 Manhattan salary buys the same standard of living as a $26,092 salary in Atlanta.[16] City living is indeed becoming a luxury only for the few.

6.2 Rent or buy?

The previous section dealt with the supply and demand for residential homes and the effect on prices. But not all people buy their own home. Some are obliged to rent theirs because they cannot afford to buy; others rent as a matter of choice. Rates of homeownership actually vary considerably across countries (see Figure 6.1). OECD studies show the Spanish and Irish have the highest rates

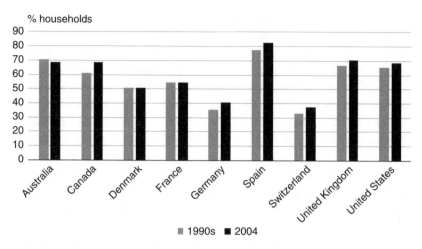

Figure 6.1 Change in homeownership rates, 1990s and 2004
Source: OECD.

of homeownership, with the United States and United Kingdom a bit behind and the Swiss and Germans at the bottom of the ranking, indicating no tight link between economic strength and incidences of home ownership. Germany's low rate of homeownership is commonly attributed to its acute housing shortage following the Second World War, which the government tackled by encouraging a thriving rental sector to rein in private ownership in order to keep the lid on prices. Germans still benefit from readily affordable housing, and the country avoided the worst of the last housing boom.

Let us begin by weighing up the costs and benefits of different forms of housing tenure. Obviously, people who own their home outright avoid rent or mortgage payments and so have more money available for non-housing consumption compared with people on the same income facing these outgoings. But most homeowners are not in this lucky position, as they will probably have had to take out a mortgage to buy the property and therefore currently face a large chunk of debt on which to make repayments. One thing to consider initially, therefore, is the opportunity cost of tying up capital in property rather than other forms of investment, such as a bank account or the stock exchange. Over a longish period, say ten years (shorter than most mortgage terms), stocks have usually outperformed property as an investment, assuming dividends are reinvested, and both beat leaving it in a bank.

But this does not necessarily make property a poor choice of investment. For sure, some people avoid stocks altogether because they do not understand financial markets and feel safer with bricks and mortar – which is not as short-sighted a reason as it might seem, as investment advisers generally counsel people to stick to what they know. But owning property also affords the opportunity to make improvements that will add value, and, last but not least, you can also live in it while it – hopefully – climbs in price.

Assuming you have the funds, or a good enough credit rating to secure a mortgage, there are other factors to consider. Transaction costs are considerable in housing and are steepest for buyers. Estate agent, legal and surveyors' fees can add many thousands to the cost of moving house, but in the rental market most fees will be covered by the landlord. These are not decisive, however, and, from a strictly financial point of view, most analysts consider buying to be a sounder decision than renting. One 2014 study by Santander, a bank, put the lifetime cost of renting in London at over £400,000 – more than enough to buy a property outright in this notoriously expensive city. A conscious decision to rent rather than buy will therefore probably be about more than just finance. A key factor is mobility. Owning a house ties you down, and so renting may suit people who move jobs a lot. In fact, unemployment is associated with higher incidences of homeownership, because of the difficulty of selling up and moving.[17]

Behavioural economists are also contributing to housing economics by pointing out that the choice of renting versus buying is not necessarily an entirely rational decision. A lot of emotion is tied up in housing to do with the warm feeling we get from owning the place we live in and, hopefully, passing it on to our kids someday. Studies that look at the actual thought processes people go through when weighing up homeownership indicate the importance of bounded rationality and use of heuristics in reaching decisions.[18] For example, homeownership reinforces feelings around entering responsible adulthood for many people, or, for immigrants to the United States, participation in the "American dream". It also seems that many individuals become overwhelmed by the amount of complex information involved in home purchases and choose to overlook the risks.

Housing tenure is also highly political, as governments get involved in private housing markets because of the impact on the wider economy, with the bias in policy generally towards encouraging homeownership. Typical policies include subsidizing mortgage costs (in the United States) and allowing tenants to buy their social housing (in the United Kingdom). They do this because of mounting evidence from economists that high rates of homeownership produce lots of "positive spillovers"; in other words, they are good for the economy and society. The most compelling reason is that, for otherwise myopic households, homeownership can create more of an orientation towards the future. The very act of pre-committing to a scheme that is costly to break through taking on mortgage debt prompts a virtuous change in spending behaviour by making people save more and fritter less away.[19]

This possibility has been undermined somewhat by the greater use of housing equity withdrawal and mortgage refinancing, with some people using their homes as collateral to get bigger loans to subsidize their errant lifestyles.[20] Following the financial crisis, policy-makers in many countries responded by clamping down on lenders encouraging risky behaviour by outlawing loans with high loan-to-value ratios (the notorious "120 per cent mortgages" offered at the height of the bubble) or loans requiring little or no collateral. The hope is that this will restore some of the positive spillovers from homeownership.

Indeed, homeownership has also been linked to better outcomes for children in terms of test scores and behaviour.[21] This may reflect the added geographic stability and improved home environment associated with homeownership compared with renting. It is not clear if the relationship is causal, however, as the risk-averse, investor-type people are likely to be exactly the kind of parents more likely to purchase a home and invest in their children.

For similar reasons, there is strong evidence for homeownership being associated with more active and informed citizens and more residentially stable neighbourhoods. Homeowners might be more likely to make political choices that favour the long-run health of their community, such as more investment in green space, while renters may favour policies bringing immediate benefits relative to long-run gains.[22] It has also been argued that homeowners take better care of their property and are both happier and healthier. We should be a bit careful about assuming this relationship is causal, however. Indeed, it could work the other way round, if homeowners face greater anxiety due to their increased financial obligations. It should also be noted that the money spent on owner-occupied housing investment might crowd out other family-specific investments that have a more direct payoff to children's outcomes. Public housing may have a positive effect on school retention, because subsidized housing allows money to be directed to other family needs.

All in all, high rates of homeownership seem to be good for society in many ways. But does this mean that governments should step in to encourage this?

6.3 Houses as casinos and piggy banks

Let us now introduce the elephant in the corner of the room: the link between the housing bubble of the early part of the last decade and the financial crisis that followed its bursting. It should be clear by now that housing is ruled by far more than the basic laws of supply and demand. Moreover, the housing market is large enough for its gyrations to have major implications for the economy and society and is therefore subject to political interference, which may introduce further distortions into the market.

An additional complication is that housing has become embroiled in financial speculation. Individuals increasingly see their home not just as somewhere to lay their hat but as part of their wealth portfolio – a financial as well as physical shelter. This interconnection attracted the interest of the financial services industry and encouraged the wall of money that flooded into the housing market in the 2000s.[23] These factors came together in the subsequent, catastrophic, housing bust, which began in the US "sub-prime" mortgage market around 2005 and quickly spread globally to other parts of the market. Although many countries experienced a housing boom in the 2000s the bubble appears to have been particularly overinflated in English-speaking economically liberal states such as the United States, United Kingdom, Ireland and Australia, which have traditionally high levels of homeownership and well-developed financial services industries.

There were also elements of unintended consequences. In the 1990s and 2000s governments in many countries sought to widen homeownership beyond the middle classes. In the United States in 1994 the Clinton administration loosened housing rules by rewriting the Community Reinvestment Act, which put pressure on banks to lend in low-income neighbourhoods. This coincided with moves to deregulate the personal finance industry that included removing restrictions on high-risk, low-collateral lending.

Some economists therefore claim that the housing boom was tolerated, if not actively encouraged, by politicians seeking private-sector-led growth. US policymakers, including the Fed, wanted rising house prices to offset the $7 trillion loss of wealth following the dotcom crash of 2000. Between the first quarters of 2001 and 2007 mortgage debt in the United States doubled from $4.92 trillion to $9.96 trillion.[24] Investment bank Merrill Lynch, a famous casualty of the financial crisis, estimated that almost a half of all American GDP growth in the first half of 2005 was housing-related, while more than half the new private sector jobs created between 2001 and then were connecting to house building.[25] By the middle of the decade *The Economist* was already warning that "[r]ising property prices helped to prop up the world economy after the stock market bubble burst in 2000. What if the housing boom now turns to bust?" (see Figure 6.2).[26]

Colin Crouch, a political economist, has dubbed the politically inspired housing boom as "privatized Keynesianism", arguing that private credit has replaced government deficit spending as the main instrument for propping up economic activity in a world plagued by low growth.[27] The instrument of this was the housing market in tandem with the financial services industry. Left-wing and Marxist economists, such as David Harvey, have drawn attention to what they call the overt "financialization" of the economy.[28] This process entails dividing capitalism into producer and consumer markets that are both then integrated into financial markets, and encourages the rise of financial engineering as an economic activity in itself. In the 1990s and 2000s mortgage markets became a key component of financialization as investors sought to tie local housing markets into global investment markets.[29] This helped to ensure that the housing crash, when it

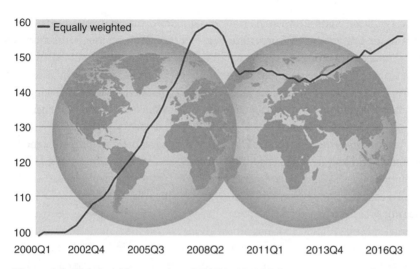

Figure 6.2 Global real house prices, 2000Q1–2016Q3
Note: 2001Q1 = 100.
Sources: Bank for International Settlements, ECB, Federal Reserve Bank of Dallas, Savills and national sources.

came, was not confined to one country, or even those that had the worst housing bubbles, but immediately went global.

Financialization was facilitated by a wave of innovation in financial services industries, which contributed to two key developments. First, people previously excluded from access to mortgage finance because of low income or a poor credit standing were now able to participate in the housing market; thus the sub-prime mortgage market was born. Second, existing homeowners were able to use the capital they had already accrued to borrow even more. Probably the key thing making this possible was the growth in so-called secondary mortgage markets. In primary markets, mortgages are a closed arrangement between the borrower and lender. Financial innovation by investment banks and local lenders prompted a growth in secondary markets, however, in which investors can buy mortgages from lenders and trade these among other investors in a process known as "securitization".

This had been going on for some time in the United States in one form or another – the government-backed "Fannie Mae" and "Freddie Mac" were created partly to provide liquidity in local mortgage markets – and the reasoning behind them, to spread the risk of default, is fairly sound. The problem was that the original lenders could thereby relieve themselves of the risk of making loans, leading to falling lending standards. In the United States and other places lenders looking to build market share resorted to selling ever riskier mortgages to ever more financially unsuitable borrowers. The increasing size and sophistication of capital markets meant more loans could be recycled, providing capital for yet more loans. Sub-prime boomed. By the time the crunch came in early 2006, in the form of a sudden collapse in prices, a vicious circle had already been created. It led from home occupiers (who could no longer finance their mortgages) through lenders (who lacked funds to support their loan book) into the world economy (whose banks no longer trusted each other enough to circulate credit) and back again to borrowers (who were unable to sell into a falling market).[30]

Housing as welfare

Let us look more at the political economy of housing. Why was all this property madness indulged by politicians and regulators alike? As indicated earlier, a vibrant and growing housing market suits politicians as well as the financial services industry, which saw the opportunity to massively increase its customer base. And, after all, why should low-income people not be able to own their own home?

But some academics argue that there is a further, underlying motive. It is that housing increasingly fills the gaps left by changing welfare states. As we shall see in Chapter 8, welfare states face cost pressures and the need to adapt to new risks stemming from structural changes to the economy and shifting family structures. Welfare is increasingly based less around offering income security on the basis of conventional labour market risks and more about actively preparing men and women for an uncertain world. These pressures affect all countries, but are particularly marked in the liberal, Anglo-Saxon nations, which, perhaps not coincidentally, had the most overinflated housing bubbles. Could people facing a more uncertain future at work and in retirement be taking refuge in housing?

Statistical analyses of homeownership rates and public welfare provision in rich OECD states show a clear correlation between the two. Countries with high homeownership rates (Australia, Canada and the United States) had more minimal welfare states, while those with low ownership rates (Sweden, Germany and the Netherlands) had highly developed welfare systems. France and the United Kingdom were somewhere in between.[31] The rationale behind this seems to be that gaps in welfare coverage undermine confidence in the ability of society to look after the elderly through public pension programmes, so people increasingly make their own arrangements and see property investment as the way to go. This may help to explain the huge attraction of homeownership, despite the risks, for many Americans on low incomes with inadequate workplace pension and healthcare arrangements. Their home became, in effect, their pension and their insurance safety net, and this magnified the incentive to gamble on future price rises. This, coupled with the eagerness of financial companies to lend to them and an absence of regulatory safeguards, could help to explain the ruinous boom that ensued.

The obvious policy response, particularly in countries burnt by the collapse of housing bubbles, might therefore be to legislate to provide greater security for those on low incomes and clamp down on predatory mortgage lending. But there is evidence that these trends are persistent and may in fact be deeply embedded in national capitalisms. For one thing, rates of homeownership affect the underlying preferences of voters, and it is voters who determine the orientation of politics. Studies find that the front loading of housing costs may make homeowners a natural constituent for a smaller welfare state.[32] There seems to be a clear trade-off in lower-income households between a preference for cash income for home purchases, and taxes for social welfare spending. In other words, people scraping the funds together for a housing down payment will vote for lower taxes and a smaller welfare state, whereas renters are able to spread their housing costs over a lifetime and may favour a more expansive welfare state.

Against this it could be objected that Sweden, a country with a generous welfare state, also suffered a serious housing bust while Germany, where welfare state retrenchment is under way, did not. Nevertheless, these kinds of arguments do suggest that residential housing and financial systems are deeply embroiled with political, economic and welfare regimes in modern capitalist democracies. Political economists also note correlations between liberal, deregulated housing markets and high levels of inequality. Herman Schwartz and Leonard Seabrook argue that housing in different countries tends to be regarded politically *either* as a social right or as a means to wealth.[33] In the latter, the initial financial commitment needed to get onto the housing ladder in the first place, coupled with the possibility for outsize capital appreciation having got there, helps to produce societies that are highly stratified by wealth. In countries where housing is seen as more of a social right, housing outcomes are less likely to be left to the market and there is political support for tax and spending policies. All this reinforces the argument that housing is deeply embroiled in national politics and society.

6.4 How to "normalize" the housing market

Even when housing is not destabilizing the wider economy, rapidly rising prices create problems over intergenerational fairness as young people and families find themselves increasingly frozen out of the housing market. It now takes 19 years for members of "generation rent" to save up a deposit to buy their first home, according to one UK study.[34] Ultra-expensive super-cities such as New York and London are also facing shortages of "key workers" – moderately paid health, maintenance and other essential staff – whose wages are insufficient to allow them to house themselves close to where they are needed. Instead, they are being shunted out to the outer suburbs, which reinforces urban social segregation and imposes long, soul-sapping commutes. Burnt by the financial crisis and under pressure from regulators, banks became much more wary about lending to low-income buyers because of more conservative underwriting standards, including higher minimum credit scores. As of 2015, homeownership rates in the United States, although recovering, were still the lowest in half a century.[35]

Policy-makers are increasingly taking note and looking at radical solutions. The obvious one, freeing up the planning system, was, as we saw earlier, too hamstrung by local politics to be easily achievable, although moves are afoot in London to loosen green belt restrictions. New construction techniques being developed may enable builders to construct homes more easily and quickly. For example, "modular housing" applies manufacturing techniques to home build-ing, with blocks of apartments manufactured off-site before being transported to their location. No matter how cheap they are to make, however, they still cannot overcome the issue of high land prices. A bolder strategy is to largely abandon the market altogether and pursue direct intervention by the state or local government to increase supply at the lower end of the market. This is the approach adopted by the Democrat mayor of New York, Bill de Blasio, who in 2014 unveiled a housing plan to build 200,000 affordable homes at a cost of $41 billion, most of this coming from the private sector.[36] The mayor justified intervention on the basis that there are over 1 million people in New York on less than the local median income of $42,000 a year for a family of four, but fewer than half that number of homes available with rents they could afford. The building plan is also accompanied by non-financial supply-side measures to change urban zoning regulations that dictate what can be built where in the city.

Towns and cities with less cash and cachet than New York are exploring more radical ways to make housing more accessible to low-income people. One is to re-examine the structure of homeownership itself. The conventional ownership model in widespread existence is to buy the home outright by taking out a long-term loan (mortgage). This imposes major upfront costs and may therefore be unavailable to people on low incomes or those whose patchy work history denies them affordable credit. Moreover, all homeowners with hefty mortgages are vul-nerable to market gyrations as repayments comprise a big part of the household budget. "Part-ownership" schemes offer a potential way around this, as buyers purchase a more limited equity stake in their property for a small initial down payment by homeowners. They share in any rise in the price of the property and can purchase a large stake when their income rises.

Academics and housing think tanks have for decades been advocating such "alternative ownership models" for the housing market. According to one, the

United Kingdom's New Economics Foundation, in conjunction with CDS Co-operatives, such forms of housing tenure need to fulfil two conditions: first, they must be stable and able to offer a regular supply of housing on uniform terms; and, second, in order to be affordable, they need to be subsidized by either the government or a not-for-profit organization. In addition, the tenancy agreement has to be designed in a way that the tenant must be able to realize some, but not all, of the capital gains from rising prices.[37] Conversely, tenants may also need an easy exit strategy from homeownership when prices are falling, not rising. Making homeownership more like a limited lease purchase can reduce the trauma around defaulting, argue American experts.[38]

There are several shared-ownership models. Community land trusts (CLTs) are non-profits that enable participants to own the physical structure of their home but not the underlying land, which they lease from the CLT. They were allegedly inspired by Vinobha Bhave, a follower of Gandhi, who persuaded a number of Indian landowners to put land into trust for poor farmers. The idea encouraged Martin Luther King, and the first US CLT was set up in Georgia in 1967 for poor African Americans.

Current variants see the CLT either repurchasing the homes at below-market prices whenever the owners decide to resell, or requiring them to resell their homes to another income-eligible household for a below-market price. Government subsidy to take the land out of the market can slice up to a third off the purchase price, and owners are also incentivized to make improvements to the property as they share the benefits with the CLT. A variation on this is limited equity housing cooperatives (LEHCs), in which residents buy a low cost share of the ownership of a building but are limited on the return from resale of the housing. Lease-purchase programmes typically allow participants, called lease purchasers, to select a home, and a local housing finance agency or non-profit buys the home on their behalf. The agency serves as the initial owner, mortgagor and property manager for the lease period of three years.

Are these a complete solution? Probably not, so long as homeownership is so deeply ingrained in our mentalities and the potential gains from owning at the right time and in the right place so great. But it is surely right that housing associations and urban theorists are looking at them. And the more light that economists can shine on the way the market operates, the better.

Conclusion: what we have learnt

- The housing market does not behave like a "normal" market, and this helps to produce its notorious booms and busts. Homes have an investment as well as consumption value and are therefore subject to financial speculation and herd-like behaviour as buyers respond to rising prices by redoubling their efforts to get onto the housing ladder.

- A further issue is limited supply. The supply of housing can be relatively inelastic, which contributes to rising prices. Urban zoning and planning laws in urban and rural areas restrict new building, and existing homeowners keen to preserve their lifestyles lobby furiously for further limits. High and rising prices are the result, and we have seen the growth of "superstar cities" where, increasingly, only high earners can afford to live. Governments continue to favour homeownership over renting because of the positive "spillovers" onto the rest of the economy and society.

- The housing markets gyrations can have a serious impact on the wider economy, as we saw in 2008 when the US sub-prime mortgage market collapsed and brought down major banks that had lent too much to buyers. Questions also need to be asked about the "financialization" of housing and the underlying conditions that drive some people to stake everything on owning property.

- Policy-makers are keen to prevent a repeat of these events while also continuing to help low-income people and key workers onto the housing ladder. Maybe adopting new forms of tenancy, such as part-ownership, is the answer?

Notes

1. J. Muellbauer & A. Murphy, "Housing markets and the economy: the assessment", *Oxford Review of Economic Policy* 42:1 (2008), 1–33.
2. S. Smith & B. Searle (eds), *The Blackwell Companion to the Economics of Housing* (Oxford: Blackwell, 2010).
3. Savills World Research, "What price the world? Trends in international real estate trading: around the world in dollars and cents" (London: Savills World Research, 2015).
4. Building Society Association and HM Land Registry.
5. Data from Standard and Poor's, cited in M. Blyth, "The politics of compounding bubbles: the global housing bubble in comparative perspective", *Comparative European Politics* 6:3 (2008), 387–406.
6. K. Scanlon, "Social housing in Europe", *European Policy Analysis* 17 (2015), 1–12.
7. Shiller produces the Case–Shiller house price index: http://us.spindices.com/index-family/real-estate/sp-corelogic-case-shiller (accessed 1 October 2016); see also R. Shiller, *The Subprime Solution: How Today's Global Financial Crisis Happened, and What to Do about It* (Princeton, NJ: Princeton University Press, 2008).
8. D. Andrews, "Real house prices in OECD countries: the role of demand shocks and structural and policy factors", Economics Department Working Paper no. 831 (Paris: OECD Publishing, 2010).
9. United Nations Environment Programme World Conservation Monitoring Centre (UNEP-WCMC), *UK National Ecosystem Assessment: Synthesis of the Key Findings* (Cambridge: UNEP-WCMC, 2011). Note that the area classified as "urban area" is higher, at 7 per cent, but this includes parks and gardens.

10. D. Andrews & A. Caldera Sánchez, "The evolution of homeownership rates in selected OECD countries: demographic and public policy influences", *OECD Journal: Economic Studies 2011* (2011), 207–43.
11. K. Barker, *Housing: Where's the Plan?* (London: London Publishing Partnership, 2010).
12. E. Glaeser, J. Gyourko & R. Saks, "Why is Manhattan so expensive? Regulation and the rise in house prices", Working Paper no. 10124 (Cambridge, MA: NBER, 2003).
13. M. Quigley & S. Raphael, "Regulation and the high cost of housing in California", *American Economic Review* 95:2 (2005), 323–8.
14. J. Gyourko, C. Mayer & T. Sinai, "Superstar cities", *American Economic Journal* 5:4 (2013), 167–99.
15. E. Glaeser, *Triumph of the City: How Urban Spaces Make Us Human* (London: Macmillan, 2011).
16. Center for an Urban Future, *Reviving the City of Aspiration: A Study of the Challenges Facing New York City's Middle Class* (New York: Center for an Urban Future, 2009).
17. A. Caldera Sánchez & D. Andrews, "To move or not to move: what drives residential mobility in the OECD?", Economics Department Working Paper no. 837 (Paris: OECD Publishing, 2011).
18. C. Reid, *To buy or not to buy? Understanding tenure preference and the decision-making process of low income households* (Cambridge, MA: Joint Center for Housing Studies, Harvard University, 2013).
19. M. Sherraden, *Assets and the Poor: A New American Welfare Policy* (New York: M. E. Sharpe, 1991).
20. W. Li & F. Yang, "American dream or American obsession? The economic benefits and costs of homeownership", *Federal Reserve Bank of Philadelphia Business Review* 2010:3 (2010), 20–30.
21. D. Haurin & L. Gill, "The impact of transaction costs and the expected length of stay on homeownership", *Journal of Urban Economics* 51:3 (2002), 563–84.
22. J. Richer, "Explaining the vote for slow growth", *Public Choice* 82:3/4 (1996), 207–22.
23. For an excellent account of how high finance took an interest in the mortgage market, see G. Tett, *Fool's Gold: How Unrestrained Greed Corrupted a Dream, Shattered Global Markets and Unleashed a Catastrophe* (London: Little, Brown, 2009).
24. K. Phillips, *Bad Money: Reckless Finance, Failed Politics and the Global Crisis of American Capitalism* (London: Penguin Books, 2009).
25. Cited in C. Morris, *The Trillion Dollar Meltdown: Easy Money, High Rollers, and the Great Credit Crash* (New York: Public Affairs, 2008).
26. *The Economist*, "In come the waves", *The Economist*, 16 June 2005.
27. C. Crouch, "Privatized Keynesianism: an unacknowledged policy regime", *British Journal of Politics and International Relations* 11:3 (2009), 382–99.
28. D. Harvey, *A Brief History of Neoliberalism* (Oxford: Oxford University Press, 2005).
29. M. Albers, "The financialization of home and the mortgage market crisis", *Competition and Change* 12:2 (2008), 148–66.
30. S. Smith, B. Searle & G. Powells, "Introduction", in S. Smith & B. Searle (eds), *The Blackwell Companion to the Economics of Housing*, 1–27 (Oxford: Blackwell, 2010).
31. F. Castles, "The really big trade-off: home ownership and the welfare state in the new world and the old", *ActaPolitica* 32:1 (1998), 5–19.
32. J. Kemeny, "Home ownership and privatisation", *International Journal of Urban and Regional Research* 4:3 (1980), 372–88.
33. H. Schwartz & L. Seabrooke, "Varieties of residential capitalism in the international political economy: old welfare states and the new politics of housing", in H. Schwartz & L. Seabrooke (eds), *The Politics of Housing Booms and Busts*, 1–27 (London: Palgrave Macmillan, 2009).
34. PricewaterhouseCoopers (PwC), *UK Economic Outlook* (London: PwC, 2016).

35. Joint Center for Housing Studies, *The State of the Nation's Housing 2016* (Cambridge, MA: Joint Center for Housing Studies, Harvard University, 2016).
36. Office of the Mayor, *Housing New York: A Five-Borough, Ten-Year Plan* (New York: Office of the Mayor, 2014).
37. P. Conaty, J. Birchall, S. Bendle & R. Foggitt, *Common Ground – for Mutual Home Ownership* (London: CDS Co-operatives & New Economics Foundation, 2003).
38. E. Graves, "Variations on an American dream: alternative homeownership models", *New England Community Developments 2011* (2011), 8–14.

7

SHOP TILL YOU DROP: SHOPPING AND CONSUMPTION

I like nice things.
    Elton John

Key questions

• What are the key influences on consumer behaviour?
• From factory to high street: how do global supply chains respond to our changing needs and tastes?
• How does what we buy drive the national and international economy?
• How are technology and the internet changing the way we shop?

Summary

We live to shop. Consumer spending comprises a major part of the economies of most rich countries, but consumers' behaviour is unpredictable and it can wreck or rescue the economy. Besides shops themselves, huge distribution chains and freight transport networks, employing millions of people, are dependent on customers opening their wallets. Consumers themselves are the targets of advertising, marketing and other forms of persuasion by retailers chasing their business. But is the growing scale and diversity of retail operations and global supply chains – while, admittedly, driving down prices and widening choice – being bought at the expense of dubious ethical standards? Some argue that our obsession with low prices in shops and supermarkets is harming workers in developing countries and cruel to animals. It could also lead to the extinction of the "high street" as consumers flock to out-of-town malls or use the internet. Do the benefits of these changes outweigh the costs?

Key topics and theories covered

The "affluent society" and consumer choice; globalization and global value chains in retail; the environmental and ethical impact of supermarkets and cheap clothing; new ways of shopping.

7.1 The economics of shopping and consumption

Shopping is one of our favourite activities and is therefore something of keen interest to economists. We certainly love to splash the cash. Private consumption spending in most advanced economies comprises a half to two-thirds of GDP and consumer sentiment is considered a critical indicator of economic vigour. Consumers spent $43 trillion worldwide in 2015, a 35-fold increase on 1965.[1] Americans, who account for more than a quarter of this total, lavished $274 billion on new cars and trucks, $24 billion on dishes and flatwear, $44 billion on breakfast cereals and $60 billion on their pets.[2] That same year the Chinese bought 25 million new cars, up from 7 million in 2008 and a third as many again as in the United States.

On one level, of course, the economic experience of shopping is pretty straightforward. You identify a want, or unmet need, and realize that your life would be made better by buying a certain good or service that helps to satisfy it. A new pair of shoes, for example, or the latest laptop computer. So you go to the store with your purse or wallet, choose and purchase the necessary item and take it home. Your life, for the moment, has been enhanced.

That simple? Well, not entirely. This chapter unpacks the whole idea of shopping and consumption, beginning with the basic economics of consumer choice. As we have seen previously in this book, and as will be outlined below, the standard NCE view is of shoppers as atomized individuals, focusing on maximizing their own utilities and largely untouched by social influences. But we will also see how this view can be counterposed against other theories that question these assumptions and point to a wider perspective on consumption: the global value chains that bring goods to market; the impact of consumption on the wider economy; and how shops and shopping are being transformed by technology.

Acknowledging this complexity, numerous authors, including many economists, often therefore refer to the "consumer society". This shifts the focus from NCE's concern with the individual shopper to a more collective, social view of the activity of consuming. The concept has a long, and rather gloomy, pedigree and embodies the idea that shopping is about much more than simply buying things but has a reciprocal effect on the shopper herself, society at large and – ultimately – the entire planet. Jean-Jacques Rousseau and Karl Marx were among the first to warn about the dehumanizing effects of chasing material possessions. Thorstein Veblen famously drew attention to "conspicuous consumption": acquiring possessions to demonstrate status rather than to satisfy genuine material wants.[3] J. K. Galbraith heralded the advent of an "affluent society" of relentless consumption after the Second World War, implying that this was something consciously fostered by planners seeking a use for redundant wartime manufacturing capacity.[4]

To its critics, therefore, the flipside of the affluent society is "overconsumption", a supposedly modern vice also implicated in rising economic inequality and environmental degradation. In his book *Richistan*, Robert Frank analyses how the lavish incomes of the top earners unleashed "luxury fever" on an envious world.[5] Millionaires and billionaires become consumed by status envy and engage in pointless competition over the size of their yachts. This obsession with luxury trickles down to the middle classes and even the poor, who go into debt to obtain prestige brands. Others question the novelty and salience of these concerns, though. Frank Trentmann, a historian of consumption, points out that taste can be upwardly mobile too (denim jeans are worn by dot.com billionaires), and a fondness for luxury is especially pronounced in relatively egalitarian societies such as South Korea.[6]

Lamenting consumerism can perhaps sometimes tip into snobbery and elitism. Critics of the consumer society are possibly on surer ground when it comes to its impact on the planet. The convention of consumer choice can too easily elide into a wanton disregard for the consequences of excess. Our consumption habits can be extremely wasteful, because in rich countries what we buy is no longer determined by what we need. "Planned obsolescence" is a genuine production strategy to make products that fall apart after a certain amount of usage so they have to be replaced.[7] Americans generate 250 million tons of trash annually.[8] The average UK family wastes £470 on uneaten food each year.[9] Humans are talented at inventing new excuses to spend money. A study of gift-giving at Christmas showed a big gap between what givers paid for their gifts and how much their recipients would have paid for them if they had chosen them themselves.[10] The roughly 10 per cent gap, or "deadweight cost", represents a colossal waste of resources when you factor in that Christmas accounts for about a quarter of yearly retail sales.

Accordingly, some economists worry about the environmental degradation resulting from our obsession with shopping and claim that consumption-based capitalism is incompatible with the concept of a sustainable economy.[11] Others, however, contend that there is no necessary contradiction, as capitalism has proved able to adapt to new challenges and will eventually solve the problems of excess waste.[12] Moreover, even those Christmas presents that no one wants keep someone, somewhere, in a job. Either way, it should be obvious by now that shopping is not merely a trivial pastime but a deeply contested activity that is nevertheless pivotal to modern economies and societies. So let us see how it is modelled in economics.

The economics of consumer choice

Consumption is central to modern economics because the final demand for goods and services – the point at which they are bought with some purpose in mind – is regarded as the ultimate point of economic activity. Even if you do not collect roomfuls of shoes you will still want to acquire food to eat, the means to cook and serve it, and nice surroundings in which to enjoy it. Adam Smith wrote that "consumption is the sole end and purpose of production and the welfare of the producer ought to be attended to only so far as it may be necessary for promoting that of the consumer".[13] For Smith, and other classical economists, the value of a good was still determined by the cost of making it – the labour and materials that went into its production. The early neoclassical economists Alfred Marshall, Léon Walras and William Jevons, on the other hand, turned this around and argued that it was above all consumers who created value through the choices they make.

That well-known phrase "The customer is always right" therefore has a firm basis in modern economics. It is embodied in the doctrine of "consumer sovereignty", which holds that individuals know best what they want, and that these wants can best be satisfied in a market in which suppliers (shops, distributors and manufacturers) respond compliantly to consumer demand. Moreover, when consumers are free to choose, suppliers are thereby able to infer their customers' tastes from these choices and can plan ahead to offer similar goods for sale at affordable prices, and the whole economy can chug along. This agreeable scenario gives rise to detailed theories of "consumer choice", which have a prominent place in mainstream economics textbooks.[14]

In view of the centrality of shopping and consumption to modern life, the concept of consumer choice is arguably a good place to start from when modelling the whole economy. As we have seen already, NCE assumes that people behave rationally and attempt to maximize their utility, or satisfaction, through the choices they make about purchasing particular combinations of goods and services. There are two main influences on this: consumers' own tastes, or preferences; and how much money they have available to spend (the "budget constraint"). These go together to determine what people will buy.

NCE's customary assumptions about individuals being rational and having access to enough information to make informed choices come out in two main ways: first, that preferences are said to be *complete* (consumers can compare all possible combinations, or "baskets", of goods); and, second, that they are *transitive* (if basket A is preferred to B and B is preferred to C, then A is also preferred to C). Completeness and transitivity simply reflect NCE assumptions about customers being rational and having good information about what is on offer. It is also assumed that if someone likes, say, apples then, up to a certain point, they will prefer to have more of them rather than fewer.

Altogether, these assumptions impose a degree of rationality and predictability on consumer behaviour, and this enables economists to model consumer choice. A system governed by consumer choice is useful for manufacturers and retailers to be able to predict demand for their products. This can be done to some extent by observing what consumers have bought in the past, but the theory of consumer sovereignty helps bring out underlying structures of markets that sharpen predictions further.

For example, the concepts of complete and transitive preferences suggest two alternative approaches to working out what consumers want. One is to focus on their willingness to substitute one good for another by modelling preferences as *indifference curves*. The shape and slope of the indifference curve indicates the satisfaction gained from various baskets of goods by showing how readily one combination would be substituted for another. This is quite a useful tool for, say, clothing companies planning next year's lines. Are pastel colours going to be preferred to this year's blacks? Skin-tight jeans may be popular at the moment, but just how much discomfort will wearers tolerate before they switch to chinos?

Box 7.1 Key terms

Supply chain. A multi-stage system for producing and distributing a good from supplier to customer.

Utility. The satisfaction a consumer derives from a good or service she has bought.

Economies of scale. When an increase in the size of a firm results in a fall in the average cost of doing business. This hands an advantage to large firms over small ones.

Search costs. Comparing the prices and specification of goods takes effort, which has an opportunity cost (you could be doing something else more interesting or productive).

Consumer sovereignty. The idea that consumers are the most important element in the economy (more important than producers).

Focusing on the readiness of consumers to substitute goods for one another is useful up to a point but it tells us little about the intensity of consumer's preferences – how much they want something. An alternative is the *utility* approach, which tries to rate the satisfaction we get from consuming particular goods. If buying three Bob Dylan CDs makes you happier than five CDs of Mozart recitals then we can quantify how much more utility you get from the folk music than the classical. For retailers and their suppliers, this might be more useful in planning stock levels than the indifference curve approach. But it is also intrinsically more difficult, as numerical differentials are ultimately arbitrary since interpersonal comparisons of utility are impossible. Economists sometimes refer instead to consumers' *revealed* preferences. A customer's willingness to slap down her money says something concrete about what she wants, and analysts can read back from this to find out more about what her underlying preferences are.

The upshot of all this is that consumption is the justification for economic activity, and consumers as a source of demand are central to the mechanisms that make economic systems function.

Consumers: not so rational after all?

The problem with the idea of consumer sovereignty and its accompanying assumptions about rationality is that tastes and preferences change and can be shaped by external influences. Behavioural economists point out that consumers' decisions are affected by bounded rationality, willpower and self-interest. In other words, they sometimes make foolish decisions and waste their money.[15] For example, NCE assumes that customers will compare the prices of many retailers in their relentless pursuit of bargains. But how systematically do they really do this? If I am in a hurry, or too lazy to scour a number of stores for the best price, I may just go with what is acceptable within my budget (the role of the internet in aiding price searching is explored in section 7.4).

In particular, individuals are present-biased and naïve as they overestimate their future capability for self-control. Gyms exploit this in their pricing by setting low discounts at the beginning of membership terms, which then increase even as the motivation to actually exercise falls off. And customers often make it worse for themselves through over-optimism by self-sorting into the more expensive gym pricing programmes (such as monthly payments rather than per visit) as they laughably believe this will "force" them to go more often.[16]

NCE also overlooks the role of fashion, peer pressure and persuasion in shaping our underlying tastes and preferences. This omission is short-sighted, as the advertising and marketing industries have become adept at working with our hidden biases to get us to buy more stuff. Their success has proved over and over again that consumers, far from being rational, do not necessarily know what they want but are always open to suggestion.

Among the numerous telling examples outlined by Vance Packard in his classic and eye-opening examination of advertising, *The Hidden Persuaders*, are the soap sellers who realized that women would pay ten times as much for face cream as for a bar of soap, even though they did essentially the same thing.[17] Soap, the advertising companies implied, merely made women clean, but face cream made them beautiful. Men, likewise, were targeted for their partiality to status symbols such as expensive cars, possession of which indicated that they were "going places", metaphorically as well as literally. Over time the "Mad-Men" of Madison Avenue also got people to overcome their pettifogging inclination to wait until products actually wore out before replacing them by instilling feelings of "psychological obsolescence" that persuaded people to upgrade on a more regular basis, increasing sales for their clients.

The effect of issues of status on the price of consumer products may be so powerful that some goods become more desirable the more expensive they are, in apparent contradiction of the laws of demand, as the high price becomes a mark of quality conferring social status on those able to afford them. These are known as "superior" or "Veblen" goods, after Thorstein Veblen, whose phrase "conspicuous consumption" described a leisured class that advertised its exclusivity through ostentatious displays of wealth. Veblen goods include items such as ultra-expensive Swiss watches that, while undeniably beautiful and supremely well engineered, still perform much the same function as the cheap, plastic watches you can pick up in your local market for a fraction of the price. This implies that consumption is a social activity, rather than a purely individual pursuit, as NCE contends. What matters for an individual's utility may not therefore be her absolute level of income and ability to acquire possessions but the level relative to other people.[18]

Does all this spending and consumption, then, actually make us happy? NCE does not really ask this question. It assumes that, so long as standard assumptions about consumer sovereignty are met, consumption must be welfare-maximizing and therefore a good thing – otherwise we would not do it. The choices individuals make about how much they need to work in order to achieve the income needed to support their desired spending level are assumed to be a simple matter of personal preferences, without enquiring into how these preferences are formed in the first place.

Much, therefore, rests on a belief in worker and consumer sovereignty – the core NCE assumption about the autonomy of individual self-maximizers. Some economists dispute this assumption. Workers in countries such as the United States have generally not been given the choice to work shorter hours for less consumption, if that is what they desire. Productivity gains have generally been taken as higher income instead, with workers adjusting their preferences accordingly as they become accustomed to the higher incomes. In place of the NCE world in which workers get what they want, which could be more leisure and less material consumption, is what economist Juliet Schor dubs the "the work and spend world", where they learn to want what they get.[19]

If this is the case, then more income and consumption will not necessarily improve welfare or happiness. "Keeping up with the Joneses", in other words, may be a recipe for unhappiness and waste. The United Nations' survey of happiness, in fact, shows that the happiest countries are rich but egalitarian, with Nordic countries taking the top three spots in 2016. The United States languished in 19th place and the Chinese were no more content than they were 25 years ago, despite enormous economic advances since then.[20]

In so far as mainstream economics tends to dismiss interpersonal comparisons of utility, it has difficulty discussing these issues of general well-being. Amartya Sen has suggested a different approach, based on people's capabilities and the extent to which institutions and policies provide them with opportunities for good, sustainable and equitable living.[21] This shifts the focus from subjective appreciations of personal utility onto objective measures of well-being and is, accordingly, popular with economists concerned with poverty and development.

There may be further, wider consequences of our love of shopping. Shops operate as part of a nexus of businesses, such as wholesalers and advertising companies. Finally, we should not ignore the manufacturers themselves, as well as logistics companies, which organize the bringing of goods to market via well-coordinated supply chains. The next section looks at how this system works.

7.2 From factory to high street: how tastes and demands are met by the global retail distribution chain

Back in the day, before global transport networks and the internet, almost all the goods in a typical home would have been produced and sold locally by farmers and craftsmen who lived and worked in the vicinity. This necessarily limited the range of merchandise on offer to what was locally available. Things changed rapidly after the Industrial Revolution, as better trading links were forged with Asia and the New World. Suddenly resources and final products could be sourced from much further away, allowing the economic specialization that made it feasible for people and nations to focus on what they were good at. Society also changed. People got richer thanks to higher growth rates from industrialization and the boom in trade, and they developed more of a taste for the exotic and

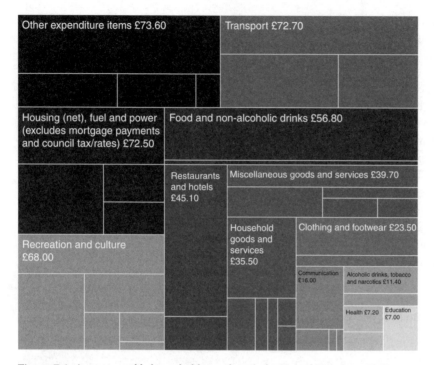

Figure 7.1 Average weekly household spending in the United Kingdom, 2016
Source: UK Office for National Statistics.

the unusual. The "consumer society" was born (see Figure 7.1 for details of how consumers spend their money).

Now we live in an age in which almost everything we could want is available to us – for the right price and, increasingly, at the click of a button. Practically every product that reaches a customer nowadays represents the cumulative effort of multiple organizations. The way these interact in bringing products to market is referred to collectively as the "supply chain". A supply chain is simply the overall process of manufacturing and distributing a product. It involves multiple and distinctive stages: from product development, to the sourcing of raw materials, production and final assembly of the good, followed by shipment to the place of sale. Complex logistics operations, relying on sophisticated information systems, coordinate all these processes. Supply chains also encompass services such as marketing and advertising and, in an age of environmental awareness, can manage how our possessions are disposed of when we have finished with them.

The length and complexity of a supply chain is determined by the scarcity and value of the good and the number of stages involved in getting it to market.[22] When products can be easily sourced locally, or perhaps are too bulky and low in value to transport long distances, it probably still makes sense to continue to supply them locally. A pint of milk, for example, is most unlikely to have been shipped across borders and will probably instead have come from a farm not a million miles away from your breakfast table. Other products are simply specific to their locality. Scotch whisky is distilled only in Scotland, otherwise it is not Scotch.

But for a staggering variety of other products the reality is that they are often produced through mind-bogglingly complex supply chains. Even simple goods that it would seem feasible to manufacture locally are most probably part of a supply chain if local provenance is not an issue. When you go to a clothes store to buy a woolly jumper, the wool for the jumper may well have come from a sheep in New Zealand (even if you live in a country with a lot of sheep farms), before being shipped to somewhere such as Bangladesh to be dyed and knitted into a jumper. Only then will it have started its final journey to your local store for purchase by you, passing through multiple distribution centres along the way. By the time you get to wear it your jumper may be better travelled than you are.

Box 7.2 How do supply chains work?

Say a Best Buy store in Minnesota has a run on DVD players before Christmas. It notifies its suppliers, such as Toshiba in Japan – which orders its factories in China to crank up production. Toshiba's Chinese contract factories place an order for chips from Zoran Corporation, which tells its own subcontractors, including TSMC, to get busy making more chips. TSMC, which is based in Taiwan, buys many of its components from California-based Applied Materials, which immediately gets on the case of its speciality machine tool services to build these. Right at the end of the chain, machine tool firm D&H Manufacturing, which mills aluminium blocks for Applied, immediately boosts production, and within weeks Best Buy is able to fill its shelves with new DVD players.[23]

Why is production organized this way? Two of the classical economists we encountered in Chapter 1 provide the answer. In *The Wealth of Nations* Adam Smith demonstrated the gains from specialization to be had through the division of labour. David Ricardo took this idea further by showing that countries could prosper through exploiting what was called their "comparative advantage".[24] Instead of striving for self-sufficiency by trying to do everything, countries should specialize in what they were relatively good at – i.e. compared to their trading partners. They could then trade with each other to acquire the goods they needed but did not produce at home because their comparative advantage was in something else. The division of labour and comparative advantage encouraged nations to trade and provided consumers with a wider variety of goods, of higher quality and at lower prices, than could be produced at home – however enticing this sounds to populist politicians.

Global trade has increased steadily, albeit with a few blips, since Smith and Ricardo's day but a couple of technological innovations have seen it accelerate over the last few decades. First, international transportation costs have plummeted. The big innovation here was "containerization", which replaced loose, bulk cargo with standardized metal containers.[25] Containerization slashed the unit cost of shipping goods long distances, making it suddenly feasible to move lower-value, higher-volume goods right across the globe. The impact of containerization was staggering. In 1965, as it was being invented, dock labour could move only 1.7 tonnes per hour onto a cargo ship; five years later 30 tonnes could be loaded in an hour. As a consequence, ships could get bigger and more efficient while still spending less time in port and cutting down on theft.

Second, huge improvements in information and communication technology (ICT) made it possible to run vast production systems across a number of countries. Supply chains involving multiple firms in different countries could henceforth be coordinated from a company's HQ far removed from the production line. Corporate HQs can remotely order supplies, coordinate production, monitor quality and ensure delivery adheres to strict timetables. In the 1980s the Japanese invented "just-in-time" (JIT) production to ship components in precise quantities as and when they are needed, cutting down on inventory costs but requiring superb logistics management. JIT techniques are now used widely and mean that huge amounts of components are now shipped around for final assembly. In Europe, total inland freight transport was estimated to be over 2,200 billion tonne-kilometres in 2013.[26]

Stages of production

Refining JIT techniques and cheap transport has enabled what is called the "decomposition" of production into many different stages. These segments of the whole can be located almost anywhere. For example, there is no longer any need to build cars near to their market; it is now so cheap to transport them that they can be assembled almost anywhere from components sourced from right across the globe (at least in principle: tariffs are often imposed on imports of high-value manufactured goods such as cars). This has had dramatic implications for the way manufacturing is done, as it allows most manufacturing firms to specialize in particular products or services. Whereas once they might have produced the

Figure 7.2 Components of the supply chain

whole good, manufacturing firms can now act as subcontractors for its final assembly by farming out all or part of the manufacturing process to other firms.

Take semiconductors, the processors that drive a PC. Firms once had to both design and manufacture them. Now only a few, such as Intel, still do this, and the rest focus either on designing or making them. In most supply chains, therefore, a "lead" firm like Intel – typically, the manufacturer whose brand name is stamped on the product – takes overall responsibility for producing it and managing the supply chain. This entails coordinating the activities of all the different suppliers and ensuring the right parts get to the right place ready for final assembly and shipment to customers.

Global supply chains put a lot of pressure on countries looking to attract investment from manufacturing firms. They have to ensure they are in a competitive "sweet spot", which means having a workforce with the right skills, and the right infrastructure to support this (see Figure 7.2). For example, Taiwan in the 1990s decided to pursue the "pure play" of situating itself as a chip maker. The Taiwanese government invested heavily to create exactly the right environment for chip makers, who flocked to the country for its cheap but skilled labour. Effectively, therefore, countries and most firms no longer trade in raw materials or finished products but, rather, specific parts of the production process in which they specialize. As supply chains have grown in importance and become more global in scope, more and more intermediate goods are being traded across borders and more imported parts and components are embodied in exports.

Two consequences stem from this that are immediately important to consumers. First, organizing production this way dramatically increases the choices available to us. I can pick from an almost bewildering variety of DVD and Blu-ray players with a huge range of features and at a price to suit my budget. Without trade and the supply chains built on this, my country might support only one or two DVD manufacturers. These would enjoy a near-monopoly and could set high prices for a probably inferior product. They would also probably innovate less, as they would have a captive market so, actually, I would probably still be watching movies on VHS cassettes. Supply chains therefore mean more competition and choice in the products we buy.

Second, supply chains drive down production costs and make goods cheaper. The decomposition of production allows work on each stage to be allocated to factories depending on how cost-effective and reliable they are, and they are forced to compete for the business. "Big box" retailers at the consumer end of supply chains, such as Wal-Mart, are able to offer their customers desirable goods at affordable prices.[27] But is all this emphasis on consumer choice in the rich world not being bought at the expense of poorer countries and the environment? Should we wonder a little more about how we get such cheap prices for our clothes and electronics?

Supply chains and consumer power

Global supply chains have numerous critics. The decomposition of production encourages manufacturers to devolve the lowest-value segments of supply chains to poor developing countries whose main comparative advantage is the very low wages their workers earn. This can lead to various forms of exploitation in poor countries, including long working hours and the use of child labour. Furthermore, the low cost base that make these subcontractors so attractive may come at the expense of workers' safety. Close monitoring of subcontractors throughout the supply chain can prevent this, but is not always done. For example, in 2013 a roof collapsed over the Savar garment factory in Bangladesh, leaving over 1,100 people dead and more than 2,500 injured.[28] The disaster prompted hard questions about whether Western chains were doing enough to check safety standards among their suppliers. Some analysts argue that indirect sourcing through cheap subcontractors is increasingly the norm in ultra-competitive industries such as clothing, in which standards are intrinsically difficult to monitor and police.[29]

Long, global supply chains – particularly those reliant on low-cost production at the bottom end – have also been criticized for encouraging businesses in rich countries to "offshore" as much of their production as possible, costing jobs and putting downward pressure on wages and costs in those that remain. Moreover, while this may be a strategy of low-cost retailers, it is not the only strategy available. Danish clothing companies have used the efficiencies enabled by supply chains to become ultra-competitive, rather than outsourcing to cheap countries. Retailers became powerful players in the Danish fashion industry and became involved in clothing design as they had good, up-to-date knowledge of fashion trends. They integrated backwards into design and distribution and set the pace for manufacturers to follow.[30]

A key factor driving complexity in supply chains is therefore the need to be able to respond to quickly changing consumer tastes. Firms supplying consumers have to keep abreast of shifting trends. But this is very difficult when managing long, complex supply chains in industries such as fashion in which tastes and demand can shift rapidly from season to season, or even month to month. Despite copious surveys and market research, the only solid indicator of demand is when customers slap down their money, by which time it is too late to alter much if forecasts prove to be wrong. Too much of the wrong items leads to discounting and lost profits; too little means unmet demand. New supply chain management techniques such as "quick response manufacturing and marketing" are being developed to slash lead times and ensure retailers can get by with lower stock levels and more frequent, small-batch ordering.[31]

Perhaps counter-intuitively, given their complexity, supply chains allow retailers to react very quickly to changes in consumer tastes. This hands more power to consumers, provided they are well informed and that the supply chain is as transparent as possible. For example, coffee fans have become very knowledgeable about the origin of the beans in their cups. Whether the beans originate in Ecuador or Ethiopia matters a lot to connoisseurs, and now they are in an increasingly better position to choose. Other consumers, besides coffee-sipping hipsters, are also educating themselves and becoming more concerned about the authenticity of products and how they are produced. The "Fairtrade" label has become a powerful indication of responsible sourcing.

Consumer pressure forcing retailers to be more transparent about their supply chains has also enabled them to pinpoint health and safety hazards before they cause harm. In 2013 the Irish Food Safety Authority tested frozen beefburgers bound for the supermarket and discovered that a third of them contained horse meat and 85 per cent contained pork, a result that horrified consumers. The episode could easily have spelled disaster for the Irish beef industry. After all, if no one could be sure what was in Irish burgers, the safest thing to do would be to eat burgers made somewhere else. The authorities were quickly able to isolate the source of the contamination, however, and removed it from the supply chain, preventing permanent harm being done.

Manufacturers have also been able to spot defective components and remove them. When Toyota was warned of defective accelerators on some of its cars in 2010 the Japanese firm was able to identify these problems and make changes without having to pull in every Toyota-built car for inspection – although, tragically, not in time to prevent several fatal crashes.

Manufacturers are also under pressure to make production processes more "sustainable" – which means not satisfying the wants of the present generation at the expense of future generations. This entails focusing on the energy and resource demands during manufacture, and disposal after use.[32] Supply chains have given rise to new "circular" business models in which the recycling of products or their components is as important as their initial fabrication.

This is increasingly the case with fast-developing products such as mobile phones, which, in rich countries at least, become obsolete after a year or two as new models come onto the market. Buyers trading up to the latest device can easily sell their old phones, whose parts are recycled through distribution networks catering to developing world consumers who want a cheap phone and do not mind being a generation or two behind.

7.3 Consumer confidence and the wider economy

Can you cause a recession just by not going shopping? It sounds like a rather self-serving excuse to break out the credit cards and spend, spend, spend. But retailing is now such a massive part of the modern economy that fluctuations in consumer behaviour can have a big impact on jobs, tax revenues and growth. In extreme cases, and usually in concert with other economic "shocks" such as the 2008 banking crisis, sharp falls in consumer confidence producing a crash in retail spending can lead directly to an economic downturn. The importance of retailing to the economy is obvious really when you look at the sheer number of people employed in it and its close linkages with related economic functions, such as wholesaling, transport, advertising, marketing and financial services. UK shops and wholesalers generated about £150 billion of economic output in 2014 and employed 4.4 million people, about 16 per cent of the total workforce.[33] In the United States, 29 million people worked in retail in 2013, plus another 13 million in related sectors – about one in five of all jobs.[34]

Clearly, then, the health of a nation's shops is crucial for its economy. Retail spending is a key component of the income flows that generate momentum for economies and contribute directly and in a big way to their growth. As well as paying for the cost of the goods themselves, the purchase price of goods and services from shops goes towards the wages of retail workers. These workers also pay taxes on their earnings, and we pay value-added or sales tax on the goods we buy. Profits made by retailers and other businesses connected with shopping are also taxed, generating revenues for the government to spend on public services. Major fluctuations in these income flows can therefore have an enormous impact on the wider economy, contributing to economic booms as well as recessions. How is this modelled in economics?

Macroeconomists have available three different measures of the economy to estimate its gross domestic product, which is the sum of all the goods and services bought and sold in the economy. These are the production, income and expenditure measures. They all focus on different aspects of the economy relying on different sources, and are reconciled together by government statisticians to produce a final "headline" GDP figure. As this chapter is about consumption, the expenditure measure is probably of most interest, so let us look at what this comprises.

The expenditure measure of GDP is expressed like this:

$$GDP = C + I + G + NX$$

The different factors measured are:

C = consumer spending/consumption
I = investment (in machinery, buildings, etc., and also residential investment by people buying property, though not financial assets)
G = total government spending
NX = net exports (export revenue minus import expenditure)

Consumption (C) goes first, as it makes up by far the largest proportion of the GDP equation (it was 68 per cent of US GDP in 2014).[35] Just to complicate things, however, consumption varies over time and according to circumstances. The crucial variable here is consumers' "disposable income", which is the proportion of their income remaining after taxes have been paid. From this is derived what economists call the "consumption function", which tries to capture the extent to which consumption will tend to rise in line with increases in disposable income. The consumption function depends on consumers' "propensity" (or inclination) to consume an extra unit of income. This simply reflects that all of an individual's disposable income is not necessarily spent but may be saved instead, which is effectively consumption deferred.

If we feel confident about the future we may be happier to save less and consume more (our propensity to consume rises). This will be good for jobs and growth, although it could lead to inflation if there is too much money chasing too few goods. Central banks may react to inflation by raising interest rates to choke off economic growth (by raising the cost of borrowing and boosting the returns to saving), squeezing consumption and possibly leading to recession. When inflationary pressures ease, the central bank can relax interest rates and consumption will, hopefully, pick up again, although there may be a time lag.

Of course, if consumers are not feeling confident, maybe because they are worried about losing their job, they may postpone their spending and save the money instead. This shows just how closely consumer spending is tied up with psychology: if we are feeling confident about the future, we will spend; if we are fearful and expect the worst, we will want to save more in preparation. All this introduces an extra element of volatility into the consumption model of the economy. When Keynes wrote about the "animal spirits" of investors increasing volatility in the economy he could just as easily have been talking about consumers.

If consumers cut spending it will have a knock-on effect on the rest of the economy as wages are cut and jobs are lost in retailing and logistics. Tax revenues from these activities will also fall and planned investments are postponed or abandoned. Because so many jobs are connected to retailing, falls in consumer spending can ripple through the economy because of what are known as "negative multiplier effects". This is because other businesses will also have to adjust investment to take account of lower activity, and so it goes on. Big falls in consumer confidence can therefore trigger a recession if consumers react by cutting their spending. Even when a loss of consumer confidence is not the main trigger of an economic downturn (as in the recent financial crisis, which originated in the US sub-prime mortgage boom: see Chapter 6), it can still amplify the other causes through its disproportionate impact on economy activity.

But too much spending in a boom can be as bad as too little in a recession if it rises more rapidly than incomes, as this means the extra spending is being financed by taking on more debt. A lot of Western countries saw household debt climb sharply during the 2000s in the period leading up to the financial crisis. In the United Kingdom it doubled to £1,600 billion between 2000 and 2008. The stock of debt tends to increase when economies are expanding, as borrowers assume their incomes will keep on rising and may borrow more. But how much debt is too much? It is difficult to say.

Economists point out that debt can be beneficial to individuals and the economy. It allows people to purchase large goods, such as cars or washing machines, which they may not be able to afford upfront. In other words, debt is a useful device to aid what is known as "consumption smoothing". Economists refer to the "permanent income" or "life cycle" model, which looks at consumption over an individual's expected lifetime income rather than at a particular point in time. It implies that it is sensible for young people to borrow money in the expectation that higher earnings in the future will enable them to pay the money back later on. On an economy-wide basis, consumption smoothing also helps economies to ride out recessions, as it means people can continue to spend even when incomes may be constrained.

The key factor here is therefore probably the *affordability* of household debt. This will be determined by a range of things: the size of the original loan, the interest rate on the loan and the length of time available to pay it off. Economists look at debt servicing costs alongside the overall level of debt, in terms of their proportion of an individual's income. If debts are rising by 2 per cent a year but incomes are increasing at the same rate then affordability is unchanged. The problem comes, of course, if personal circumstances change, such as someone losing his job, which make it impossible for an individual to keep up payments on his debts, and so he may default.

All in all, it is no wonder that consumer spending is one of the most closely monitored areas of the economy. Keeping watch on all of this, which is the job of financial regulators, is incredibly complex, and mistakes can be costly. Central banks were accused of taking their eyes off the explosive growth of personal debt in the run-up to the financial crisis. But the volatility of consumer spending is not the only potential danger. Policy-makers are also worrying about the effect of changes in retailing itself on jobs and the character of our towns and cities.

7.4 Developments in retailing: "big box" stores and the growth of e-retailing

So far we have considered the tastes and behaviour of individuals and how these are satisfied. But bringing goods to market is a complex operation that also requires retailers, who act in many ways as "middlemen" between producers of goods and their ultimate users. In modern economics the retailer is viewed as a "producer" of retail services, which are supplied to customers who "consume" the service.[36] The retailer takes a cut, or margin, from this activity. Retailers compete externally by offering a range of services tailored to the needs of consumers, and innovate internally by trying to operate more efficiently. Assuming prices are set competitively by market forces may therefore overlook the role of shops as important actors in their own right. John Stuart Mill was one of the first to observe that retailers often largely disregard the need to compete and instead set prices among themselves.[37]

Retailing is a highly competitive business subject to constant change. As time goes by, established retailers with particular ways of doing business find themselves unable to compete with newcomers and they may go out of business or be forced to adapt. An example of this is the rise of e-commerce giants such as Amazon and the inability of many high street stores to compete. Indeed, a lot of the changes that have occurred in retailing have been to do with getting customers to do things that retailers previously did themselves so they can focus on logistics.

Of course, on the surface, the basic experience of purchasing goods as an economic exchange between buyer and seller is roughly the same as it always was: you hand over your money and you get the product in return. But the manner in which this occurs is changing rapidly. It is being transformed by culture, technology and, of course, the changing economics of competition.

Economists argue that retailing develops according to whether the innovation in question creates economic competitive advantage in given market conditions – i.e. driven by efficiency but also heavily subject to changing customer culture, and demand. The two key developments we consider here are the growth of out-of-town, "big box", stores at the expense of the traditional high street, and the impact of the internet. Underlying both developments is probably the fact that, despite the existence of a few unfeasibly expensive Veblen goods, retailing is ultimately driven by consumers' desire for low prices, and both these trends are facilitated by our search for value.

The death of the high street?

In many town and cities the high street is being transformed as shops increasingly gravitate towards cheaper sites on the edge of town. Traditional high streets composed of small, specialist retailers still survive in many places, of course, but physical shopping is increasingly being done either online or in big box outlets. The big stores increasingly crowd out their smaller town centre rivals, which are less profitable. The result has been a sort of "division of labour" between larger stores, offering a bit of everything at low prices, and small shops, which increasingly focus on niche sections of the market for customers prepared to pay just a little more for a particular item.

Why have so-called "big box" stores been so successful? The main reason is that they enable retailers to maximize economies of scale. These occur when an increase in the size of the enterprise leads to it becoming more efficient, producing a fall in the average of cost of doing of business. For example, if my high street shoe store has overheads of £10,000 a year and sells 1,000 pairs of shoes, that is £10 coming out of my profit for each pair sold. If your "Shoes R Us" superstore faces overheads of £50,000 a year but shifts 100,000 pairs that falls to 50 pence a pair. When feasible, economies of scale therefore encourage businesses to get bigger. At a certain point they simply outgrow the high street and find it logical to move out.

While the big box store loses out from the decline in footfall of being on the high street, where people come to shop, they probably gain more from lower business costs and less congestion. In fact, the new location may actually be better, as it may be near a motorway and have extra room for parking.

Big box retailers are able to drive down prices in lots of other ways. First, they can develop expertise in logistics, enabling them to eliminate the need for wholesalers. This means they can source their products direct from suppliers, and in bulk, putting them in a good position to drive a hard bargain. Second, they develop the technical expertise to buy and sell difficult-to-handle products, such as frozen foods. Third, they can use their economic power to strike good deals with local authorities, exploit new technologies and keep wages low.

Big, out-of-town stores have actually been around for a century or more. In the 1920s retailing in the United States began to be dominated by "department stores" in the big towns and cities – that is, a series of stores under one roof offering wide choice in one place – such as Macy's in New York and Marshall Fields in Chicago. Outside the big cities, mail order firms such as Sears Roebuck catered for customers in the rural hinterland who wanted a choice of goods but without travelling far. These retailers relied on huge distribution complexes and vertical integration (supplying, selling and distribution within one firm) to sell goods more cheaply than smaller shops with higher overheads. Urbanization and cheap personal transportation eventually doomed the mail order companies and so Sears moved into suburban high streets but maintained its supply network so as to maintain its ability to keep prices low.

So what went wrong? One suggestion is that Sears miscalculated by focusing on the "middle class", which split between prosperous professionals, who abandoned it by moving upmarket and were therefore not primarily motivated by low costs, and a poorer, more insecure tranche, chasing ever lower prices.[38] This left an opening for giant companies such as Wal-Mart, which doubled down on the efficiency savings made available by focusing on supply chains rather than the "customer experience", and has come to dominate the lower end of the market.

Wal-Mart is probably the archetypal big box store. There are other examples of the breed, such as Home Depot and Best Buy, but none of these offer the range of merchandise and so are not in as good a position to enjoy the additional economies that come with huge size. Indeed, the business strategy of its founders, the Walton family, arguably revolves around the application of economic and supply chain management concepts to aspects of its business in a relentless drive to bring down costs and prices.

One of Wal-Mart's key advantages is that its size enables it to cut out a number of costly middlemen in the distribution chain. Those it cannot avoid dealing with are loaded with as much of the costs and risks as possible. If they want the business, they have to comply. As a massive retailer selling just about everything it can deal directly with suppliers, rather than going through wholesale distributors. By sourcing products in bulk it is in a good position to drive down prices, and the toughness of Wal-Mart's product buyers is legendary. Doing without wholesalers also means dispensing with large, costly storage warehouses, as stock can be moved through Wal-Mart's own distribution centers with minimal fuss.[39]

But the technology of retailing has also changed enormously, which has contributed to big changes in how shopping is done and, again, benefits the big stores more than the small ones. The key development over the last century was the move from shops where customers were served by staff to a self-service environment where the customers help themselves to what they want and bring it to the checkout to make their purchase. Self-service transfers staffing costs onto the customer but it required a number of technological innovations to make it possible – not just the standardized packaging of goods but also different shelving systems and new types of tills. From the 1990s onwards information technology became the key driver of innovation. So, for example, manually operated tills became electric tills, which – when plugged into the store's computer mainframe – became, effectively, networked computers. Soon afterwards scannable electronic barcodes on the goods allowed tills to be linked with the inventory systems run from head office and integrated into supply systems.[40]

IT in retailing has been like a performance-enhancing drug for an industry otherwise known for low productivity and wafer-thin margins. Studies have found that productivity levels and growth rates of retailers have been driven heavily by their investment in IT.[41] The most recent step has been for retailers to divert the focus away from themselves and their inventory chains to learning more about the tastes and habits of their customers – consumer sovereignty in action, perhaps. Tesco, a UK grocery store, pioneered the use of loyalty cards, which are scanned at the till with every purchase. In return for customer discounts and promotions these enabled Tesco to gather detailed, real-time information about purchases. Tesco's heavy investment in IT to crunch the mountains of data was a valuable tool in helping it to respond to changes in customer demand.

Other retailers were quick to see the potential in the digitization of shopping, and continual advances in IT have enabled them to integrate all parts of the supply chain, even linking up with outside firms. For example, major suppliers to big box retailers, such as Procter & Gamble (P&G), are wired up to the stores so they can respond instantly to demands for restocking. So, when a tube of toothpaste is sold in a Wal-Mart store, P&G knows about it instantly and can decide whether it needs to ramp up production and increase deliveries without waiting for an order from the retailer.

Wal-Mart's structural economic power is certainly enormous, making it legitimate to ask how readily national or local governments would defy it. According to CNBC, if Wal-Mart was a US government department it would be ranked fifth by spending, behind only health, social security, treasury and defence. And, if its 2.2 million "associates" were an army, Wal-Mart would rank behind only the army of the People's Republic of China and well ahead of the US army.[42] Campaigners therefore worry that its size hands it too much power. The company has been accused of brutalizing employees, who are prevented from joining trade unions. Very low wages, in many cases only just above the legal floor, and minimal benefits such as healthcare appear to be a central part of its strategy to keep costs and therefore prices low.

All this has sparked debates about how to calculate the welfare gains from Wal-Mart's strategy. Is it ultimately justifiable, in other words? Left-wing critics argue that low wages impoverish entire communities, as the arrival of a

Wal-Mart store generally spells doom for smaller retailers, who are unable to compete.[43] Others, on the free market Right, take the view that the relentless pursuit of productivity gains by companies such as Wal-Mart raises the real purchasing power of people on low incomes, who are Wal-Mart's main customers.[44]

Internet shopping

The biggest technological change of all affecting shopping over the last few decades has undoubtedly been the rise of the internet and emergence of "e-commerce". The growth of selling over the internet has excited economists because, by increasing product information and allowing easy price comparison, it is assumed to provide many of the features necessary for "perfect competition". Is this the case?

On the demand side, internet shopping offers some crucial advantages to consumers, which help to explain its growth. Internet search tools make researching products much easier, as their features can be examined and prices compared entirely online. In economic parlance, the internet lowers search and transaction costs and increases information. These problems can be significant in normal modes of shopping, especially if you live on the edge of town or beyond with little choice of retailers. One stubborn source of friction in online shopping, though, is the delay between purchasing an item and it being delivered. In a conventional store, it is yours to take away as soon as you hand over your money, but online there is a delay while you wait for it to arrive, and you may need to be at home to sign for it. E-retailers are addressing this by investing heavily in their stock-picking and delivery capabilities, with Amazon, for example, offering next-day or even hourly delivery and investing in drones to make deliveries.

On the supply side (the retailers themselves), e-retailing can mean doing away entirely with "bricks and mortar" stores, which are costly to run as they have to be located near centres of population, where rents and taxes are high. E-retailers have only to invest in their distribution networks. Only the largest of these, such as Amazon, feel the need to own physical distribution centres, and these can be located in cheap locations outside town. Many smaller e-retailers dispense with warehouses entirely and act simply as middlemen between manufacturers and consumers. Despite the low wages paid to staff, productivity tends to be much higher in e-retailing than regular retailing, because they are in a much better position to exploit technology.

Of course, e-commerce firms do not have it all their own way, and there are some problems with buying online that are hard to surmount. One is the information asymmetry related to buying something you cannot see, smell or touch. How can quality be gauged by the customer at a distance? This may be one reason why buying fresh food, or clothes, over the internet has caught on a lot less than books and CDs.[45]

E-retailers have investigated two solutions to this. One is to make product returns as easy as possible, offering free and no-questions-asked exchanges if the customer is unhappy. Another is to address the information problem directly by providing as much quality-relevant detail as possible before the customer makes the purchase. For a car, this can include data on mileage, service history and all the relevant features of the vehicle. An alternative way of doing this is to focus on establishing a prior reputation for quality so people will intrinsically trust the e-retailer. Sellers on eBay, the online auction site, are rated by previous customers for their veracity and the information displayed prominently alongside the price. This incentivizes sellers to treat their customers well and overcomes the information asymmetry, as dishonesty will be instantly punished with a bad rating.[46]

Does the internet spell the end for "bricks and mortar" stores? The rapid growth of e-retailing has certainly been disruptive. Amazon began as an online bookseller and transformed the market. Barnes & Noble, its main rival, has seen its market share fall dramatically. Borders, the other big US bookseller, went out of business. But there is hope yet for physical stores. E-commerce gets a lot of attention in the business press but it is still a relatively small part of retailing. Between 2000 and 2014 its share of all US retail sales grew 11-fold. But this was from a relatively low base, and online shopping still only accounted for 6.4 per cent of the market by then, although this is projected to rise to 20 per cent by 2024 in non-food categories.[47] Internet customers tend to be younger, more affluent and better educated than the norm – just the sort of shopper demographic that retailers fight over.

What seems to be happening is that retailing is being pulled in two directions: towards e-retailers, on the one hand, and the out-of-town big box retailers and "warehouse clubs", on the other – such as Costco, which saw a bigger rise in sales between 2000 and 2013 than the dominant e-commerce retailer, Amazon. Increasingly, both sets of retailers are looking to have a foot in both camps. Costco and Wal-Mart now have large online operations, and Amazon is opening physical stores where customers, rather than taking their purchases to the till, can simply walk out through the door and have their online account billed automatically.

The big loser has been the high street. Stores here face higher overheads, as they lack the economies of scale of the big box and online retailers and are unable to provide the range of goods likely to tempt customers. Towns are suffering because money and trade is therefore taken out of town centres. The United

Kingdom lost some 15,000 town centre stores between 2000 and 2009, and nearly one in six stores stands vacant.[48]

A report for a worried government suggested ways for small shops to fight back. One strategy is to make physical stores as enticing and distinctive as possible.[49] Shopping is, after all, an enjoyable leisure activity. A good defence against "showrooming" – when people browse goods in the store but buy them online – is to stock exotic, own-label items not available elsewhere. The high street's fightback may ultimately take the form not of competing with the big players but of offering something completely different: more relaxed and convivial, and not just concerned with ever lower prices.

Conclusion: what we have learnt

- Economics suggests that "consumer sovereignty", whereby customers' tastes and preferences are catered for by retailers, will produce an efficient outcome that allows the market to respond quickly to changing tastes.
- Globalization and the growth of global supply chains have meant an explosion in the variety of goods available and brought down prices. Some claim the costs of this fall on workers in the developing world, who toil for low wages in dangerous factories to meet the demand for cheap goods.
- Shopping is a massively important activity that supports numerous functions elsewhere in the economy. "Consumer confidence" is critical, therefore, in keeping the macroeconomy ticking over.
- The traditional high street is under threat from the internet and out-of-town stores, which offer lower prices and greater convenience. Internet shopping, in particular, is offering something increasingly close to economists' dream of a "perfect" market.

Notes

1. World Bank statistics.
2. US Department of Commerce, Bureau of Economic Analysis.
3. T. Veblen, *The Theory of the Leisure Class* (New York: Modern Library, 1934).
4. J. K. Galbraith, *The Affluent Society* (New York: Houghton Mifflin Harcourt, 1958).
5. R. Frank, *Richistan: A Journey through the American Wealth Boom and the Lives of the New Rich* (New York: Crown, 2008).
6. F. Trentmann, *Empire of Things: How We Became a World of Consumers, from the Fifteenth Century to the Twenty-First* (London: Penguin Books, 2016).
7. J. Bulow, "An economic theory of planned obsolescence", *Quarterly Journal of Economics* 101:4 (1986), 729–49.

8. US Environmental Protection Agency.
9. See www.lovefoodhatewaste.com (accessed 1 May 2017).
10. J. Waldfogel, "The deadweight loss of Christmas", *American Economic Review* 83:5 (1993), 1328–36.
11. J. Speth, *The Bridge at the End of the World: Capitalism, the Environment and Crossing from Crisis to Sustainability* (New Haven, CT: Yale University Press, 2008).
12. N. Stern, *The Economics of Climate Change: The Stern Review* (Cambridge: Cambridge University Press, 2007).
13. A. Smith, *The Wealth of Nations* [1776] (New York: Modern Library, 1937), 625.
14. For a clear and only mildly technical treatment of this topic, see the relevant chapters of R. Pindyck & D. Rubinfeld, *Microeconomics*, 8th edn (London: Pearson, 2012).
15. S. Mullainathan & R. Thaler, "Behavioral economics", Working Paper no. 7948 (Cambridge, MA: NBER, 2000).
16. S. Vignier & U. Malmendier, "Paying not to go to the gym", *American Economic Review* 96:3 (2006), 694–719.
17. V. Packard, *The Hidden Persuaders* (New York: David McKay, 1957).
18. J. Duesenberry, *Income, Saving and the Theory of Consumer Behavior* (Cambridge, MA: Harvard University Press, 1949).
19. J. Schor, *The Overworked American: The Unexpected Decline of Leisure* (New York: Basic Books, 1992).
20. J. Helliwell, R. Layard & J. Sachs (eds), *World Happiness Report 2017* (New York: Sustainable Development Solutions Network, 2017).
21. A. Sen, *The Idea of Justice* (London: Allen Lane, 2009).
22. T. Sturgeon, "Global value chains and economic globalization: towards a new measurement framework", report prepared for Eurostat (Cambridge, MA: Industrial Performance Center, Massachusetts Institute of Technology, 2013).
23. This example is described in *The Wall Street Journal*: "Clarity is missing link in supply chain", 18 May 2009.
24. D. Ricardo, *On the Principles of Political Economy and Taxation* [1817] (Timeless Books, 2014).
25. M. Levinson, *The Box: How the Shipping Container Made the World Smaller and the World Economy Bigger* (Princeton, NJ: Princeton University Press, 2008).
26. Eurostat, "Freight transport statistics" database.
27. R. Vedder & W. Cox, *The Wal-Mart Revolution: How Big-Box Stores Benefit Consumers, Workers, and the Economy* (Washington, DC: AEI Press, 2006).
28. A. Westervelt, "Two years after Rana Plaza, have conditions improved in Bangladesh's factories?", *The Guardian*, 24 April 2015.
29. S. Labowitz & D. Baumann-Pauly, *Business as Usual Is Not an Option: Supply Chains and Sourcing after Rana Plaza* (New York: NYU Stern Center for Business and Human Rights, New York University, 2014).
30. K. Jensen & R. Poulsen, "Changing value chain strategies of Danish clothing and fashion companies, 1970–2013", *Erhvervshistorisk Årbog* 62:2 (2013), 37–56.
31. B. Lowson, R. King & A. Hunter, *Quick Response: Managing the Supply Chain to Meet Consumer Demand* (Chichester, UK: Wiley, 1999).
32. J. Linton, R. Klassen & V. Jayaraman, "Sustainable supply chains: an introduction", *Journal of Operations Management* 25:6 (2007), 1075–82.
33. C. Rhodes, "The retail industry: statistics and policy", Briefing Paper no. 06186 (London: House of Commons, 2015).
34. PwC, "The economic impact of the US retail industry", report prepared for the National Retail Federation (New York: PwC, 2014).
35. For a full explanation of this model of the economy, see O. Blanchard, *Macroeconomics*, 7th edn (Boston: Pearson, 2017).

36. K. Tucker & B. Yamey, *Economics of Retailing* (London: Penguin Books, 1973).
37. J. S. Mill, *Principles of Political Economy with Some of Their Applications to Social Philosophy* [1848] (Indianapolis, IN: Hackett, 2004).
38. N. Lichtenstein, *The Retail Revolution: How Wal-Mart Created a Brave New World of Retail* (New York: Holt, 2009).
39. P. Bloom & V. Perry, "Retailer power and supplier welfare: the case of Wal-Mart", *Journal of Retailing* 77:3 (2001), 379–417.
40. R. Jessen & L. Langer, *Transformations of Retailing in Europe after 1945* (Aldershot, UK: Ashgate, 2012).
41. M. Doms, R. Jarmin & S. Klimek, "IT investment and firm performance in US retail trade", *Economics of Innovation and New Technology* 13:7 (2004), 595–613.
42. See www.cnbc.com/2016/02/18/putting-wal-marts-numbers-in-perspective.html (accessed 23 February 2017).
43. A. Bianco, *The Bully of Bentonville: How the High Cost of Everyday Low Prices Is Hurting America* (New York: Crown, 2009).
44. G. Reisman, *Capitalism: A Complete and Integrated Understanding of the Nature and Value of Human Economic Life* (Ottawa, IL: Jameson, 1996).
45. J. Bronnenberg & P. Ellickson, "Adolescence and the path to maturity in global retail", *Journal of Economic Perspectives* 29:4 (2015), 113–34.
46. E. Lieber & C. Syverson, "Online versus offline competition", in M. Peitz & J. Waldfogel (eds), *The Oxford Handbook of the Digital Economy*, 189–223 (Oxford: Oxford University Press, 2012).
47. A. Hortaçsu & C. Syverson, "The ongoing evolution of US retail: a format tug-of war", *Journal of Economic Perspectives* 29:4 (2015), 89–112.
48. Department for Business, Innovation and Skills, *Understanding High Street Performance* (London: Department for Business, Innovation and Skills, 2011).
49. M. Portas, *The Portas Review: An Independent Review of the Future of Our High Streets* (London: Department for Business, Innovation and Skills, 2011).

8

FROM CRADLE TO GRAVE: BENEFITS AND WELFARE

A hungry man is not a free man.
Adlai Stevenson

Key questions

- Why do we have collective insurance solutions to personal risks, rather than leaving people to make their own arrangements?
- Should welfare be delivered by the state, or privately?
- How can we ensure that the welfare bill does not grow inexorably and undermine self-sufficiency?
- How do we ensure "generational equity" when the old vote in greater numbers than the young?

Summary

Life springs surprises, and sometimes these are not pleasant or welcome. Unemployment and sickness can come out of the blue to upset our carefully laid plans. But even life events that are more predictable, such as getting old, can be difficult to prepare for on our own. This is why collective social protection, or welfare states, can sometimes come to the rescue by allowing us to pool our risks and resources to deal with unexpected events. Modern welfare states are designed to take care of us "from the cradle to the grave": from helping with childcare to maintaining an income for pensioners and the unemployed. One of the biggest drivers of increasing costs is medical progress in producing greater longevity. Having and raising children is a big expense for families, and a particular focus for policy-makers is how to help people deal with this in ways that will not disrupt their participation in the labour market, for example. The trouble is, if the state, or my private insurance scheme, will always take care of me, however I behave, why should I work hard, take care of my kids properly or look after my own health? Welfare states therefore face challenges in overcoming moral and other hazards to keep the lid on affordability. Although a well-designed and fully resourced welfare state, such as Denmark's, helps the economy stay competitive, some others, such as Greece's, are a huge drag on the economy. And, with so many vested interests bound up in welfare states, they can be very difficult to reform.

Key topics and theories covered

Social insurance and risk pooling; moral hazard and welfare state design; children and the welfare state; old age and pensions; poverty and inequality; welfare and the public finances; "worlds of welfare capitalism".

8.1 Welfare as a form of "social insurance", or risk pooling

Capitalism is inherently unequal, and so most rich countries have developed welfare states to shield their citizens from the social dislocation produced by market society. These have massively expanded in size since the Second World War, and spending on social programmes is now typically the largest item in the government's budget, dwarfing health and education. Their size and ubiquity mean that virtually all of us, even the most self-reliant, are likely to encounter the welfare state at various points in our lives. This is most likely to happen when we retire and draw a state pension, or require care to deal with declining health. But it may be at other times as well; help with starting a family, for example, or financial assistance in getting by after losing a job. In some countries, such as Sweden and Denmark, the welfare state plays a particularly active and central role in building and managing society and is seen as integral to national identity. In others, such as the United States, it is more contentious, even though millions rely on it for a lifeline. But what exactly is the welfare state for? Is it getting too expensive? Do welfare states even work?

One of the leading justifications for welfare states was set out in the 1970s by John Rawls, an American political philosopher who was concerned with reconciling fairness with individual freedom.[1] Rawls described a thought experiment in which no one knew at the outset how well set up they were to get on in life. Behind this initial "veil of ignorance", Rawls thought people would, together, rationally choose a society that protected its weakest to guard against the possibility that they might find themselves at the bottom of the pile. Social reformers build on this insight to advocate universal welfare provision that both tackles inequality and shields individuals from unexpected calamities. Latterly, the focus of thinking on welfare policy has shifted further, from "freedom from want" to "freedom to act", implying the need to look beyond basic survival to find ways to help people to flourish.[2]

Critics of "welfarism" on the political Right counter that welfare states are inefficient and expensive. They undermine self-reliance and create client groups that block any reform, no matter how sensible, that might threaten their entitlements. This objection has some force. The business of transferring money from rich to poor (or the lucky to the unlucky), which is, effectively, what welfare states do, has been compared to a "leaky bucket". The bucket moves money around society but some of it inevitably spills onto the ground, in the form of damage to incentives, bureaucratic inefficiencies, etc. The question is: how much spillage are we as a society prepared to put up with?[3]

Economics obviously cares about wastage but is not blind either to the need for market societies to consider the worst off in society. The concept of "Pareto optimality" encountered in Chapter 1 sets out clear grounds for judging the fairness of policy changes in market societies – principally, that no one should be made worse off. But Pareto-optimal outcomes can still be highly unequal, and in any case provide little in the way of policy advice to tell us what do to construct a fair society. Moreover, while the market can provide protection against many of life's contingencies, it is also replete with failures, particularly to do with information, and these failures provide an initial rationale for collective measures via a welfare state. The analysis of market failures pinpoints many of these gaps, and in the last few decades the sub-field of welfare economics has emerged to apply theories of information problems and behavioural economics to the issue of welfare states.

Welfare economics sidesteps many moral and political arguments by showing that there are powerful *efficiency* arguments for welfare states as well. When they function well, welfare states can make the economy work better. Even when the economic benefits are ambiguous the application of rigorous economic analysis can help to ensure they are at least cost-effective. Nevertheless, we still cannot ignore the politics. The boundaries between market and state concerning "welfare" are not easy to delineate, and this provides an opening for either private or public provision for the ideologues to fight over. Welfare states are also having to shift to accommodate the radical changes to economy and society we have been discussing in previous chapters of this book. The rest of this chapter examines these arguments from economics and political economy and looks at how welfare states are changing.

Welfare and welfare states

Welfare states are commonly understood as having two main functions: as "Robin Hood", to provide poverty relief and redistribute wealth; and as a "piggy bank", to provide insurance against life risks. We will deal with the Robin Hood element later, but for now let us focus on the idea of risk sharing.

Welfare states serve to pool risks that might otherwise be difficult to manage if individuals were left to bear them on their own. These are "life risks" associated with working, growing old, raising a family and possibly falling on hard times. The term "risk" might sound pejorative (why view raising a family as a risk?), not to mention odd (is not growing old a sure thing – assuming we do not die young, which is surely the bigger risk?). But all it is meant to convey is the sense that we can and should prepare for these life events but cannot exactly be sure how or when they will affect us and our loved ones, inhibiting our ability to plan for them. And this is the key point: as a society we *can* prepare for these events, in many cases much better than individuals are able to, through insurance. The mechanism that makes this feasible is *risk pooling*. By using statistical methods based on colossal amounts of data, insurers (which may be private insurance companies or government agencies) can spread risk across a large number of people. They do this by calculating a premium that all insurance policyholders have to pay in order to cover their individual risks at a much lower tariff than if individuals had to save for the risky event themselves.

Consider this example of insurance in operation. There is a risk that your house will burn down, and if it does you will be financially ruined as well as homeless. It might therefore make sense to put aside some money for this possibility. The trouble is, we are talking about a large amount of money, which could be better deployed elsewhere to prepare for an event that is still (let us face it) rather unlikely. This is a classic case of a low-likelihood, high-impact event for which risk pooling makes enormous sense. Although you cannot predict whether your house will burn down, you can look at 1,000 random houses in the neighbourhood and estimate from this the probability, or risk, of any of them catching fire. From this, you construct your risk pool. For example, you note that over the last ten years there have been on average five house fires a year requiring compensation. If each house is worth $200,000, then everyone needs to pay $1,000 (i.e. the 0.5 per cent probability of a fire multiplied by the value of a house) to achieve an insurance pot of $1 million – enough to compensate five people for losing their home.

Setting the necessity of keeping aside the $200,000 cost of rebuilding your house against the $1,000 annual insurance premium it is abundantly clear that insurance is worth it. And insurance for *social* risks, based on identical principles of risk sharing, makes just as much sense. We know we will get old someday. But we do not know what physical state we will be in – for example, whether we will get sick and require expensive long-term care in a nursing home. Your job might seem secure, but supposing your employer goes bust or decides to replace you with a robot? How will you manage? You want kids, ideally one or two, but what if you end up with five and one of them has special educational needs? Risk sharing in all these instances is as worthwhile as insuring your next skiing holiday. The question is: who will organize it?

One obvious candidate is the market. If private insurance companies can make money from insuring against risks like this then why not let them? They also have a lot of experience in generating actuarial risk models for all sorts of eventualities: crashing your car, getting your laptop stolen, etc. Social insurance might seem to be a special case requiring government involvement, but in welfare provision the boundary between the market and the state is actually often blurred; many people have private pensions alongside state pension entitlements, for example. So how do we decide whether public intervention is necessary? When, in other words, do social welfare issues require a welfare state?

The field of welfare economics provides a set of criteria for judging this. Welfare economists operate on the assumption that market provision is fine if certain factors are present. Many of these mirror the standard assumptions of NCE outlined in Chapter 1. First, markets need to be competitive, peopled by utility-maximizing individuals with all the information they require to make good decisions. Second, there must be no problems with externalities, public goods or increasing returns to scale. If these conditions apply, then the market operating alone can produce a Pareto-efficient, welfare-enhancing outcome. Debate in economics therefore centres on exactly when these conditions are met. Welfare economists interested in market failure, such as Nicholas Barr of the LSE, point out that many areas of social insurance do not conform to these principles.[4] In other words, the market frequently fails, providing a potential rationale for state provision (note that this does not necessarily mean that the state will intervene, or that it will intervene only when these market failures exist).

Box 8.1 Key terms

- *Risk pooling.* Insurance works by spreading risks among a large and diverse group of clients who "pool" their risks.
- *Bounded rationality.* The idea that individuals often fail to make rational decisions because of patchy or unreliable information and their limited ability to make sense of it.
- *New social risks.* Emerging challenges for welfare states bound up in changing labour markets, demographics and family structures.

Here are some examples. Take unemployment insurance. Why do not individuals organize this themselves by taking out a policy privately instead of relying on the state? The main problem here is known as moral hazard. This follows from my ability to game the system by influencing the probability of my gaining employment. If insured, and thereby guaranteed an income regardless of whether I work, I might take longer to find a job than otherwise. I could even arrange with an employer to work for free for a week so he can make me redundant and I can collect the insurance money. This is very difficult for an insurance company to monitor, so it may not offer insurance at all – despite there being a clear need for this given the likelihood that I will face unemployment at various points in my career. Public, state-provided unemployment insurance is often the solution, as the government is obliged to deal with the wider repercussions (externalities) of jobless, uninsured workers (poverty, social unrest, lack of demand in the economy) and is also in a position to force people to look for work.

An additional issue is that unemployment is a systemic, as well as individual, risk. In other words, it can hit a lot of people at the same time – during a recession, say. A private company would need huge reserves to deal with this, requiring high premiums, whereas the government can go into debt to pay for mass unemployment. You can look at this problem in another way, as one of *asymmetries* of information: one side knowing more than the other. I know much more about myself than insurers do, especially my work ethic and competence at the job, which makes it hard for them to calculate my risk of unemployment and easy for me to pull the wool over their eyes.

Again, a diligent insurer can uncover this information from my past – but only at a cost, pushing up premiums. Low unemployment risks – highly skilled and motivated workaholics – would effectively be subsidizing riskier prospects and so may not bother insuring themselves. This would lump the insurance company with the high-risk, work-shy and incompetent clients, and it may just exit the market, or be forced to charge exorbitant premiums if it remains. This particular market failure is also known as adverse selection, and is prevalent in healthcare as well, as we saw in Chapter 4. Public welfare provision – a welfare state – can overcome adverse selection by making membership of collective risk-pooling schemes compulsory for all in society, preventing the good (low) risks from opting out, and also by being able to insure all, the good as well as bad risks, at a lower cost.

Behavioural economics also has a lot to say about welfare and insurance markets. Pensions provide a clear example of the information and rationality issues at play here that undermine the market. If I want a good retirement income in my old age then it pays to begin saving at the start of my career. Thanks to the beauty of compound interest, the earlier I begin saving, the longer my money will have to work for me and the bigger my retirement pot at the end. Advertisements for financial companies scream this basic fact at potential pension scheme customers, but does anyone listen? Some do, of course, but the problem is that being this sensible requires workers to make a lot of complex, rational decisions about the long term quite early in their careers, at a time when money may be tight and they face other demands on their limited finances – saving up for a house or starting a family, for example. With the best will in the world, many people simply decide to cross that particular bridge when they come to it, often too late. This is known as "bounded willpower"; we know something is a good idea but just cannot seem to force ourselves to do it right now.

"Bounded rationality" is another, related, problem. Suppose we decide to be sensible and plan ahead. The trouble is, pensions and annuities are complicated, and many people lack basic financial literacy. Even if we regard saving for retirement as important and want to educate ourselves, doing so is time-consuming and difficult; transaction costs, as economists would say, are high, and a particular problem for low-income groups.[5] Information is also available asymmetrically, in that pension companies know more about the pitfalls of their products than their clients, creating the potential for mis-selling. Finally, even if we make all the right decisions for all the right reasons, markets may still fail to provide the requisite products. For private insurance to be viable, it must be possible to calculate the risk and benefit based on "actuarial" principles. These equate a known, or estimable, risk against an agreed payout if the insured incident occurs, enabling the insurance company to adjust premiums to ensure it makes a profit. But the market may fail in the many instances when the risks are intrinsically unknowable (the future rate of inflation, important for any insurance product to replace lost income) or the terms of the contract are hard to specify (what constitutes an acceptable level of care in an old people's home?), for example.

Box 8.2 What are welfare states?

Welfare states have various *purposes*.[6]

- Consumption smoothing: for example, old age pensions redistribute income from our younger to our older selves; unemployment benefit softens the financial impact of losing one's job.
- Risk sharing: many life risks are more financially manageable if pooled – e.g. the risk of unemployment.

They can *perform their function* in a number of ways.

- Cash benefits: for example, unemployment benefit, old age pensions, sickness and disability benefits, child benefits.
- Services, or benefits in kind: education (Chapter 2), or healthcare (Chapter 4).

They can be *financed* in different ways.

- Contributory: payment is tied to a specific benefit, for example through workplace insurance, and may be voluntary.
- Non-contributory: payment is compulsory through general taxation or national insurance contributions (though there may be opt-outs available).

They can be *delivered* in different ways.

- State-funded and state-delivered, such as the United Kingdom's National Health Service.
- State-funded and privately delivered, such as Canada's healthcare insurance.

These examples indicate that relying always on the market is neither obviously just (the needy may end up with no cover) nor even efficient (bad risks driving out the good, leading to an under-provision of insurance cover). Welfare states can address many of these problems by filling in gaps where market provision is lacking or using government authority to force people to participate. Of course, the resulting arrangements may not be perfectly actuarial in public insurance, as the link between premium and individual risk is broken and the contract usually less strict than with private insurance. But the political, economic and social benefits of collective insurance are likely to be such that it is seen as worth doing anyway. There may be also instances when some redistribution may be intentionally factored into insurance schemes, such as survivor benefits for families with lots of children, and women who never had enough market earnings to save for a decent retirement.

Market failure and politics

Welfare states can therefore step in when the market fails to deliver. But they are obviously about much more than correcting market failures; otherwise, we might expect them to be organized in much the same way. That is, unless you buy into the idea that the French are sicker and need to retire earlier, or Americans are lazier and so require minimal unemployment insurance cover to motivate them – two possible conclusions from observing the design of their national welfare states, which are flatly contradicted by the evidence. And yet welfare states are very different. Welfare spending varies hugely across advanced nations, as does the design of social programmes and the groups seen as most deserving of intervention.

Why are national systems so different? Obviously, there are many factors at play besides the state rushing in where the market fails, and so the welfare economics approach – let alone the basic assumptions of NCE – is clearly not enough. One explanation for diversity is that there is no optimal design of a welfare state, although some systems are clearly better than others. Welfare economics is good at pointing out problems with market provision but can only offer broad guidelines for designing institutions to correct them. So, when it comes to explaining how welfare states have evolved into what we have today, history and politics are equally important.

Karl Polanyi, a Hungarian political economist, argued that welfare states emerged symbiotically with capitalism as a "counter-reaction" to protect society from the market.[7] Employers were initially concerned about schemes such as unemployment benefits and old age pensions because of the cost, but they came eventually to see that these produced a healthier and more motivated workforce.[8] Polanyi's followers suggested that welfare states were most advanced and comprehensive when political coalitions at the moment of their foundation between left parties and trade unions were strongest – in Scandinavia, for example.[9] Path dependence, the tendency for initial conditions to determine later development, is very influential in studies of how welfare states develop and maintain their character in the face of pressures to change.[10]

But welfare states also clearly vary holistically by function. For instance, welfare programmes can be targeted (at the very poorest, or pensioners) or universal (treating everyone in need the same way). They can drastically affect how people are affected by participation in labour markets, and have implications for the role women play in society. Gøsta Esping-Andersen, a Danish political economist, has divided up modern welfare states into three main categories, according to how far they reduce the impact of market forces on citizens' lives ("decommodification") and modify or preserve existing social relations ("stratification").[11]

The three "types" are clearly abstractions, but they indicate the guiding ideology of each system. Other logics, such as political traditions, will clearly also be at play.[12] Esping-Andersen's first type, the "Anglo-Saxon" welfare state, is geared mainly towards making the labour market operate effectively by removing all possible impediments to work, such as high unemployment benefits. It is "residual" – i.e. not very generous – and does not go out of its way to preserve social stratification. The United Kingdom and Ireland are the main European examples, and the United States is clearly also organized on similar lines. The second, "social democratic" type, found in the Nordics, is also universal but much more generous and explicitly decommodifying. Social democratic welfare states also make great efforts to provide help for women to combine care responsibilities with a career. The third type is known as the "Bismarckian" welfare state and is found in continental Europe, particularly Germany and France. Here, welfare provision is tied up with your job through social and/or private insurance, so it is highly stratifying and concerned with status preservation. All three types are under pressure from changes in the economy and society and are responding in different ways, as we will see next.

8.2 All change in society: families, pensioners and the poor

As we saw at the end of the last section, welfare states were originally set up to deal with the social dislocations around industrialization and the changes this wrought on societies. After the Second World War there were political pressures for measures aimed at poverty reduction and providing dignity in retirement. We can use the techniques of welfare economics to examine how well they address these goals and explore the unintended side effects. But because welfare states are so bound up with politics they are also quite difficult to change and reform, and so sometimes what we observe about welfare states are structures set up to deal with a particular set of social needs that have now become obsolete. We can look at these societal changes through the prism of "new social risks", a term that welfare and political economists use to explain emerging pressures on welfare states.[13]

The foundations for most welfare states were laid in the early twentieth century and were designed to deal with a set of what are now referred to as "old" social risks. These concern traditional welfare policies that revolved around the world of work. It was assumed at the time that there would always be plenty of jobs to go around and people would live only a few years after retirement. Early to mid-twentieth-century welfare states embodied what was sometimes referred to as the "male breadwinner, female carer" model, as family life was organized around a division of labour between the husband and wife. The man's role was to go out and earn a living, leaving his wife to take care of their extended family.

Welfare systems organized around the male breadwinner model relied on most social care (including childcare and looking after sick relatives) being provided privately within the home, and the thrust of policy was directed towards smoothing the family's income in the face of the father's potential (temporary) joblessness and eventual retirement. The focus was on cash transfers rather than the provision of services, and women were treated as dependants, with gender issues subordinated to the need to ensure the father was able to take care of his family financially. Not surprisingly, the male breadwinner model has been heavily criticized by feminists, who blame it for denying women choices and equality.[14] Combatting poverty or reducing income inequality were also not seen as central tasks of the welfare state, as jobs at this time were usually plentiful.

Important elements of this system remain, of course, with unemployment insurance still a central plank of all welfare states. But, as we saw in Chapter 3, there have been enormous changes in labour markets, such as an end to the "job for life" and the growth of insecure employment contracts. Welfare states have therefore had to deal with unemployment that is much more likely to be long-term or even permanent. International competition has pushed down wages, meaning that even a full-time job may not be enough to make ends meet. Rapidly changing technologies mean skills may become redundant and need to be refreshed.

The final nail in the coffin of the male breadwinner model is that many more women now go out to work. The decline of manufacturing and rise of services have vastly increased opportunities for female employment, and welfare states have had to adjust to the fact that things such as childcare and caring for elderly relatives are now increasingly provided outside the home. A further issue is demographic change, especially rising life expectancy. The fact that we are living longer is an unambiguously good thing and should be celebrated. But it means that pensions systems predicated on us enjoying a long working life followed by a short spell of well-deserved retirement are out of date.

How are welfare states dealing with these "new social risks"? Education and healthcare, which are generally considered to be part of the welfare state, are dealt with fully in Chapters 2 and 4, respectively. So let us look now at the Robin Hood function of welfare: tackling poverty and inequality. The key dilemma for policy-makers is whether to help the very poor, who are also the hardest and most expensive to help, or achieve a quicker hit by doing something about inequality, which can often be achieved relatively easily by directing resources at those just below the poverty line.

The dilemma is not helped by difficulties in arriving at a workable definition of poverty. Should it be regarded as an absolute or relative concept? Absolute poverty is generally agreed to be a situation in which a person is unable to earn enough to stay healthy. It is possible, therefore, to arrive at a relatively objective definition of this in principle, and few governments in rich countries would be content with a situation in which this predicament was widespread. Relative poverty, or inequality, is different, however, as it is more subjective, and is generally taken to mean that a person's low income sets him apart from the rest of society. Inequality can be measured by something called the Gini coefficient, which expresses it as a number between zero and one, with zero being total equality and one when a single person owns all the wealth (see Figure 8.1).

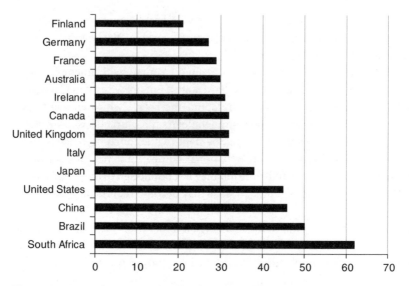

Figure 8.1 Inequality as measured by the Gini coefficient
Notes: Data is for latest year available. Highest = most unequal.
Source: OECD.

The Gini is a good way of comparing inequality across countries but it does not tell us the optimal level of inequality or the maximum we should tolerate. Some inequality is arguably a good thing in the interest of preserving incentives, and it is not even necessarily bad in itself. Theoretically, you could have a society of millionaires and billionaires in which the former would be considered (relatively) poor. But it is a moot point whether they would they be deserving of much sympathy, let alone serious effort to redistribute wealth to make them feel better about their situation. Too much inequality erodes social cohesion and is ultimately bad for growth, however, as the rich tend to save rather than spend their income, reducing consumption. But, again, this is probably as much of a political and moral question as an economic one. Measures of inequality such as the Gini are pretty unreliable, though, as they omit non-money income and take no account of life cycles; students tend to be poor when at college, for example, but the education they receive there enhances their human capital and so they should earn more than the average in the future.

Helping families

A key target of welfare policy is that modern political cliché: "hardworking families". Family policy scarcely existed in its own right under the male breadwinner model but now it is a key plank of modern welfare states. The task has been complicated by a number of changes to labour markets and family structures over the last few decades. As we saw, the end of the male breadwinner accompanying the decline of manufacturing and rise of service industries saw many more women enter the labour market. Men's labour force participation in EU countries fell from 89 per cent in 1970 to 78 per cent by 2001, while that of women rose from 45 per cent to 61 per cent.[15] Female employability is paramount to making welfare states sustainable. It also gives rise to new challenges, however. Women's greater financial independence, as well as changes to the law to make divorce easier, have led to a big rise in the number of single-parent families, 90 per cent of which are headed by mothers. Governments are also worried about declining fertility rates, because working women are delaying having children until they feel they are established in their careers, which means they tend to have fewer children than previous generations.

Much social policy is therefore aimed at helping women to work while preventing child poverty. Having children is strongly correlated with poverty because of the financial demands involved in raising a family, and the danger of this is magnified if the family is headed by a lone parent. Families at risk of poverty can be helped in several ways. Most OECD countries have introduced universal child benefit. This consists of direct cash payments that lift family income and can be means-tested if funding is tight to focus on the very poorest, as in the United Kingdom. Child policies are therefore an important means of tackling absolute and, as importantly, *intergenerational* poverty – as children who grow up poor face a lifetime of underachievement. Moreover, in two-parent families, as the benefit is usually paid to the mother, it can assist intra-family income distribution and is also more likely to find its way to the child. Most European countries offer some form of child benefit, although not the United States. Family tax credits do much the same thing but favour those in work, so they may be a good policy if the focus is more on income inequality. Welfare packages for families can also help with housing costs, and waiting lists for social housing increasingly prioritize those with children.

The other main focus of family policies is to help mothers stay in touch with the world of work. The welfare state can help women by "defamilializing" care policies, with states and markets absorbing care responsibilities and freeing mothers to seek part-time work.[16] These can include providing public childcare or subsidizing it through the market. Generous parental leave schemes can also encourage women to take a long break from their job to have a family but without giving up work entirely and risk having to start again at the bottom.

An emerging issue for policy-makers is "homogamy", the tendency for highly educated professionals to marry their social counterparts, and for poorer people with low educational attainment and more precarious employment prospects to do likewise. This is leading to a concentration of welfare problems – low wages, redundant skills, child poverty – in a subgroup of usually low-income families. At the moment, it is not altogether clear how to deal with this – short of telling people who they can marry. But possible policies in the future might include more of an emphasis on promoting social mobility and subsidies for schools in poorer areas.

8.3 Why welfare may change our behaviour and how to design a system to encourage good habits

This section focuses on the impact of welfare states on behaviour. It addresses a key microeconomic critique of welfare programmes: that they discourage people from working and make them dependent on government handouts. High spending on welfare is probably one reason for this disquiet, and this trend is examined in section 8.4. But another is undoubtedly rooted in our understanding of human nature; surely, policies that cushion us against life events must have an effect on how we prepare ourselves for these? A particular concern is whether benefits intended to help the unemployed maintain a decent standard of level discourage them from working. The first part of this section explores the "dependency" critique, the second looks at government responses.

Let us start with a few examples of how welfare can change behaviour.

- Tom has a full-time job and Tara is thinking about giving up being a housewife and taking part-time work. But this would bring their joint income over the threshold for higher rates of tax, leaving them little better off. Tara elects to stay at home.
- Marcella survives a car accident but is paralysed from the waist down. Neither Marcella nor her husband Dave, who works in a small business, has health insurance. Because US means-tested assistance programmes are designed for the poor, the couple is forced to spend down assets to near the poverty level before qualifying for help. To remain eligible, they will have to stay under these restrictions for the rest of their lives (that means no saving for retirement, no tax-free college savings, etc.).[17]
- Diane, mother of a family of three, has the chance to get promotion at her retail job. She would have to work many more hours, but her gross income would double from $20,000 to $40,000. This means that she would lose access to several income-based programmes, however, including publicly subsidised childcare for low-income parents. As a result, her take-home income would remain exactly the same. Should she refuse the promotion?

The claim that welfare policies shape decisions and create dependency forms an influential critique of welfare states and builds on numerous real-life examples resembling the above. The key allegation is that welfare pushes up unemployment and does nothing to tackle poverty.[18] The reasoning behind this is that if unemployment benefit replaces a pay cheque then this creates an incentive to reduce any work effort that is financially motivated. NCE highlights two reasons why unemployment benefits increase unemployment, based on standard microeconomic assumptions about incentives. First, they create "frictional" unemployment: we all change jobs from time to time, but if our search effort is cushioned by high benefits we are less likely to rush to find a new position. Second, since welfare is financed by employer taxes or social insurance deducted from payrolls it increases employment costs, which decrease real wages and discourage firms from taking on workers. In general, the narrower the gap between your income in work and out of work, the less attractive work becomes; after all, why slave away for little or no extra money?

Of course, there are many reasons why we work besides money. Maybe we enjoy getting out of the house and interacting with colleagues. Perhaps we find a sense of purpose in what we do professionally. Economics does not discount these non-financial motivations entirely, as they comprise part of an individual's utility function. Particularly at the low end of the income scale, however, where money is tight and the work probably dull, they are likely to be very much of secondary concern. Primarily, work is about earning money to live, and so the key question is whether sacrificing our time and effort to do a job makes us materially better off, given alternative means of support available.

The tax and benefits systems can interact in various ways to exacerbate this dilemma. Income tax rates in most countries are progressive, in that they are graduated in order to ensure proportionately more tax is levied on higher earners. The trouble is, there are often steep jumps rather than a gentle transition between tax rates as successively higher earnings thresholds are reached. Welfare systems are often organized in the same way, so benefits tend to be withdrawn suddenly rather than gradually as the individual achieves a certain income. Together, these can result in a sharp and substantial loss of income as people move from unemployment into work, or from part-time towards full-time work.

These factors produce several types of "traps".[19]

- "Unemployment trap": when the benefits paid are high relative to paid work, making taking a job financially unattractive.
- "Poverty trap": when you have a job but benefit withdrawal means working more hours will not make you much better off.
- "Inactivity trap": similar to the unemployment trap, but this applies to people not receiving any unemployment benefits. For example, when Tom and Tara's

income is taxed jointly, her extra earnings from taking a job would lift their family income into a higher tax bracket, and so it may not be worth her while.

These examples make sense in theory, and they mesh to some extent with conceptions from NCE about how humans respond to incentives. But how can we accurately gauge the extent of welfare dependency? It is surprisingly difficult to tell for sure. At a very general level, countries with basic "safety net" welfare systems, such as the United Kingdom, United States and Canada, have tended to have slightly lower unemployment than countries where benefits are more generous, such as France or Italy. But there could be many reasons for this besides levels of unemployment benefit, such as a country's ability to generate low-paid, entry-level jobs. A large number of quantitative studies have been carried out[20] but these are unreliable on account of statistical and measurement problems, and there appears to be no clear and unambiguous link.[21] The key issue is establishing causality, as it is tricky to isolate the external effect of benefits from hidden, personal characteristics: did I turn down the promotion and pay rise because it left me no better off financially, or because I am lazy and shirk responsibility? Studies that look at the welfare system holistically tend to conclude that it is the *duration* of benefits, rather than their generosity, that has the bigger impact on unemployment.[22] Maybe knowing there is a strict time limit on how long I can draw benefits might be a more powerful incentive to find work than cutting these to the bone to force me into the labour market? And, anyway, if the demand for labour is deficient then tinkering with benefit levels may not provide much of a solution.

Overcoming welfare dependency

Simply because the link between unemployment and benefit levels is weak does not mean that policy-makers should not try to minimize any possible disincentive effects from unemployment benefit. One common finding from the vast academic literature on the economics of welfare dependency is that well-designed policy can have a big impact on choices and outcomes. The "old" approach to welfare, which focused on minimizing disincentives by keeping benefits low relative to wages, is being superseded by "new" welfare policies, which address benefit structures and labour markets holistically and place more reliance on positive incentives. These are also beginning to incorporate insights about human motivations and hidden biases from behavioural economics, developed inside government "nudge" units to prod people towards more constructive behaviour.

Policies using such positive incentives work in various ways. Tax credits are a popular way of topping up the incomes of the low-paid to incentivize them to stay in work. Although unemployment benefit subsidizes the unemployed, tax credits do the reverse by assisting those in employment and are thus popular with governments under political pressure to "make work pay". The growing use of tax credits can also be seen as a response to the rise in the number of low-paid, insecure jobs, often in services sectors. They work by providing a cash payment once a threshold of working hours is reached – say 15 hours a week. The trouble is that tax credits are often withdrawn at a steep rate once recipients increase the number of hours, which can be a disincentive to work more (see section 8.3). There are also suspicions that they merely subsidize "low road" employers who are content to offer low wages in the expectation that these will be topped up by the government. And, in any case, the really poor have little contact at all with the job market, so this is not the best way of tackling entrenched poverty.

Another approach is to use carrots as well as sticks to get people into work. Traditional unemployment benefits based around cash transfers to the jobless are largely passive, in that they focus on preventing unemployed people becoming destitute or suffering a catastrophic drop in income that might harm their families, while doing nothing to get them back into work. In the early 1990s a number of Scandinavian countries, faced with big budget deficits and mounting unemployment but politically unable to slash benefits, developed a set of "active" welfare policies in response. Active welfare policies do more than merely cushion against the income loss of unemployment; they also focus on helping the unemployed back into the labour market and are being drawn up with increasing input from behavioural economists, who are advising politicians on how to make people *want* to work.

Nordic-style active welfare policies still include stick elements aimed at making unemployment less comfortable, but these act in less punitive ways. Typical measures include reducing replacement rates (increasing the gap between incomes inside and outside work), being stricter about job search criteria (you will need a better reason for rejecting that toilet-cleaning job…) and placing time limits on how long you can claim for. The carrot side, on the other hand, is about improving your employability through training and reskilling, so you will have more chance of being offered alternatives to a career as a "public waste technician". Policies aimed at encouraging female carers into the workplace can also involve help with childcare provision.

The exact balance between carrot and stick varies across countries. Continental European countries, and particularly Scandinavian ones, are keener on persuasion and adopt a more "enabling" approach, with the focus less on coercion and more on the development of human capital (see Chapter 2). Perhaps the most highly developed (and very effective) example of the enabling approach is Denmark's "flexicurity" system. Denmark integrates welfare and labour market policy by offering generous, but time-limited, benefits and training options to the jobless while incentivizing employers to take on workers through easy rules on hire and fire. Flexicurity is interesting because it combines a weak workfare approach, representing a slight softening of traditional Scandinavian norms of "social citizenship", with strong enabling elements. Other countries that previously emphasized the enabling approach, such as Germany, are moving more towards coercion, however.

On the other hand, the economically liberal Anglo-Saxon nations opt instead for a tough love approach sometimes dubbed "workfare", as it makes social rights conditional on the obligation to look for work. The administration of Bill Clinton in the United States developed extensive workfare policies in the 1990s and the "New Deal" policies pursued by the government of Tony Blair in the United Kingdom combined workfare policies with some more activist elements. These policies could be viewed as more stick and less carrot versions of the Nordic schemes. The political focus on incentives and unemployment benefits is understandable; no one likes the thought of being taken advantage of. But we must not lose sight of the fact that unemployment benefits account for a relatively small amount of welfare spending compared with other areas – pensions, for example.

8.4 Reforming welfare: why pensions, not unemployment, are the cause of welfare state expansion

This section focuses on the second big criticism of welfare states: that they are just too costly and are bankrupting countries. Angela Merkel, the German chancellor, famously quipped at the start of the Eurozone crisis that the European Union has 7 per cent of the world's population, produces 25 per cent of its GDP, but has to finance 50 per cent of global welfare spending.[23] She was immediately jumped on by supporters of welfare states, who argued that this generosity was a mark of Europe's civilized values, not a badge of shame. Nevertheless, large and sometimes employment-unfriendly welfare states were implicated in the budgetary problems EU countries faced during the crisis. Harsh austerity measures were prescribed to deal with these, which some economists claim made the situation worse.[24] So who is right? Let us start by examining the facts, then move on to some of the reasons why, before asking whether welfare states are sustainable in their current form.

Welfare spending has undeniably crept up steadily over the last few years (see Figure 8.2). Critics say it has actually begun to crowd out other areas of government spending. One analysis indicates that welfare's share of total government spending in Europe has increased from 39 per cent in 1980 to well over 52 per cent in 2005. In other words, more than half of every euro spent by European governments now goes on welfare.[25] Even when governments have been forced to cut overall government spending, as happened under austerity measures following the Eurozone crisis, welfare spending has proved relatively immune to

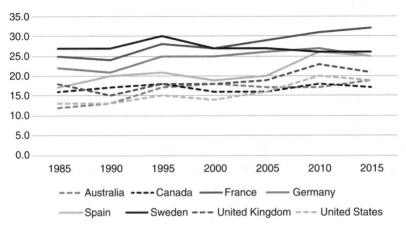

Figure 8.2 Social spending as a percentage of GDP, 1985–2015
Source: OECD.

these pressures. Southern European countries such as Greece and Italy spend proportionately more on cash transfers than services, with a lot of this going on old age pensions and less on families and the jobless, despite big increases in unemployment. Northern European countries, by contrast, spend big on activation policies to aid retraining, and the liberal, Anglo-Saxon nations focus their smaller budgets on basic poverty alleviation.

Welfare spending varies according to the demand for it – what is happening in the economy and society – and so financial pressures on it vary by time and place. During the financial crisis and recession of 2008–9 spending on unemployment benefit in Europe and the United States predictably soared (see Figure 8.3). But this increase was cyclical, driven by the poor economic conditions, and fell again when employment recovered. Spending on pensions follows a different dynamic; it is driven by demographics and politics. Western societies are ageing, and official retirement ages decreeing when you can start drawing a pension are increasing at too slow a rate to keep pace. The result is a steady rise in the dependency ratio, which is the number of workers whose taxes pay for pensions divided by the number of retired people drawing pensions. Many economists argue this ratio is unsustainable in the long term: too few workers to pay for the growing population of retirees.

This is leading to complaints about "generational unfairness" – a feeling that the young are losing out to the old financially. For example, in 2010 the UK government introduced the "triple lock", a guarantee that pensions rise by the same as average earnings, the inflation rate or 2.5 per cent, whichever is the highest. The result? The state pension in the United Kingdom, which is already equivalent

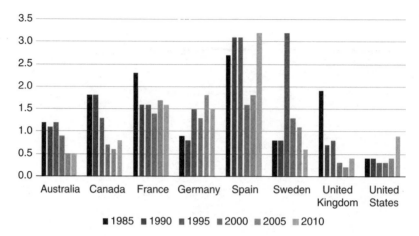

Figure 8.3 Spending on unemployment as a percentage of GDP, 1985–2010
Source: OECD.

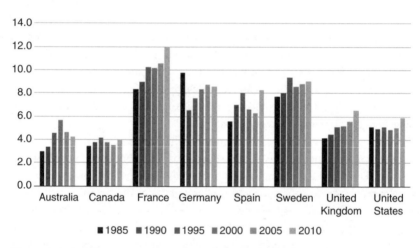

Figure 8.4 Spending on pensions a percentage of GDP, 1985–2010
Source: OECD.

to 6.6 per cent of GDP, is forecast to rise to 8.6 per cent by 2060.[26] At the same time the UK government has cut tax credits for working families and kept the lid on unemployment benefit. UK government spending on state pensions was £92 billion in 2015–16, but only £23.6 billion on housing and unemployment benefit combined. In the United States, spending on families accounts for just 17 per cent of pensions spending (see Figure 8.4 for details of spending on pensions).[27] Shifting spending from pensions to other parts of welfare that benefit young families seems to be the solution, but is it happening?

Why are welfare states difficult to reform?

Money-saving moves to raise the retirement age or make pensions less generous have, predictably, been resisted by both retired people and those saving for
a pension. Older people tend to vote in greater numbers than the young, and
they form a powerful interest bloc that politicians ignore at their peril. Politicians
are generally reluctant to intervene because of the perceived unfairness of tam-
pering with the incomes of people who have already exited the labour market
and so lack the means of replacing the lost income. But the wider point is that
welfare spending in all its forms tends to create political constituencies behind
it that resist reform. People know well what they stand to lose personally, but
the costs of high welfare spending in the form of higher taxes are shared more
widely. This may explain why Margaret Thatcher and Ronald Reagan, for all their
talk of fostering self-reliance, found it so difficult to cut welfare bills.[28] Expanding
welfare states is politically popular but cutting them is tricky, as this imposes
concrete costs while the benefits (lower taxes) are more diffuse. It is hard to
present this in a politically attractive manner, so elected politicians have tended
to dodge the issue.

Thus, welfare reform, when it happens, tends to be done in the most boring
and glacial fashion possible. Over the longer term it is possible to cut the pensions budget by, for example: linking increases to inflation rather than income
(which rises at a slower rate); increasing the retirement age, but phased in over
decades rather than years to defer the blow; and delegating decisions about
reform to extra-political technical committees and public inquiries. Forward-
thinking governments have been using these devices, as they give people time
to adjust to change and defuse inevitable opposition. But this is rarely as easy
as it sounds, and some countries find it harder than others. Welfare systems
financed through payroll and insurance contributions, such as those in many
continental European countries, are harder to roll back as contributions are
clearly earmarked for benefits.[29] These have tended to approach the affordability
issues by hiking contributions, which runs the risk of making business uncom-
petitive and increasing unemployment. The reform task is easier in tax-funded
systems, in which revenues disappear into general government spending, making cuts seem less unfair. The United Kingdom and Scandinavian countries take
this approach, while the United States has a mix of the two systems, and their
attendant problems.

Ultimately, however, welfare reform is, ideally, less about spending totals than
maximizing efficiency. "Expensive" welfare states, such as those in Scandinavia,
can still be very cost-effective in tackling social ills while those in the low-tax
United States achieve more modest aims at a still substantial cost. America gets
away with an inefficient tax and spending system because the overall tax burden

is quite low. Welfare in Scandinavian countries, on the other hand, is forced to be efficient because the stakes are much higher.[30] Ultimately, it is about the society you want to achieve as well as how much you are prepared to pay for it.

Conclusion: what we have learnt

- Welfare states have grown in importance since the Second World War and have two main functions: as "Robin Hood", redistributing from rich to poor; and as a "piggy bank", smoothing out the impact of life's risks.
- The field of welfare economics points to failures in market provision that justify the state provision of welfare through welfare states. Welfare economics also shows that well-designed welfare policies contribute to efficiency as well as social justice.
- Ultimately, however, it is politics that dictates how welfare states are organized, and there is huge variation in purpose, generosity and quality across countries.
- Economists and other social scientists suspect that welfare policies may change behaviour in some ways; for example, generous unemployment benefit may increase voluntary unemployment. But the link is not clear, and most societies are happy to tolerate a certain amount of "leakage" in welfare spending.
- Although welfare spending is creeping up, the big sums are directed towards pensions rather than families or the unemployed. This is proving increasingly unaffordable but it is politically very difficult to reform welfare because the costs of high spending are diffuse and the benefits concentrated.

Notes

1. J. Rawls, *A Theory of Justice* (Oxford: Oxford University Press, 1972).
2. A. Sen, *The Idea of Justice* (London: Allen Lane, 2009).
3. A. Okun, *Equality and Efficiency: The Big Tradeoff* (Washington, DC: Brookings Institution Press, 1975).
4. N. Barr, *Economics of the Welfare State*, 5th edn (Oxford: Oxford University Press, 2012).
5. O. Mitchell & A. Lusardi, *Financial Literacy: Implications for Retirement Security and the Financial Marketplace* (Oxford: Oxford University Press, 2011).
6. N. Barr, *Economics of the Welfare State*.
7. K. Polanyi, *The Great Transformation: The Political and Economic Origins of Our Time* (Boston: Beacon Press, 2002).
8. P. Swenson, *Capitalists against Markets: The Making of Labor Markets and Welfare States in the United States and Sweden* (Oxford: Oxford University Press, 2002).
9. W. Korpi, *The Democratic Class Struggle* (London: Routledge, 1983).
10. P. Pierson, *Dismantling the Welfare State? Reagan, Thatcher and the Politics of Retrenchment* (Cambridge: Cambridge University Press, 1994).

11. G. Esping-Andersen, *The Three Worlds of Welfare Capitalism* (Cambridge: Polity Press, 1990).

12. W. Schelkle, "Collapsing *Worlds* and *Varieties* of welfare capitalism: in search of a new political economy of welfare", Europe in Question Discussion Paper no. 54/2012 (London: LSE, 2012).

13. P. Taylor-Gooby, *New Risks, New Welfare: The Transformation of the European Welfare State* (Oxford: Oxford University Press, 2004).

14. M. Daly, "Families versus state and market", in F. Castles, S. Leibfried, J. Lewis, H. Obinger & C. Pierson (eds), *The Oxford Handbook of the Welfare State*, 139–51 (Oxford: Oxford University Press, 2010).

15. Eurostat data.

16. J. Lewis, "Gender and the development of welfare states", *Journal of European Social Policy* 2:3 (1992), 159–73.

17. This real-life example is drawn from A. Campbell, *Trapped in America's Safety Net: One Family's Struggle* (Chicago: University of Chicago Press, 2014).

18. R. Moffitt, "Incentive effects of the US welfare system: a review", *Journal of Economic Literature* 30:1 (1992), 1–61.

19. OECD, "Increasing financial incentives to work: the role of in-work benefits", in *OECD Employment Outlook 2005*, 125–72 (Paris: OECD Publishing, 2005).

20. For a good survey of these, see N. Bonoli, V. George & P. Taylor-Gooby, *European Welfare Futures: Towards a Theory of Retrenchment* (Cambridge: Polity Press, 2000).

21. For a review of these studies, see Barr, *Economics of the Welfare State*.

22. A. Atkinson, *Incomes and the Welfare State: Essays on Britain and Europe* (Cambridge: Cambridge University Press, 1995).

23. These remarks were made at the World Economic Forum meeting in Davos in 2013 and were widely reported.

24. M. Blyth, *Austerity: The History of a Dangerous Idea* (Oxford: Oxford University Press, 2015).

25. H. Obinger & W. Wagschal, "Social expenditure and revenues", in Castles *et al.* (eds), *The Oxford Handbook of the Welfare State*, 333–52 (Oxford: Oxford University Press, 2010).

26. Department for Work and Pensions, *Long term projections of pensioner benefits* (London: Department for Work and Pensions, 2013).

27. J. Bradshaw & N. Finch, "Family benefits and services", in Castles *et al.* (eds), *The Oxford Handbook of the Welfare State*, 462–78.

28. P. Pierson, *Dismantling the Welfare State?* (Cambridge: Cambridge University Press, 1994).

29. P. Manow, "Trajectories of fiscal adjustment in Bismarckian welfare systems", in B. Palier (ed.), *A Long Goodbye to Bismarck? The Politics of Welfare Reform in Continental Europe*, 279–300 (Amsterdam: Amsterdam University Press, 2010).

30. P. Lindert, *Growing Public: Social Spending and Economic Growth since the Eighteenth Century* (Cambridge: Cambridge University Press, 2004).

INDEX

Note: Page numbers in **bold** indicate tables.